Mediating Dangerously

Mediating Dangerously

The Frontiers of Conflict Resolution

Kenneth Cloke

JOSSEY-BASS
A Wiley Company
www.josseybass.com

Published by Jossey-Bass
A Wiley Imprint
989 Market Street, San Francisco, CA 94103-1741   www.josseybass.com

Jossey-Bass books and products are available through most bookstores. To contact Jossey-Bass directly call our Customer Care Department within the U.S. at 800-956-7739, outside the U.S. at 317-572-3986, or fax 317-572-4002.

Jossey-Bass also publishes its books in a variety of electronic formats. Some content that appears in print may not be available in electronic books.

Library of Congress Cataloging-in-Publication Data

Cloke, Kenneth, date.
   Mediating dangerously: the frontiers of conflict resolution/by Kenneth Cloke.
      p. cm.
   Includes bibliographical references and index.
      ISBN 0-7879-5356-3
   1. Conflict management. 2. Mediation. I. Title.
HM1126.C558 2001
   303.6'9—dc21   00-063895

Printed in the United States of America
FIRST EDITION
HB Printing   10

Other Books by the Author

By Kenneth Cloke and Joan Goldsmith:
Resolving Conflicts at Work: A Complete Guide for Everyone on the Job
Jossey Bass, 2000

Resolving Personal and Organizational Conflict:
Stories of Transformation and Forgiveness
Jossey Bass, 2000

Thank God It's Monday! 14 Values We Need to Humanize the Way We Work
McGraw-Hill/Irwin Professional Publishing, 1997

Self-Directed and Empowered Teams: An Owner's Manual
Center for Dispute Resolution, 1997

By Kenneth Cloke:
Mediation: Revenge and the Magic of Forgiveness
Center for Dispute Resolution, 1994

Contents

*For Joan, whose loving support, indomitable spirit,
and countless contributions have made this a better book,
me a better person, and the world a better place;
and for Nick and Elka, who taught me to follow
the path of the heart.*

Preface

The dangers of life are infinite, and among them is safety.
GOETHE

When conflicts occur, things fall apart, turn, transform themselves, and come together in new ways. As conflict resolution professionals, we work at the edges, the frontiers, and boundaries, the dark places where everything we know crumbles and disintegrates. But we also work in the bright places at the center where what we did not know coalesces and becomes something new.

Conflicts mark the frontiers, the places where we weaken and divide. Yet these same frontiers embody the forces that strengthen us, bring us together, transform us, and dissipate our differences. Conflicts probe both our innermost natures and the outermost limits of our being. They provoke cruelty and compassion, competition and collaboration, revenge and reconciliation. Mediation is the *dangerous* magic that moves us from one to the other.

This book is about the edges and boundaries, possibilities and peripheries in mediation practice. How do we impart precisely what we risk when we imagine forgiveness? How do we advance beyond traditional accounts of mediation, which focus on steps, procedures, and techniques, to unveil its invisible heart and soul? How do we speak of the subtle, sensitive engine that drives the extraordinary process of personal and organizational transformation?

We need to explore the limits of this process and search out the places where mediation begins to break down, so we can see why, how, and what changes when it does. We need to contemplate what happens when mediators confront fascism, oppression, fear, apathy, insanity, dishonesty, hierarchical power, resistance, revolution, systems, and revenge. We need to explore the dangers we encounter mediating at the inner heart and outer edges of conflict.

This book is about the center, the hub and core, the spirit and soul of mediation practice. It describes the quality of energy that is released in resolution, transformation, and forgiveness. It unravels what happens when people reveal their authentic selves to one another. It explores the ways conflicts are miraculously stripped away, revealing the simple, stark beauty of human love and kindness.

This book is also about structures and systems, politics and philosophy, law and justice. It is about the art and science of transformation through conflict. It looks beyond personal disputes to those that grip families, communities, schools, commercial organizations, governments, political parties, societies, cultures, and nations. It is about what happens when these systems begin to change or trigger conflicts by resisting it. It is mainly about taking risks and about being *dangerous* in small and large ways. It is about translating big ideas into small, petty, everyday actions, and vice versa. It is about bringing a deep honesty and a deep empathy to every human encounter. It is about the perilous, immensely satisfying journey of the spirit. When we live cautiously, we retreat from life's challenges, from doing what is right, from authenticity and relationships. Without danger, there is only stasis, status quo, and anticipation of death.

A *Dangerous* Approach to Mediation

I believe our role as mediators is not simply to settle conflicts or fashion agreements, but to create choices. I believe the choice of whether to agree or settle a dispute belongs to the parties, not the mediators. At the same time, I recognize that people in conflict have difficulty comprehending the full range of choices available to them. They may not have genuinely listened or revealed themselves to each other. They may have failed to look deeply enough into themselves. They may have been blinded, hypnotized, and seduced by their conflicts and unable to see them clearly.

As mediators, we help people choose to surrender the illusions, mirages, and fantasies they have accepted about themselves, about others, and about their conflicts. We encourage them to recognize a diversity of truths and to clarify and infuse their conflicts with meaning. We allow them to abandon stories that cast themselves as victims and others as demons. We assist them in recognizing their interconnectedness. We support them in overcoming their fears. We address their subconscious beliefs that if they admit their fears, they will be standing alone, naked, unprotected, and unsupported; that their compassion will lead them nowhere; that they will be unloved and unlovable. We aid them in moving to the center of their conflicts, where they can discover that reaching the center *anywhere* in their lives allows them to locate the center everywhere.

Conflicts are immense sources of stress and pain, which we try to avoid. At the same time, they are indicators of areas in our lives and organizations that require immediate attention, deep thinking, and willingness to change. In facing our conflicts, opening our hearts, and locating the center of what is not working, we pass through to the other side, uncovering hidden choices and transformational opportunities that ask us to develop, grow, and learn more about our inner selves.

By personal transformation, I do not mean forcing people to change or be someone they are not, but helping them become more authentically who they *really* are. Transformation works on the undeveloped, rejected parts of the self. By organizational transformation, I mean bringing group cultures and systems into congruence with the wishes and desires of the people who work in them, who are served by them, and who are the true reasons for their existence. By transcendence, I mean that a conflict no longer bothers us and that we must now address conflicts at a higher level.

Because every conflict is an opportunity for transformation that can fundamentally impact our lives, it is dangerous for mediators to uncover hidden choices and reveal transformational openings. People easily become addicted to their conflicts and to the dysfunctional systems that generate them. This makes it frightening to even suggest the possibility of recovery to someone locked in conflict, because it means every rationalization and accommodation they have relied on to support their addiction is now at risk. This is what I mean by mediating *dangerously*.

An Invitation

I invite you to look beneath the surface of your own assumptions, to examine the limits you have accepted or created, to step outside your ideas about what you can and cannot do. I invite you to mediate dangerously, to take the risk of exploring your own heart and spirit, and to test the limits of what is possible.

The German philosopher Nietzsche wrote: "When you look into the abyss, the abyss looks into you." Looking deeply into the abyss of conflict means investigating where it came from, exploring the hearts and spirits of those trapped in adversarial conflict. Yet it is not possible to look deeply into others without looking with equal depth into ourselves. We cannot resolve conflict without looking it directly in the eye and understanding how our own history with conflict, our biases, vulnerabilities, and assumptions affect our skills and choices. Our lives and conflicts thus form a private, personal, and professional database from which each of us can learn.

I invite you to start this exploration into the frontiers of mediation. I challenge you to hunt for what happens when you become deeply honest and empathic, when you test the limits of process, try to alter the systems that generate conflicts, or encourage people to change the way they fight. I invite you to mediate from your heart, to seek authenticity, to approach conflict as a spiritual path, and to mediate dangerously, as though your life depended on it. In fact, as I have discovered, it does.

My Experience with Conflict

Like many of you, I have played different roles in relation to conflict at various stages of my life. I spent many years as a child learning how to avoid, accommodate, provoke, compromise, and settle conflicts. During the 1960s, I actively instigated and encouraged conflicts, in order to extend civil liberties, civil rights, and peace.

Over the last thirty years, I have worked with thousands of individuals and hundreds of organizations to resolve seemingly unresolvable conflicts. At various times, I have been a mediator, arbitrator, fact finder, university professor, voluntary settlement judge, judge pro tem, administrative law judge, hearing officer, community organizer, counselor, regulation-negotiation facilitator, political agitator, organizational investigator, public policy mediator, law school professor, group dialogue facilitator, mentor, consultant, public speaker, coach, process manager, and designer of conflict resolution systems for groups and organizations.

During this time, I have resolved thousands of complex, multi-party, organizational, interpersonal, and public policy disputes, ranging from grievance and workplace issues to wrongful termination, discrimination, sexual harassment, and neighbor-hood, community, divorce, family, business, public policy, labor-management, partnership, intraorganizational, commercial, and other kinds of conflicts. For fifteen years, I have taught mediation certification classes twice a year, for individuals, schools, and orga-nizations seeking training in mediation and conflict resolution. I have worked with private and public sector organizations to design conflict resolution systems, including peer mediation programs for employees and students in public and private schools. I have helped set up and train staff and volunteers for victim-offender mediation and reconciliation programs and community mediation programs. I have coached, mentored, trained, and developed orga-nizational leaders and have tried to model conflict resolution behaviors. I have educated thousands of school teachers, princi-pals, staff, and parents in conflict resolution techniques. I have conducted thousands of classes and workshops for organizations on mediation, effective communication, conflict resolution, col-laborative negotiation, team building, strategic planning, organi-zational change, leadership, prejudice reduction, family issues, forgiveness, and personal transformation.

In the process, I have observed firsthand the rage, shame, per-sonal loss, and irretrievable damage experienced by individuals and organizations as a result of conflict. And I have seen miracles of transformation, people moved to forgiveness and reconcilia-tion, groups revitalized, lives renewed, and relationships reclaimed.

How the Book is Organized

I have divided this exploration of dangerous mediation into two sections. The first section investigates the *inner frontiers,* the hidden personal recesses that limit our effectiveness. The second half examines the *outer frontiers,* the systems and structures that restrict our capacity to act on what we learn internally.

Each of the chapters explores a different kind of danger. Each addresses an aspect of mediation that takes us to the limits of our experience. Each offers fresh possibilities for approaching systems and circumstances that are largely unexamined in the literature of mediation. Each identifies potential openings, creative techniques, and unusual or untried approaches.

Acknowledgments

I cannot adequately express my gratitude and appreciation of Joan Goldsmith, who comediated many of the conflicts dissected in these pages, and who edited, sharpened, and nurtured this text. My appreciation also goes to Alan Rinzler, who critiqued and helped clarify, enrich, and hone it. A special thanks to Miriam Goldsmith, Grace Silva, Solange Raro, Anne Roswell, and Matt Kramer, who made it possible for me to write.

Center for Dispute Resolution   KENNETH CLOKE
Santa Monica, California

Part One

The Inner Frontiers

Chapter One

The Dangers of Mediation

Only someone who is ready for everything, who doesn't exclude any experience, even the most incomprehensible, will live the relationship with another person as something alive and will himself sound the depths of his own being. For if we imagine this being of the individual as a larger or smaller room, it is obvious that most people come to know only one corner of their room, one spot near the window, one narrow strip on which they keep walking back and forth. In this way they have a certain security. And yet how much more human is the dangerous insecurity that drives those prisoners in [Edgar Allen] Poe's stories to feel out the shapes of their horrible dungeons and not be strangers to the unspeakable terror of their cells. We, however, are not prisoners.
RAINER MARIA RILKE

The words *mediating* and *dangerously* do not often appear together in the same sentence. The ostensible purpose of mediation is to ameliorate danger, pacify hurt feelings, and create safe spaces within which dialogue can replace debate, where interest-based negotiation can substitute for a struggle for power. We are aware that conflict is dangerous, but we expect mediation to be safe.

We can all recognize that in order to resolve our conflicts we have to move towards them, which is inherently dangerous because it can cause them to escalate. It is somewhat more difficult for us to grasp that our conflicts are laden with information that is essential for our growth, learning, intimacy, and change, that they present us with multiple openings for transformation and unique opportunities to let go of old patterns. Why should this make mediation dangerous?

The Danger of Mediation

Novelist Norman Mailer is said to have remarked that "there is nothing 'safe' about sex. There never has been and there never will be." The same can be said about communication and change. Every honest communication poses a risk that we will hear something that could challenge or change us. All significant change, whether in how organizations are structured or who makes family decisions or how we live our lives, will be perceived as dangerous, because we do not and cannot fully understand where it will lead.

Even the most destructive patterns, dysfunctional ruts, and painful routines seem safer than doing something different that could result in change. Every pattern repeats itself, whereas change could result in things becoming worse. The known, even when it is painful, is measurable and reassuring. There is danger in the uncertainty of change.

Yet there is also danger in trying to hold on to things as they are. Everything is always in flux, and efforts to freeze the status quo or return to an earlier, imagined safety cannot succeed. Rather, these efforts succeed only in sparking an eternal conflict between those who strive to move forward into the danger of the new and those who try to stand still or steal backwards into the safety of the old.

The same tension occurs in every dispute. Most people prefer the conflicts they know to the resolutions they cannot completely imagine. Once they have learned how to accommodate a particular conflict, it becomes part of their routine, and they know what to expect. The script is invariant, calculable, and sure, even when it results in misery and pain.

Everyone intuitively understands that genuinely resolving conflict means getting to the bottom of what is not working. The role of the mediator is to locate the wellspring of the quarrel and dam the source that is feeding it. It does not fundamentally matter whether that system is emotional, intellectual, familial, relational, organizational, political, economic, or social. The closer we get to the heart of *any* system, the greater the possibility that something fundamental could shift and therefore the greater the resistance.

Deeper still, every authentic communication demands openness, honesty, and vulnerability to others. Being vulnerable means risking pain and disillusionment, while anticipating the same honesty in return. The outcome of every open, honest encounter is therefore unpredictable and risky. It means facing parts of ourselves we would rather avoid. It means no longer demonizing our opponents as a way of asserting our own virtue but confronting our demons directly, as the only way of escaping them.

The greatest danger we face is our tendency to retreat from conflict, to accommodate and adapt to it. We quickly learn to expect nothing from our conflicts, to tolerate or anticipate them in our lives, to engage in them without self-reflection. This adaptation to conflict means abandoning all possibility of growth, awareness, learning, improved relationship, deeper intimacy, better results, and personal or organizational transformation, all of which are lost when we are unwilling to risk open communication.

The only way to escape the gravitational tug of a conflict to which we have grown accustomed, even addicted, is by honestly and energetically confronting the reasons we got into it, that kept us in it, that allowed us to accommodate and adapt to it. When we realize what we have gotten and lost by engaging in it, and what will happen if we remain trapped in it, we quickly discover which is the greater danger.

As mediators, we need to be willing to bring a deep, *dangerous* level of honesty and empathy to the dispute resolution process. Otherwise, we become characters in other people's scripts, rationalizing their torments, fears, and avoidance. As mediators, we need to avoid producing agreements that do not resolve conflicts, but merely suppress, silence, or settle them, that result not in growth, but in reluctant acquiescence and enduring discord.

To resolve any conflict, we need to trust that what will happen if we discuss it is better than what will happen if we do not. This inevitably means opening Pandora's box and not really knowing what will fly out. It is the depth and clarity of our own honesty and empathy, and our willingness to explore conflicts that are always just slightly out of control, that allows us to mediate dangerously.

Defining Conflict in New Ways

Most people think of conflicts as disagreements based on differences over what they think, feel, or want. Yet most arguments have little or nothing to do with the issues over which people battle. If we are going to support parties in using their conflicts as opportunities and guides to transformation, we need to deepen our understanding of the nature of conflict.

How we define conflict is critical to creating deeply honest and empathetic communications and achieving lasting resolutions. If our definition of conflict is superficial, we may resolve the wrong issues, communicate at an ineffective level, or address concerns that distract us from resolving core problems.

In every conflict, the parties appear to have nothing in common, yet they fit together like interlocking parts in a system. The masochist seems to have nothing in common with the sadist, or the optimist with the pessimist, yet they have their differences in common. There are no free-standing masochists, and if there is a single masochist in a crowd of a thousand people, he will find or create the sadist he needs in order to be whole. And he may have become so addicted or identified with his role that it will feel *dangerous* to discuss anything that might change it.

To better understand the rationale for a dangerous approach to mediation, consider the following alternative definitions of conflict. Each calls for a different set of strategies to probe the inner logic of the dispute, and a different set of questions to elicit honesty and empathy.

Alternative Definitions of Conflict

• *Conflict represents a lack of awareness of the imminence of death or sudden catastrophe.* As the parties become more aware of the finite quality of each others' lives, their conflicts become less important.

• *Conflict arises wherever there is a failure of connection, collaboration, or community, an inability to understand our essential interconnectedness and the universal beauty of the human spirit.* Everyone behaves in ugly ways when they are in conflict, hiding their essential beauty and interconnectedness. When they notice these qualities, their conflicts tend to diminish. When they act together, their conflicts become mere disagreements.

- *Conflict is a lack of acceptance of ourselves that we have projected onto others, a way of blaming others for what we perceive as failures in our own lives. It reveals a need to hide behind roles or masks that do not reflect our authentic feelings so we can divert attention from our mistakes.* People escalate their conflicts by not being authentic. As they accept themselves more fully, they become more accepting of others.

- *Conflict represents a boundary violation, a failure to value or recognize our own integrity or the personal space of others.* As people recognize and respect each others' boundaries, they experience fewer conflicts.

- *Conflict is a way of getting attention, acknowledgment, sympathy, or support by casting ourselves as the victim of some evil-doer.* If the parties secure the attention, acknowledgment, sympathy, and support they need, they experience fewer conflicts as a result.

- *Conflict represents a lack of skill or experience at being able to handle a certain kind of behavior.* As the parties become more skillful in responding to difficult behaviors, they cease being drawn into conflict.

- *Conflict is often simply the continued pursuit of our own false expectations, the desire to hold on to our unrealistic fantasies.* When the parties give up their false expectations of each other, they surrender the conflicts they have created by trying to get the other side to become someone or something they never were.

- *Conflict represents a lack of listening, a failure to appreciate the subtlety in what someone else is saying.* As the parties listen closely to the metaphors and hidden meanings of their conflict, they discover its true content, and feel less like counterattacking or defending themselves and more like responding constructively.

- *Conflict is often a result of secrets, concealments, confusions, conflicting messages, cover-ups, and what we have failed to communicate.* Conflict hides in the shadows. When one of the parties throws a light on it, it disappears.

- *Conflict represents a lack of skill, effectiveness, or clarity in saying what we feel, think, or want.* When the parties are able to tell each other clearly and skillfully what they need, they are often able to have their needs met without creating conflicts.

- *Conflict is a way of opposing someone who represents a parent with whom we have not yet resolved our relationships.* If the parties can recognize that the other person resembles or is behaving like someone from their family of origin, they may see they are really angry with someone else.

- *Conflict is the sound made by the cracks in a system, the manifestation of contradictory forces coexisting in a single space.* Many interpersonal conflicts represent the points of weakness in an organizational or family system. When the parties address these weaknesses, the conflicts they create usually disappear.

- *Conflict is the voice of a new paradigm, a demand for change in a system that has outlived its usefulness.* The need for change always announces itself in the form of conflict, including increased interpersonal conflict. The introduction of needed changes often reduces the level of conflict in an organizational or family system.

- *Conflict represents an inability to grieve or say goodbye, a refusal to let go of something that is dead or dying.* Many divorcing couples and surviving relatives get into fights as a way of saying goodbye to each other, or as a way of mourning someone they loved.

- *Conflict is a way of being negatively intimate when positive intimacy becomes impossible.* Most parties prefer anger over indifference until they are really ready for the relationship to be over. This is because anger strips away their masks, permitting negative intimacy that results in boundary violation.

- *Conflict is the expression of one-half of a paradox, enigma, duality, polarity, or contradiction.* Many of the conflicts people experience are actually polarities in which each person plays the role of *yin* while the other plays *yang*.

- *Conflict is often a fearful interpretation of difference, diversity, and opposition, which ignores the essential role of polarity in creating unity, balance, and symbiosis.* As the parties learn to see their differences and disagreements as sources of potential unity or strength, their conflicts tend to disappear.

- *Conflict is a result of our inability to learn from our past mistakes, our failure to recognize them as opportunities for growth, learning, and improved understanding.* Conflicts are often simply requests for authenticity, emotional honesty, acknowledgment, intimacy, empathy, and communication from others—in other words, they flow from the desire for a better relationship.

What is common to all these definitions is that our conflicts begin and end with us, as well as with the systems in which we operate. They have little to do with our opponents. As mediators, we can assist the parties in defining their conflict in alternative ways that allow them to perceive its deeper, more accurate meanings. We can define their conflict as a story, a culture, a set of bitter conversations or nasty words, or just feeling stuck. Through a dangerous process of definition, recognition, and acknowledgment, paths open to personal and organizational transformation. Each definition allows parties to redefine their conflict at a deeper level than would be possible, based on the surface issues over which they are arguing. To realize this in practice, we need to understand it in theory.

Searching for Relational Truth

If we focus for a moment not on the parties, but on ourselves as mediators, we can see that the roles we play in mediation are largely defined by our own attitudes, expectations, and styles. These roles, in turn, depend on a set of assumptions about human nature, the nature of conflict, and the nature of change that have reverberated throughout Western political and philosophical thought for centuries, resulting in radically different definitions of mediation.

These assumptions, in their starkest, most polarized form, separate the principle of Logos, representing science and reason, from the principle of Eros, representing art and pleasure. They contrast order with freedom, masculinity with femininity, work with play, discipline with enjoyment. They are reflected in the differences between Aristotle and Plato, Hobbes and Rousseau, Hamilton and Jefferson. They concern discipline versus permissiveness, hierarchy versus heterarchy, autocracy versus democracy. They separate those who believe people are bad and need controlling from those who believe people are good and need freeing.

There is, of course, a third approach that represents a combination of science and art and takes the form of ordered anarchy, disciplined permissiveness, and controlled freedom. This approach views yin and yang as parts of a whole that is greater than the sum of each. It seeks to promote the different interests of both in a victory that is without defeat. As Heraclitus wrote centuries ago: "Opposition brings together, and from discord comes perfect harmony."

There are several consequences of this approach. First, it means mediators need to reconcile what appear to be opposite truths into a single framework. We need to accept the notion that there can be no fixed answers to emotional or artistic questions. This does not mean that there is no objective or scientific truth, or that one or another answer might work better in a given circumstance. It means that it is impossible to determine scientific truth in mediation, not only because there is always some indeterminate, emotional, or artistic truth, but because consensus precludes it. The word *consensus* trivializes what actually takes place, which is more a search for a third, higher, more profound, relational truth, than a compromise over facts. Isolated, adversarial, individual truths, in this sense, are less exact than relational truths. This allows us to walk with the person, but not with the literal truth of what they say. We communicate this to people through tone of voice, through intensity of attention, and by not deserting or silencing them. More deeply, as philosopher Martin Buber discovered: "I can only become I through my relationship with you, so truth is never just mine or yours, but ours."

A second consequence of this approach is that mediators must always be open to change, because answers always depend on a unique set of ever-changing conditions requiring continuous modification. Third, this combined approach means no truth, no story, no claim, can ever prevail over its opposite, except by disappearing altogether, or combining in some new synthesis. Good can never defeat evil, life can never conquer death, and the sacred and the profane are one.

In mediation, it means there are no victories without defeat. Mediators who assume one party is right and the other is wrong have ignored the fact that, in mediation, being right is a form of being wrong, just as being wrong is a form of being right. Mediators who want to reach a deeper level of truth have to begin by *dangerously* examining their own underlying assumptions about right and wrong, and see how these result in approaches to mediation that reinforce adversarial thinking. Philosopher Humberto Maturana wrote:

> When one puts objectivity in parenthesis, all views, all verses in the multiverse are equally valid. Understanding this, you lose the passion for changing the other.

Alternative Definitions of the Role of Mediator

Each of these polarized philosophical systems corresponds to a different approach to mediation. Accordingly, if people are basically bad, mediators need to be forceful, evaluative, and directive. If people are good, mediators need to be facilitative, nondirective, and conciliatory. If people are basically good but behaving badly, mediators need to be elicitive and transformative. If people are both and neither, but just human, mediators need to be all of the above. We need to transcend notions of good and evil, allow for paradox, affirm the unity of opposites, and identify the real enemy as none other than ourselves.

The evaluative or directive model of mediation regards conflict as something to be ended, the parties as incapable of ending their conflicts by themselves, and the mediator as responsible for directing them toward a settlement that need not come to grips with the underlying, essentially unresolvable issues that gave rise to the conflict in the first place. This model is commonly used in litigation and by attorneys and judges.

The facilitative or conciliatory model of mediation views conflict as something to be overcome, and the parties as capable of doing so through active listening and describing their feelings. The mediator becomes a largely inactive supporter of the process, who empathetically models and facilitates their interactions. It is the parties' responsibility to reach settlements that may or may not address the underlying issues, depending on their interest in addressing them. This model is commonly used in community and public policy disputes, as well as by psychotherapists.

The transformational or elicitive model of mediation, as described by Bush and Folger in *The Promise of Mediation,* views conflict as something to be learned from, and the parties as ready for introspection and fundamental change. The mediator becomes an empathetic yet honest agent, whose role is to elicit recognition and empower the parties to solve their own problems.

In the transformational model, the mediator typically facilitates and does not suggest solutions or direct the parties toward resolution. Yet many parties require assistance in developing options, and no one trapped in a system willingly authorizes their own transformation. Personally, I use a modified version of the transformational model, based on a more intuitive, integrative, dangerous approach to mediation. I neither direct nor stand apart from the conflict, but interact with the parties and reflect on possibilities, based on intuitive assessments at the time.

There are occasions when the parties need honest feedback, external coaching, or recommendations for action, and are unable to move forward on their own. There are times for mediators to be silent, times to be elicitive, and times to be dangerous. While process as well as content decisions should be open to the parties, there is a danger of mediators abdicating to superficiality. Problems arise whenever tactics solidify into strategies. The real difficulty is knowing when, why, and how to use each approach.

In our experience, mediators need to elicit, conciliate, and facilitate, yet also to evaluate and direct parties in seeking resolution or transformation. They need to inquire about deeper underlying issues and relationships. With the tacit permission of the parties, mediators can recommend concrete steps that will break the participants' system. While directive and facilitative styles rarely result in transformation, transformational and *dangerous* styles easily produce settlements.

As mediators, we need to recognize that while people act in ways we call good or bad, these categories have no existence in nature. They are polarities, like up and down, hot and cold, forward and backward, that cannot exist or be thought of without their opposites. Human nature is not fixed or eternal, but changes with culture and conditions. No two parties are alike, no two conflicts are alike, no two mediators are alike, and no one is the same from one moment to the next. What succeeds for one mediator with one party at one moment may fail for another mediator with a different party or at a different moment. What is needed is not proscription, but skill, intuition, flexibility, and the ability to be dangerously honest and empathetic.

Mediation and Neutrality

In directive, facilitative, and transformational models, mediators are frequently described as "neutrals." There are several difficulties with this notion. In the first place, there is no such thing as genuine neutrality when it comes to conflict. Everyone has had conflict experiences that have shifted his or her perceptions, attitudes, and expectations, and it is precisely these experiences that give us the ability to empathize with the experiences of others.

Nor are there any genuine neutrals in courts, workplaces, organizations, and government offices, including judges, CEOs, managers, and human resources representatives, all of whom have biases and points of view, including the bias of wanting to protect the organization from being disrupted by conflict. Judges have the most intractable bias of all: the bias of believing they are without bias.

Even outside observers cannot really be neutral. They inevitably become part of whatever they observe, trivially or fundamentally altering both themselves and what they are observing. When mediators "merely" listen, they may still have a profound, even a *directive* impact on the parties, the conflict, and themselves, ending all possibility of neutrality.

What is most useful to mediators in the concept of neutrality is not its emphasis on formality, perspective, objectivity, logic, or dispassionate judgment, but its concern for fairness and lack of selective bias. Parties most often want mediators to be honest, empathic, and "omnipartial," meaning on both parties' sides at the same time.

The language of neutrality creates an expectation that mediators will act fairly once they erase their own past experiences. But real fairness comes from using the past to gain an open, honest, humble perspective on the present. Worse, neutral language is bland, consistent, predictable, and homogenous; it is used to control what cannot be controlled. When confronted with something unique, or with paradox, contradiction, or enigma, a stance of neutrality makes us incapable even of observing without denying or destroying the very thing being observed, which is often a conflict that is riddled with paradoxes, contradictions, and enigmas.

The idea of neutrality originates in the law, as a result of a superficial similarity between the role of settlement judge and mediator, together with a lack of appreciation for the central differences between them. What is called neutrality or objectivity in the law exists neither in the solitary decision-making power on the part of the judge, nor in the partiality and subjectivity that flow from an adversarial, advocacy-based system.

In mediation, there is no judge, no power to decide in anyone other than the parties, no process other than consensus, and no victory other than a rough equality of loss. Both sides have the right to veto any outcome they perceive as unequal. For this reason, it is not neutrality that is important, but the ability to reach out, use subjectivity, and deepen empathy and honesty between adversaries.

Because conflicts produce distrust, polarization, and passion, people become caught up in their stories. They have no doubt that any fair person will side with them, and that once the mediator does so, it will be impossible to remain neutral. They sometimes see neutrality as a mask for partiality or indifference. Yet it is not actually neutrality they desire, but the *appearance* of neutrality, empathy, and the ability to find the inner connection between both sides' stories.

Because neutrality implies objectivity and distance from the source of the conflict, it cannot countenance empathy or give the mediator room to acknowledge or experience grief, compassion, love, anger, fear, or hope. Neutrality can paralyze emotional honesty, intimate communication, vulnerability, and self-criticism. It can undermine shared responsibility, prevention, creative problem solving, and organizational learning. It can ignore the larger systems in which conflict occurs. It can fail to comprehend spirit, forgiveness, transformation, or healing, which are essential in mediation. As a result, it can become a straitjacket and a check on our ability to unravel the sources of conflict.

It is dangerous to give up the protective cover of neutrality for something uncertain, emotional, unpredictable, and unsettled. Yet, as Ralph Waldo Emerson observed: "Everyone wants to be settled. But only insofar as they are unsettled is there any hope for them."

Chapter Two

Suppression, Settlement, and Resolution

The whole history of the progress of human liberty shows that all concessions yet made to her august claims have been born of earnest struggle. Find out just what people will submit to, and you have found the exact amount of injustice and wrong which will be imposed upon them; and these will continue until they are resisted with either words or blows, or with both. The limits of tyrants are prescribed by the endurance of those whom they oppress.
FREDERICK DOUGLASS

Having proposed ways that mediation might become more successful, we need to examine the reasons it is not. One reason has to do with a habituation to power and oppressive relationships, and a consequent reliance on aggression and suppression, or compromise and settlement, rather than collaboration and resolution.

The Tendency Toward Suppression

We get into trouble as mediators when we try too hard to put an end to conflict. If our objective is to make conflict disappear, we may produce settlements that result in a surrender of important values, a loss of integrity, a continuation of oppression, or a discounting of deeper, underlying issues. The desire for peace is not always a desire for resolution. Sometimes, beneath the surface of a willingness to mediate, there is a desire for suppression, or for the conflict to simply go away. The danger is that the search for res-olution, willingness to negotiate collaboratively, and openness to dialogue, will be seen by brutal, aggressive, manipulative people as signs of weakness, or even surrender.

The opposite is true. Conflict resolution does *not* require relin-quishment of forceful advocacy, principled opposition, or resis-tance. The positive consequences of conflict, including learning, change, better solutions, and improved relationships, only occur when we accept conflict as a teacher. In this way, resolution means seeking transformational results. It does not mean being silent or neutral, but engaged and dangerous.

The Price of Suppression and Settlement

Anthropologist Laura Nader has written a critique of alternative dispute resolution practitioners, arguing that they induce passiv-ity, are willing to "trade justice for harmony," and seek pacification rather than peace. Certainly, there are forms of dispute resolution and individual dispute resolvers who, out of fear of conflict, pur-suit of personal profit and privilege, or lack of sensitivity to the suf-fering of others, are willing to promote peace at any price.

There are two fundamental reasons for wanting to resolve con-flict, leading to two very different methods or approaches to reso-lution. First, we may be frightened of conflict, or expressions of anger and confrontation, and wish to avoid, minimize, or suppress them. Second, we may desire opportunities for growth, learning, resolution, and transformation that open when we engage our ene-mies and communicate, listen, dialogue, solve problems, and nego-tiate our differences.

The first approach seeks to pacify or mollify the opposition without discovering or correcting the underlying reasons for the dispute, and it desires settlement purely for settlement's sake. The second pursues a deeper level of empowerment and under-standing through honest communication about the source of the dispute, allowing the parties to decide how and whether to end it. The first creates temporary settlements; the second lasting resolu-tions. The first leads to sullen acceptance, suppressed anger, revolt, and revolution; the second leads to joint participation, collabora-tion, reconciliation, and closure.

Those who adopt the second approach recognize that princi-pled engagement and value-based opposition are not destructive, futile, or debilitating. They are opposed to unnecessarily hostile, combative, and violent enemy-making, which confuses the person with the problem, substitutes self-righteousness for dialogue, and magnifies hatreds.

Conflict suppression leads to a tolerance of evil and acceptance of injustice, which is itself repressive. The fear of change, conflict, and opposition, of standing up for what is right, of demanding what is needed, of articulating what is believed in, whether in fam-ilies, organizations, or societies, leads to the overthrow of integrity and the destruction of human values.

Conflict settlement, while not actively engaged in suppressing conflict or denying its underlying causes, strives to silence outrage, and enforce—through civility—a perfunctory peace. Settlement is linked with suppression through a self-replicating system. Media-tors who seek settlement rather than resolution ignore the under-lying reasons for the conflict, silence voices entreating to be heard, and plug up the transformational process. Mediators who seek to suppress conflict settle for half-measures, squelch honest ideas and true feelings, and undermine the values that lie at the heart of the process. Settlement is thus a form of suppression, and suppression a form of settlement. Those who promote suppression and settle-ment consider conflict an unnecessary evil.

Nonetheless, the active suppression of conflict is also qualita-tively different from the effort, even out of fear, to settle, and make it go away. Promoting settlement is often a frightened response to suppression in which mediators try to hush conflict up, so the mediators and parties will not be hurt in the fray. In this sense, set-tlement accepts the superior power of suppression and the inferi-ority of the silenced.

Conflict resolution recognizes the inevitability of conflict, and its potential to generate positive outcomes. This requires media-tors to equalize the negotiating power of disputing parties, fully surface underlying concerns, encourage equal ownership of outcomes, negotiate collaboratively, and fix systems rather than people.

Most of the positive changes in our lives are linked to working through conflicts, rather than suppressing or settling them. Every major organizational, social, political, and economic advantage we enjoy, from racial equality to democracy, was won not through avoidance, but engagement in conflict. Dr. Martin Luther King, Jr., accurately pronounced, "Our lives begin to end the day we become silent about things that matter." He reminds us that conflict resolution is part of a larger human endeavor about which we cannot be neutral or silent. Silence spells the death of resolution, relationship, collaboration, and community.

Mahatma Gandhi's creed was not one of nonengagement, but nonviolent *resistance* to oppression. Neither Gandhi, Dr. King, Jane Addams, César Chávez, nor any of the great leaders of nonviolent protest movements advocated capitulation in the face of evil. On the contrary, they saw their methods as ones of active confrontation. Gandhi described the main component of nonviolence as *satyagraha,* or "speaking truth to power." Yet doing so is dangerous.

Rather than coercing, manipulating, conciliating, or abdicating, in dangerous mediation we encourage parties to dig deeper. Rather than trying to fit round pegs into square holes, we value uniqueness, diversity, and the clash of opposites. At the same time, we elicit the unity of these opposites, the wholeness that links their disparate parts. Dangerous mediation thus reflects a "species consciousness" and a "golden rule." It reveals the ground state of our interconnectedness, the central importance of relationships, the humanity of our enemy.

Conciliating Slavery

Consider, for example, the work of antislavery activists before the Civil War who intentionally created conflicts with southern slave society and, through opposition, expanded possibilities for emancipation. To have suppressed or settled these conflicts over slavery in order to win a temporary peace, as many sought to do, would have meant peace *within* the context of slavery; and in effect, continuation of a slavery status quo.

Had it been possible to draw slave owners into open public dialogue *with slaves* over whether slavery ought to continue, the ground would have shifted from suppression and denial of underlying issues, or from settlement by negotiating a kinder form of slavery, to resolution by direct abolition. This approach would have used the conflict to bring about an alteration in the underlying reasons that created it. Dialogue and negotiation lay outside the assumptions of slave culture and society, and were therefore in dangerous opposition to the status quo, which always encourages settlement and suppression.

Pursuing this example, if we were to mediate a dispute between a master and a slave, it would clearly matter whether the slave were permitted to speak—not only for reasons of empathy and formal equality, but because the process of communication *encodes* and recapitulates the content of their relationship. If the slave is not allowed to speak, as was the case in federal proceedings under the Fugitive Slave Act, slavery has succeeded. Whereas if the slave is permitted or invited to speak and given equal time, slavery has already been abolished, or irrevocably impaired.

To fully resolve conflicts over slavery and completely end them, more is required. Slave owners would need to understand why slavery was wrong, apologize for and fully repair the damage they caused, and rediscover how to live humbly and respectfully as equals with their former slaves. Slaves, on the other hand, would need to find empathy for slave owners as people, accept their apologies and reparations, and learn to live without the assumption of oppression. Together, they would need to discover how they were twisted and estranged by the system of slavery and to commit to a protracted process of reconciliation.

I cite slavery as an example because the lessons are so clear. However, there is no qualitative difference between slavery, which we all condemn, and the authoritarian, hierarchical, coercive systems that generate conflicts today in millions of families, workplaces, political speeches, government bureaucracies, and corporations. The issues for mediators are similar.

Mediation as Resolution

Part of the success of mediation lies in the fact that, as a process, it encourages resolution and reconciliation. Simply by agreeing to meet on an equal footing with one's enemies in dialogue, negotiation, or informal problem solving, reconciliation begins. For example, in South Africa, a Truth and Reconciliation Commission under the leadership of Archbishop Desmond Tutu probed political crimes of violence committed during apartheid. An informal pamphlet issued by the Truth and Reconciliation Commission promised profound transformation:

> Instead of revenge, there will be reconciliation.
>
> Instead of forgetfulness, there will be knowledge and acknowledgement.
>
> Instead of rejection, there will be acceptance by a compassionate state.
>
> Instead of violations of human rights, there will be restoration of the moral order and respect for the rule of law.

While full reconciliation did not occur, the commission brought penetrating honesty and public awareness to prior crimes committed by both sides. As perpetrators were confronted by victims with the personal reality of what they did, acknowledging and taking responsibility for their acts, they received genuine forgiveness and reconciliation, and a new contract was forged between them and the new multiracial society. As victims detailed their suffering, they gained a quality of closure and release that only took place once those who caused it directly heard and acknowledged their pain. Through this arduous process, many conflicts were resolved. By addressing everyone's stories, the complex experience of apartheid was confronted, rather than denied or suppressed. In the process, the truth became richer, multifaceted, and human.

Resolution is the translation into practice of truth and reconciliation. Its power comes from recognizing that war and hatred create inhumanity and unhappiness, even for the victors, and that peace without justice is a cause of and a prelude to war. The great problems for peacemakers arise when a greater inhumanity results from settlement than from shouting, from peace than from war.

These dilemmas are, of course, not restricted to conflicts involving slavery or apartheid, but can be found in small-scale conflicts, where the everyday reality of values and ethics reside. Most conflicts have less to do with large-scale issues, or problems of ethics and justice, than with the seemingly infinite sources of human miscommunication and misunderstanding.

The problem for mediators is the same: How do we know, even in petty conflicts, whether we are silencing the disempowered or achieving a temporary peace by suppressing someone's desire for justice? How can we be sure we are not promoting peace to reinforce an unfair status quo or petty tyranny? What do we do when we discover that our efforts at settlement have turned into a form of suppression?

The Danger of Condonation

When we mediate dangerously and encourage parties to act on their values, we run the risk of aggravating conflict or blowing it out of proportion. It is easy for parties to rationalize aggression or inaction by demonizing their opponents, to cast themselves as innocent victims acting on principle, and to mistake simple differences for baseness or evil. Most conflicts are petty, personal, and filled with miscommunications, misunderstandings, and missed opportunities for dialogue between well-meaning individuals who are rarely as horrible as they are made out to be. By demonizing others, they compromise their own humanity and capacity for understanding.

There is also the opposite danger of slipping into avoidance, condonation, capitulation, and cowardice in the face of evil. As Albert Camus wrote eloquently in *Reflections on the Guillotine:*

> I do not believe . . . that there is no responsibility in this world and that we must give way to that modern tendency to absolve everyone, victim and murderer, in the same confusion. Sentimental confusion is made up of cowardice rather than generosity and eventually justifies whatever is worst in this world. If you keep on excusing, you eventually give your blessing to the slave camp, to cowardly force, to organized executions, to the cynicism of the great political monsters; you finally hand over your brothers.

The difference between cowardice and collaboration, condonation and forgiveness, surrender and negotiation, is identical to what distinguishes resolution from suppression. What is common to all accommodating behaviors is that they trade justice for peace and harmony. In the former, peace is the sole value, while in the latter, equal value is placed in fairness, honesty, equity, and getting to the root of the problem. It has often been the case in history that advocacy of peace has masked a hidden agenda of maintaining an oppressive status quo.

It is one thing to silence complaints about slavery or smaller injustices by asking those offended to drop their complaints in the interests of peace. It is quite another to get to the core of these problems and resolve them. Blaming the complainer is like shooting the messenger rather than solving the problem that needs to be eliminated if they are to live together in a respectful, synergistically diverse community.

The Limits of Conciliation and Compromise

The principal techniques employed in conflict settlement are conciliation and compromise. *Conciliation* means calming and placating the person who is most obstinate, emotional, or irrational, by "cleansing" proposals, processes, or ideas of anything that might give offense. Conciliation can be useful, provided the mediator does not encourage or validate unconscionable behavior by rewarding or accommodating to it. Attorneys and powerful parties often use aggressive, bullying behaviors to intimidate people into conciliating and meeting their demands.

It is always tempting for mediators to split the difference as a quick way to settle a dispute, and this is not wrong when the issues are inconsequential. But conflict is often, like fever in disease, symptomatic rather than causal. Compromise and conciliation mask the disease, temporarily relieve the suffering, postpone medicating the problem, and allow it to fester and grow.

Compromise means mutual give and take, which is also useful in mediation. There are two major problems with compromise. The first occurs when mediation becomes indistinguishable from capitulation. The second transpires when parties are asked to compromise over matters of principle, which is like advocating a happy medium between truth and lies, freedom and slavery, peace and war.

Compromise is often advanced as a cure-all, a superficial solution to ills as diverse and deep-seated as those between hostile family members, nations, races, classes, religions, and personalities. While compromise is often beneficial in ending bloodshed or creating a temporary peace, there are times when it is not, when conflict is preferable to compromise and conciliation. Mary Parker Follett, one of the early twentieth-century founders of the field of mediation, argued against the cult of compromise:

> Compromise too is temporary and futile. It usually means merely a postponement of the issue. The truth does not lie 'between' the two sides. We must be ever on our guard against sham reconciliation. Many, unfortunately, still glorify compromise.

> I have just read that the spirit of compromise shows the humble heart. What nonsense. In the first place it doesn't, as you will find if you watch compromise; in the second place that kind of humility, if it existed, would not be worth much. Humility needs to be defined: it is merely never claiming any more than belongs to me in any way whatever; it rests on the ability to see clearly what does belong to me. Thus do we maintain our integrity.

All compromises, however small, signify a balance between ethics and survival, struggle and release, war and peace, meaningful and meaningless, which are always in flux. These difficulties arise when someone who has been sexually harassed decides whether to report it, when someone who has been insulted considers whether to express his feelings, when someone who has been lied to weighs whether to tell the truth.

We need to broaden our definitions of conflict resolution to include ending disputes, *as well as* helping people actively and effectively express them. This means inviting them to open up, expose their underlying rationale, encourage principled opposition, support emotional authenticity, elicit diverse interests, and sustain honest dialogue.

Through these efforts, we can assist less-empowered parties to become more productive, intelligent, and successful in completely ending their conflicts by addressing the underlying reasons that created them. In the long run, we will end disputes quicker with less damage and at lower cost than if we push for compromise, conciliation, and settlement for settlement's sake.

Compromise versus Collaboration

The chief difference between bringing opposing parties, ideas, feelings, or systems together to compromise and bringing them together to collaborate is that compromise routinely produces nontransformational results. It blends opposites without transforming them, as when black and white are merged to produce gray, as opposed to combining them to create a third alternative that is neither, both, and beyond.

Compromise produces results that are intermediate, lukewarm, mediocre, vague, average, and ordinary. Collaboration produces results that are unexpected, synergistic, transformational, unique, creative, and amazing. For every opposite, there are simple and complex forms of combination. Simple combination consists of adding, averaging, or blending two parts until they disappear into one. Complex combination consists of bringing opposites into creative tension, and multiplying or recombining them until they become something new and different.

In a typical conflict over who will perform a task, compromise has one person perform it one day and another the next, while collaboration has them do it together. By collaborating, a social bond is forged that did not exist before. It is something new that could result in an improved relationship. It allows creative solutions to be found. It represents a tangible sharing of burdens, an equality of labor, and a respectful acknowledgment of partnership that cannot be found in compromise.

There is nothing wrong with tactical compromise. For example, compromise is useful when one's goals are not particularly important, when one faces a powerful opponent who is strongly committed to contradictory goals, to achieve a temporary settlement of complex issues, or as a back-up when collaboration has failed. The problems with compromise occur when it is used as a strategy rather than as a tactic, and when it becomes a substitute for principle in the face of oppressive relationships.

This means, paradoxically, that there are times when it is more productive to *increase* the level of conflict. This is especially the case when one side has more power and is unwilling to listen or negotiate. Here, engaging in conflict becomes the only way of bringing the issues to the table, and allowing the underlying conflicts to be resolved fully, fairly, finally, and effectively. This requires a unique combination of honesty and empathy.

Chapter Three

Honesty and Empathy: Speaking the Unspeakable

You've got to be moving toward the heart of the matter, got to burn people's souls. You've got to get inside of people. That's where it all is. And you can't get inside of them unless you open yourself up to be got inside of. Follow what I'm saying? The key to other people's hearts is finding the key to yours. You've got to give to receive, got to open up yourself to get inside somebody else.
JESSE JACKSON

The primary purpose of mediation is to create a controlled "chain reaction," in which the conflict is allowed to explode and implode without damaging the parties. The implosion fuels self-awareness, while the explosion allows them to identify the dysfunctional systems that cause the conflict. The chain reaction starts with deeply honest, empathetic questions that defuse or disarm the parties' defensive mechanisms, allowing truth and positive feelings to reach their target.

In this way, mediation is a way of combining the passion and learning that transpire during warfare with the introspection and listening that take place during peacetime. It links empathy for parties who are suffering with honesty about how they are contributing to it. Transformation and learning require awareness and listening, just as empathy and honesty require each other.

The Marriage of Empathy and Honesty

Honesty without empathy becomes brutal and judgmental, while empathy without honesty turns sentimental and ineffectual. To reach deeper levels of honesty, greater empathy is required to disarm defensiveness and judgement. To build greater empathy, deeper honesty is needed, to keep it from feeling false and make it practical.

Empathy is not readily available to most parties in conflict. By modeling empathy, mediators encourage each side to experience the feelings, thoughts, and inner logic of the other, to walk a while in their shoes and see the world through their experiences. The purpose of empathy is not to excuse destructive behavior, but to separate the person from the problem, disarm judgments, and consider what might lead them to do the same. In this way, empathy helps each side understand and grow into a part of themselves they have ignored or suppressed.

Mediators are often confused about the distinction between empathy and sympathy. Psychiatrist Dr. Norman Paul, in an essay in *Parenthood: Its Psychology and Pathology* carved a clear distinction between empathy and sympathy:

> Empathy is different from sympathy: the two process[es] are, in fact, mutually exclusive. In sympathy, the subject is principally absorbed in his own feelings as they are projected into the object and has little concern for the reality and validity of the object's special experience. Sympathy bypasses real understanding of the other person, and that other is denied his own sense of being. Empathy, on the other hand, presupposes the existence of the object as a separate individual, entitled to his own feelings, ideas, and emotional history. The empathizer makes no judgments about what the other *should* feel, but solicits the expression of whatever he *does* feel and, for brief periods, experiences these experiences as his own. The empathizer oscillates between such subjective involvement and a detached recognition of the shared feelings. The periods of his objective detachment do not seem to the other to be spells of indifference, as they would in sympathy; they are, instead, evidence that the subject respects himself and the object as separate people. Secure in his sense of self and his own emotional boundaries, the empathizer attempts to nurture a similar security in the other.

Dangerous empathy consists of recognizing your enemy as yourself, being vulnerable in the presence of someone you do not trust, recruiting your own best self, taking an appreciative approach to disagreement, and becoming "the best of enemies." The limit of empathy is reached in compassion, when we take on the suffering of others.

The Importance of Being Honest

Mediators have developed a large body of technique for promoting empathy through active listening, but little for encouraging honesty. Many mediators "play it safe," using active listening and process skills to defuse or simply settle conflicts, as opposed to resolving or transforming them. In doing so, they cheat the parties out of opportunities to learn and grow, which only arise when those in conflict confront each other, and reveal their own contributions to the conflict.

Conflict resolution differs from conflict suppression and its less objectionable cousin, conflict settlement, in its use of honesty as a means of focusing, even intensifying the conflict—not as judgment, but as *meaning*. Most honesty is heard as judgment, but that is usually because inadequate attention has been paid to preparing the way with empathy.

While empathy consists of discovering the other within the self, honesty consists of discovering the self within the other. This means seeing conflict as a reminder, not only of opposition, but the unity of all opposites. Practically, it means *owning* the conflict—not by halves, but entirely. Relationships are nourished when both sides become 100-percent responsible for making them work.

When couples divorce, they routinely blame each other for the breakup of their marriage. Real growth and learning, however, are triggered when each person assumes full responsibility for not letting the spark disappear. Through honesty, mediators trigger a process of dialogue and self-improvement that is beneficial regardless of anything the other side chooses or refuses to do.

Agreed, it is difficult to be deeply honest. It is risky. It can backfire, and mediators can lose the empathic connection that encourages deep listening. Yet to settle disputes without ever touching the underlying reasons for them hinders the parties' ability to learn from their conflicts. When self-justifications take the place of self-examination, and a downward spiral of rage and shame blocks real communication, mediation becomes superficial, without risk or opportunity for fundamental change.

Why do people so rarely discuss what is really going on directly, immediately, and honestly with their opponents? Why do they want to be kind more than they want to be honest? Why do lies, secrets, and silence seem less risky and more powerful than honesty, sharing, and communication?

One reason is because aggression, self-protection, and the "fight or flight reflex," are instinctual. Another is because the negative behavior that parties direct at others festers inside, requiring them to either "pass it back or pass it on." Another is that anger makes them simultaneously overly sensitive to the failings of others and insensitive to their own failings. Another is that it is difficult to listen, speak coherently, or reach a common understanding when someone is attacking them or being defensive.

Reasons for Honesty and Empathy in Mediation

To begin with, everyone in conflict has a different perception of what happened, who caused it, and why. Each side tells stories that are accurate and honest—for themselves, as requests for communication, empathy, and authenticity. Both sides also tell stories that are inaccurate and dishonest—for each other, as literal facts, and as requests for surrender or acceptance of blame.

In other words, everyone in conflict views the world from the inside out, and finds empathy and honesty difficult with those they detest or by whom they feel detested. Their willingness to accept responsibility is distorted by their need for sympathy and support, or their desire to make themselves appear right by making others appear wrong.

Everyone in conflict wears a mask that can only be observed from the outside. They respond to attack egocentrically and suffer from silent self-doubt, poor self-esteem, and denial. Their intentions are always honorable, yet at odds with the effects their actions have on others. Their feelings are too important to risk discussing openly, so they repress or externalize their emotions.

Everyone in conflict takes deliberate steps to protect themselves from the truth, because they know the consequences could compel them to leave the comfortable, albeit dysfunctional patterns they have created. They easily forget what it is like *not* to be in conflict, and adjust to living in environments that are rife with dissension.

Yet everyone in conflict can use their distress and suffering to open their doors of perception. They can communicate honestly about what happened, explore what they contributed to the conflict and why, accept responsibility for what they could have done better, and discover within themselves not only their opponents, but deeper, more authentic parts of themselves.

Everyone knows it is dangerous to speak honestly, because doing so means accepting the possibility that the other person will speak honestly in return. Hence, a conspiracy of banality and nonengagement is forged, encouraged by the fear that honesty and passion will not be held in check by either side. What results is an unspoken agreement to speak only superficially, either because of a lack of courage, or lack of skill at controlling the chain reaction honesty could trigger.

As a result, fears are anointed and timidity canonized, all with a few simple rationalizations. People tell themselves that there is no need to be deeply honest. They don't want to hurt the other person's feelings. The other side could misinterpret what they say, and they probably wouldn't be receptive anyway. It could put their relationship at risk. It is possible to reach a settlement without taking risks. It could backfire and the problem could get worse. They will be out on a limb and they won't be supported. It could leave them open to retaliation and counterattack. And nothing is going to change anyway.

It is easy to formulate an opposite set of rationalizations that encourage honesty. Being honest can encourage others to follow suit. It is possible to communicate honestly and not hurt anyone's feelings. If they are accurate there will be less possibility for misinterpretation. The other side won't be receptive unless they try. Their relationship is at risk without honesty. They will create better solutions if they are honest. The problem will get worse if there is no honest communication. If they risk being honest, others may support them. They could be open to retaliation and counterattack if they don't speak honestly. And things only really change when people communicate honestly.

Mediators, acting on these arguments for honesty, will develop skills and techniques to encourage honest, empathetic communication. We will learn how to obtain permission to be deeply honest from the parties; how to confront them in ways that do not increase their defensiveness or animosity; and how to model what we advocate and risk being deeply honest with ourselves.

Encouraging Deep Levels of Honesty

Any truth we seek to elicit from others requires an equal openness to hearing the same truth about ourselves. In our experience, people intuitively apprehend whether mediators are willing to be deeply honest. If they sense we are not, they will interpret our requests for honesty as manipulation or prying. In this way, mediation is less a third party, than a *three-party process,* in which the mediator joins the conflict to model empathic listening, honest questioning, and equanimity in accepting painful answers.

When the mediator remains outside the conflict, little is risked and honesty remains superficial. But when the mediator *enters* the conflict, focusing attention on the underlying issues, creating an empathic connection with both sides and affirming a dangerous honesty, the parties grow more open to hearing painful yet truthful information about themselves.

Increasing the depth and quality of empathy and honesty encourages both sides to accept responsibility for their lives and choices, based not on what the other party says or does, but on their own values and integrity. While integrity requires honesty, honesty does not necessarily require integrity. Integrity means acting consistently with values, even when it runs counter to one's immediate self-interest. While nearly everyone in conflict espouses collaborative values, they nonetheless demonize their opponents and offer excuses for themselves. Mediation reminds them of their integrity, which forces them to abandon defenses against learning and growth, if only to avoid similar problems in the future.

As mediators, we need to begin by giving *ourselves* an honest appraisal. Doing so automatically encourages parties to see mediation as a source of self-discovery. If we model doing so, they will not take critical comments personally, become more willing to reassess their statements and actions, and be less apt to engage in covert or manipulative behavior.

We can encourage growth and learning, deepen dialogue, and increase the possibility of resolution and transformation by asking intensely honest questions and searching for sources and underlying issues. We can seek permission to impart honest feedback, present it as though we were the ones receiving it, support and applaud their willingness to give or receive it, and model how to receive it ourselves. This is done mostly through eye contact, body language, energy, and tone of voice. We also advance honesty between parties when we:

- Listen to, normalize, and acknowledge deeply honest responses.
- Assist parties in taking "baby steps" toward honesty and dialogue.
- Tell the truth and speak the unspeakable.
- Trace anger backwards into self-awareness.
- "Unhook" parties from judgments about each others' personalities, intentions, and motivations.
- Describe the parties' behaviors in nonjudgmental terms.
- Identify specific examples of problem behaviors and ways of correcting them.
- Help to clarify differences between intent and effect.
- Allow each actor to explain their intent or motivation, then probe deeper.
- Share our perception of the effects their behavior might be having on the other party.
- Surface and discuss covert behavior.
- Suggest alternative ways of achieving the parties' true desires.
- Search for forms of honest expression that allow them to save face.
- Look for ways of reconnecting and reintegrating them after honest communication.

Overcoming the Fear of Honesty

We have seen many parties refuse to resolve conflicts when workable solutions were presented, so they could continue to describe themselves as victims, hide behind hateful judgments about each other, or hang on to defensive or aggressive postures. In these situations, honest communication and complete resolution meant abandoning some crucial element of how they defined themselves. This possibility was simply too frightening to consider.

There are obvious dangers in advocating deeper honesty to mediators who are not themselves open to emotional understanding, or who are not experienced in the sensitive, empathetic art of intimate, painful conversation. Taking risks with honesty is not easy and should not be done casually, clumsily, or without being willing to work completely through the issues. For this reason, only small risks should be taken at the beginning, and only after a long, deep look inside.

Every technique in mediation can be more or less hard-hitting, and the best way of softening honesty is by blending it with empathy or self-interest. I mediated a dispute in which I asked each side to agree to a cease-fire for one week until we could meet again. One of the parties said, "I wouldn't give them the satisfaction." I responded by saying, "I'm not asking you to do it for them. I'm asking you to do it for you." Her response was: "Oh. Okay then." All I did was reframe the request as an effort to support the self-interest of the listener, and it became a way of releasing her from her fear of humiliation or defeat. Virtually every communication can be handled in a similar way.

Drop the Pose and Cut the Act

Most people in conflict strike a variety of poses or "acts." These melodramatic affectations are highly effective in capturing other people's attention. None, however, describe who they really are, or allow others to see them as multifaceted, complex individuals. In this way, each pose keeps them locked in conflict. Mediating dangerously means helping them drop the pose and cut the act.

The ultimate problem with any pose is that it takes on a life of its own, and prevents parties from resolving their disputes. Oscar Wilde wrote:

> A man whose desire is to be something separate from himself,
> to be a Member of Parliament, or a successful grocer, or a
> prominent solicitor, or a judge, or something equally tedious,

invariably succeeds in being what he wants to be. That is his
punishment. Those who want a mask have to wear it.

Wearing a mask or striking a pose transforms the person
assuming it, and calls forth a sympathetic response from others
that reinforces and locks it in place. The dramatic intensity of listening sparked by the pose provides the actor with attention, a
rush of adrenaline, and a clear identity that may otherwise be
absent from his life. The audience is mesmerized, welcomes the
show, and *wants* it to be true.

In conflict, these poses dance and play off one another. For
each pose, there is an equal, opposite one that is called into existence as a partner. Together, they form a *system,* a whole that is
greater than the sum of its parts. In addition, within each conflict
pose and its supporting story, we can identify an accusation, a confession, and a request.

For example, a common pose in conflict is that of the victim,
or "Innocent Sufferer." This affectation, designed to elicit sympathy from an audience, allows the player to wallow in self-pity, and
to be released from responsibility for solving the problem that produced their pain. Yet it is possible to interpret their pose either as
an accusation of cruelty, a confession of vulnerability and poor self-
esteem, or a request for respect, acknowledgment, and empathy.
While the first results in defensiveness, the second triggers empathy, and the third transforms the relationship by eliminating the
need for the pose and supporting story.

For every pose there is a counterpose that binds them in conflict. The counterpose to the victim is the aggressor, or "Righteous
Enforcer." These poses mutually reinforce each other, spiraling
into a kind of sadomasochistic dance. Some common conflict poses
include the "Poor Innocent Victim Who Did Nothing Wrong," the
"Indignant Avenger of Wrongs," the "Screw-up Who Can't Do Anything Right," and the "Perfect Person Who Never Does Anything
Wrong."

Each pose is less a statement than a concealment, keeping the
actors' authenticity, vulnerability, desire, and pain well hidden. People strike conflict poses to achieve three primary purposes. The
first is external, to gain attention, sympathy, and support by asking
the listener to interpret it as though it were a fairy tale, a dramatic

conflict between good and evil, and to reward the hero and punish the villain.

The second is internal, to disguise the *opposite* of the pose, which is what the actor really feels. Poses are masks that cloak and camouflage what the actor perceives as ugly. For this reason, the details of their design reveal what they are meant to cover up, allowing mediators to move from the mask to the confession, then to the request, need, interest, or desire. For example, anyone who poses as self-confident *only* does so because they do not feel it internally. Knowing this, we can probe deeper to discover the sources of self-doubt within.

The third purpose, hidden even from the actor, is to lead a caring listener to search for their authentic self, to ask questions that allow the actor to strip off the mask, drop the pose, cut out the act, and reveal who they really are. The hidden request behind every mask, the secret pleasure they stimulate in audience and actor, their tease and sport, is the desire to disrobe, and see or reveal what lies beneath.

Yet probing beneath conflict masks is dangerous, because those who put them on fear taking them off. Poses are struck and masks are donned because people find it difficult to be authentic. For most people in conflict, their masks reflect a fear that they will be judged and found wanting. Their true desire is for others to see what lies beneath, and find it beautiful.

Often beneath one mask or pose lies another, entreating us to probe even deeper. Under the pose of the victim, for example, one finds uncommunicated or unacknowledged pain. Beneath that lies another, less identifiable guise, which is that of the speaker's unrecognized best intentions. These subtler masks and poses are designed to conceal a deep sense of shame, guilt, or fragile self-esteem, hiding actions that lack integrity.

In other words, the more righteous the pose and more angry the mask, the more likely it is that the actor feels bad about himself and what he did. His masks simply express his desire to conform to an ideal of who he should or ought to be, together with a sense of shame about not being it, and about having to use masks to hide who he naturally is.

From Intention to Effect

In this way, people's poses can be read as *requests* to communicate deeper and be perceived as having honorable intentions. Yet the noble intentions of people in conflict are usually contradicted, undermined, and distorted by what they actually do and say to their opponents, who see their poses as indications of insincerity, insensitivity, defensiveness, or lying, yet who respond with equally inaccurate poses. The more adversarial the conflict, the more people adopt contradictory poses that, when added up, equal zero.

The intentions people have are usually quite different from the effects of their behaviors on their opponents. For example, we often hear people say: "That's not what I meant," or "I didn't intend . . . ." Their opponents meanwhile disregard intent and focus on the effect the other person's statements or behavior had on them.

While everyone in conflict wants others to acknowledge their virtuous, blameless intentions, their opponents experience only insensitivity, disrespect, pain, and untrustworthiness. Each pose they adopt represents a new failure to recognize the truth of what they have done, an unwillingness or inability to acknowledge the negative effects their behaviors had on others, regardless of their good intentions.

As long as parties hold on to their poses, whether of injured virtue, anger, or self-righteousness, honest communication will be blocked and conflicts left unresolved. The mediators' role is to assist parties in dropping their poses, communicating honestly and empathetically, and taking responsibility—not only for their intentions, but their words, actions, and effects they have on others, regardless of intention.

People who adopt poses need to be helped to find language to apologize for the pain they cause, without adopting an equally self-defeating pose of being a "Bad Person." Yet, as the brilliant philosopher Ludwig Wittgenstein found, what can be expressed *through* language cannot be expressed *by* language. Only an honest, authentic, balanced *intention,* together with open communication, will allow them to drop these poses, see themselves clearly, and be seen for who they are.

As parties experience their opponents using empathy and honesty and taking responsibility for their actions, they drop their poses and listen to who the other person is, often for the first time. They behave virtuously without posing as the "Personification of Virtue," and become more authentic themselves. How else can we explain the fact that when parties resolve their conflicts, the one described as "Evil Incarnate" is somehow transformed into a living, breathing human being?

The Authenticity of Deeply Honest Questions

People who adopt poses and masks are lost not only to others, but to themselves as well. They can only emerge from these false identities by honestly accepting the truth of who they are, without judgments or blame, and open themselves to authentic, deeply honest levels of communication. A broad set of poses and masks are readily available through professional titles, organizational hierarchies, and corporate identities. It is common for people to pose as managers, or irresponsible employees, or mediators. These poses distance us from honesty and authenticity.

As an illustration, I worked with a team manager (A) who yelled frequently, issuing loud, angry commands, causing others around him to behave like harassed employees. One day, one of his subordinates (B) yelled back in front of other team members: "Stop being such a bully." The manager initially responded by denying he was being a bully, then by counterattacking and accusing the person who shouted at him of making irresponsible statements and being insubordinate.

If you mediated this conflict, what deeply honest, *dangerous* questions might you ask? An easy response would be to ask B to reframe the comment so A does not feel labeled or personally attacked, as in: "I feel intimidated when you yell at me." This shifts the focus of the communication from being about A to being about B. It specifically identifies what B can do to solve the problem without feeling judged by A. You might also encourage A to react nondefensively to B's response, as in: "Are you saying you feel intimidated when I yell at you?" When you ask this question, A refocuses the conversation on what B experienced, rather than judging or labeling A or A's intentions.

It is extremely difficult, if you are A or B and have just been labeled a bully or felt bullied, not to respond angrily or defensively. On the other hand, if you ask questions to discover the effect your behavior is having on others, you may be able to hear their response differently, reduce their need to use insults as a way of getting attention, and improve the effectiveness of your communication and relationship with them.

Here are some additional questions you might consider asking. They reveal progressively deeper and more honest interventions, so they need to be approached gently, with empathy, making sure each question is asked as though you were the one being asked to answer it. By modeling asking these questions, the parties are encouraged to ask them of each other.

Before asking these questions, create a safe environment that accepts all answers, including "I don't know" or "I don't want to say," without judgment. You might begin by asking permission to pose some questions that might be difficult to answer. You will then have their consent to start the process and can continue moving to deeper levels of honesty until you encounter resistance.

- "What specifically did A do that you consider to be bullying?" "What made that feel like bullying to you?"
- "What did it feel like to be bullied by A?" "Did you feel ashamed, insulted, angry, or humiliated?" "Say more about how you felt."
- "What would you have liked A to have done instead?" "How could A have made the same point, but in a way that would not have been experienced by you as bullying?"
- "Has this ever happened to you before?" "How many times?" "Why have you allowed yourself to be bullied?"
- "Can you think of anything you did that encouraged A to engage in what you call 'bullying'?" "What could you do in the future that might encourage A to act differently?"
- "What do both of you think are some of the reasons people bully others?" "What are some of the rationalizations people offer for allowing themselves to be intimidated?"
- "What do you think A wants to *get* through what you call bullying?" "If you talk about those issues, do you think A will still feel a need to push so hard for what he wants?"
- "Why did you yell at B?" "Why didn't you just ask politely?"
- "Can you understand why A felt intimidated or bullied by what you did?" "Why do you think B felt afraid of or intimidated by you?" "With hindsight, how could you have handled it better?"

- "Would you be willing to try that approach right now and see if it works?"
- "Was there anything you did that encouraged B to think it was acceptable to yell back at you?"
- "Did B do anything that led you to feel that he consented to or accepted your behavior?"
- "Was there anyone who was a bully or was bullied in the neighborhood or school where either of you grew up, or in your family of origin?" "How did you respond to it then?" "Would you respond the same way to it now?" "Why?" "Why not?"
- "Can you both agree that you can have a better relationship if you do not engage in or accept bullying behavior?" "What are some of the ways your relationship could improve if you moved away from these behaviors?"
- "Can you agree as a ground rule for your communication or relationship in the future that neither of you will act in a way that leaves the other person feeling intimidated?" "Can you also agree that it is OK to refuse to accept bullying behaviors, and to say so?"
- "Can you agree that you will both listen to what the other person is saying and not engage in or accept bullying behavior?" "Will you let each other know in the future if you feel intimidated?" "How would you like each other to do that?" "Would you like to try that out right now and see how it works?"
- "Did this conversation you just had work better than the one that brought you here?" "What made it work better?" "What have you learned from this conversation?" "What are you going to do differently as a result?"

Similar questions can be asked in any conflict, whether the issue is bullying or any other behavior. You should not use questions to force your views on the parties, but to get closer to the center of the conflict and seek the answers that could lead to resolution and transformation. If you are simply curious without having an axe to grind, the parties will be less offended as you probe deeper.

Designing Dangerous Questions

Deeply honest and empathetic questions clarify each side's interests and desires, challenge their poses and assumptions, and increase their capacity for listening. With deeply honest questions, you can help them reframe their communications and reveal the elements in their conflict stories that rely on demonization or victimization, or result in defensive, aggressive, or passive poses. As they reframe each other's concerns, you can raise or lower the emotional temperature of the conflict, and open a door to deeper, more honest, and empathetic communication. You can ask questions that defuse demonization, for example: "What did he do that you disliked?" "What would you like him to have done?" "What would you like him to do now?" "How should he start?" "What should he say?" "How would you respond if he did?"

High-risk questions often appear as follow-ups to ambiguous or somewhat vulnerable answers that reveal how to move the interaction to a deeper level. For example: "What price have you paid for that behavior?" "What were you afraid would happen if you did or didn't do that?" "What would it take for you to give up that behavior?" "Why do you feel that way?" "How is this conversation working right now?" These types of questions all deepen the dialogue.

As you intervene, try to sense your own bias or need to hear a particular answer. The object of each question is to lead people to their *own* answers, not the answers you want them to reach, or preordain. To succeed, you need to let go of your own masks and poses, expectations and ideals, the answers you would give, and the ones you know are right.

There is a danger in asking rhetorical questions that manipulate people into accepting the mediator's point of view. Your object should simply be to encourage the parties to discover, without blame or shame, their own honest answers, to reveal their authenticity to you and each other. The best way to encourage them is to model the behavior you seek. Invite them to ask you some deeply honest questions, and answer them with as much integrity, authenticity, and commitment as you can. If you set the tone by responding at a deeply authentic level, the chances are good that they will answer in kind.

From a place of anger or blame, it is difficult to stimulate anything but counterattack or defensiveness. But from a place of openness and authenticity, vulnerability and honesty, empathy and introspection, it is possible to discover a different perception, gain a clearer sense of the other person, learn, and find common ground. I leave it to you to decide which is more dangerous: vulnerability or masks, authenticity or poses, honesty or triviality, empathy or distance. The answer will depend on your willingness to explore the conflicts within yourself.

Chapter Four

When Helping Becomes a Hindrance

If one more person had tried to help me, I would have committed suicide.
MEMBER OF ALCOHOLICS ANONYMOUS

Tolstoy wrote that everyone thinks of changing the world, but no one thinks of changing himself. Many mediators are drawn to conflict resolution because of its potential to change *other* people, but they fail to perceive that unless they change themselves, the very help they offer may limit or confine the people they are trying to support.

Helping, including mediation, is considered the opposite of selfishness, and a high moral value. Yet there is a point where helping turns into its opposite, and becomes what Freud labeled "counterfeit nurturance," and D. H. Lawrence referred to as "the greed of giving." This is where mediation turns dangerous for the mediator, because it requires a deep level of honesty about the reasons for helping others.

The opposite of helping is hindering, and, as with all opposites, it becomes difficult in the gray areas to discern which is which. Helping and hindering are both efforts that are directed *at* another person. Both are inducements to action or inaction on their behalf. Both are expressions of concern and need. Both occur when there is some action on the part of the helper, together with some absence of action on the part of the helped.

And each can suddenly become the other, turning helping into hindering through a small shift in either party's intention.

In helping, which comes from the outside, there is nearly always an element of egocentrism or cultural bias. An African proverb states: "'Let me help you or you will drown,' said the monkey, placing the fish safely up in a tree," revealing that helping takes place within the cultural context and assumptions of the helper, rather than the helped. The helpers' unexamined subjective needs and single-minded myopia can result in the opposite of what the person being helped needs or wants.

Who is the Helper, Who the Helped?

Some of the reasons people become mediators have to do with their own hidden needs. There are secret desires in many helpers:

- To be helped themselves in ways they never were, or by parents who never did.
- To find in other people's distress ways of satisfying their own needs for gratitude or assistance.
- To feel powerful or successful, or to mend their own poor self-esteem.
- To find companionship, but one that depends on failure, since, with success, the helped are enabled to succeed by themselves.

Helping becomes hindering through a kind of *moral imperialism* or coercive good will, in which the helped become objects to be manipulated to satisfy the suppressed needs of the helper. Erich Fromm wrote in *The Art of Loving* that our deepest need is to overcome our separateness, to leave "the prison of our aloneness." And South African novelist Nadine Gordimer wrote, "The true definition of loneliness is to live without social responsibility." Helping and hindering are both attempts at social responsibility. They are both ways of being together in the presence of adversity. While helping tries to end the problem, hindering covertly works to keep it alive.

Helping becomes hindering, in conflict resolution as in other professions, through an *arrogance of giving*, when helpers do not acknowledge their own need to help. As a result, they find themselves superior to those they are helping. More often, they disguise their inner sense of superiority by assuming a mask or pose of humility, generosity, even inferiority. Yet beneath false humility and calculated self-deprecation lies a well-concealed arrogance that appears whenever the helped develop a will of their own.

Helping becomes hindering through *official giving* and through the mechanical application of ethical principles, which is the same as their substantive denial. This happens whenever helping is dishonest, manipulative, or bureaucratic; when it lacks empathy and integrity; when it is one-sided and asks nothing in return; when it asks something in return for which it has no right to ask; when it is clouded in mystery; and when all the mystery has been taken out of it. Nearly everything that happens to welfare recipients fits into this category.

The danger of hindering, both in mediation and in law, is that it protects people in conflict from the idea that they might be able to resolve their disputes themselves. This is done by *negative nurturing*, which arises when people become frightened that positive nurturing will not be possible. Pity then suffices, because it is assumed that respect will not be given freely. At bottom, the hindered find themselves wanting, and feel they do not deserve to be helped. The flip side of pity is contempt.

Mediators need to watch themselves carefully to avoid slipping into negative forms of nurturing, particularly in cases where one party has adopted the pose of victim, labeling the other a perpetrator. Most people who choose the role of victim believe they will be supported only as long as they are in pain, unhealed, and oppressed by someone evil. Their persecutor, meanwhile, is generally some other oppressed person playing the role of victim to some other would-be rescuer. The rescuer gets to be the nurse or hero only so long as someone else is the injured or victim.

When this happens, the helper, rescuer, or mediator becomes part of the victim's self-replicating system, fueling a self-fulfilling prophecy in which each person plays a role in allowing the persecution to continue. For this reason, genuine helping requires that each participant in the system question their role in it, and cultivate autonomy and collaborative partnership.

Hindering is distinguished from helping partly by the way it is carried out. Hindering is usually accomplished either as an *imposition,* in which all fundamental decisions are made by the "helper" from outside; or as a *manipulation,* in which all decisions made by the "helper" are assumed to be those of the helped, as though their interests were identical.

Collaborative Partnerships

Partnership, on the other hand, is a collaboration between equal, independent people, one of whom is engaged in giving while the other is receiving. In partnerships, the autonomous contributions of both parties form the basis for an alliance, and are openly acknowledged, allowing them to negotiate collaboratively to resolve their conflicts.

Collaborative partnerships require relationships that are transparent and elastic. Both sides need to be sensitive, skillful in managing the relationship, and committed to honest, responsive, and empathic communication, ethics and values, and the integrity to act on them. The goal of all partnering relationships is to build the capacity of those receiving assistance to help themselves.

Helping and hindering are relational systems that require each side to play its' part. When one side refuses to participate in unilateral helping, it becomes far more difficult for the other to remain passive, dependent, and irresponsible. In this way, mediators can alter the dynamics in conflict systems by being willing to intuitively, collaboratively, and *dangerously* examine themselves and the assumptions they bring to the process, while building the capacity and independence of those they wish to support.

An advanced declaration of human rights might articulate the right of people being helped to choice, transformation, and self-discovery:

- The right to see, hear, and become aware of what is really happening around and inside us.
- The right to own all the consequences of our actions and failures to act.
- The right to take risks, tell the truth, play, feel passionately, and act on our convictions.

- The right to ask for exactly what we want.
- The right to change, let go, and move on.
- The right to accept and be accepted for who we really are.

The self-discovery required in dangerous mediation, fortunately, is also encouraged by it. The practice of listening actively, empathetically, and responsively to others automatically increases our skill and motivation to listen to our inner voices. Just as there is no end to our need to understand the dynamics of conflict in others, there is no end to our need to bring honesty and empathy, clarity and compassion, precision and kindness, awareness and equanimity into our own inner lives. The more honest and empathetic we are with ourselves, the more we are able to display these qualities—not on demand, but as an integral part of who we are. Character, someone remarked, is what we do when no one is looking.

As we do these things, we become more authentic. This allows us to mediate from the heart, and exercise a deep level of empathy and honesty without appearing unprofessional. It allows us to partner without hindering, build positive self-esteem in ourselves and others, and address the dangerous issues that arise in connection with fear, apathy, insanity, and dishonesty.

Chapter Five

Exploring the Conflicts Within Ourselves

It doesn't interest me if there is one God
or many gods.
I want to know if you belong or feel
abandoned.
If you can know despair or can see it in others.
I want to know
if you are prepared to live in the world
with its harsh need
to change you. If you can look back
with firm eyes
saying this is where I stand. I want to know
if you know
how to melt into that fierce heat of living
falling toward
the center of your longing. I want to know
if you are willing
to live, day by day, with the consequences of love
and the bitter
unwanted passion of your sure defeat. . . .
DAVID WHYTE

Because dangerous mediation is more difficult to learn and demanding to practice, it asks more of the mediator. The danger in David Whyte's questions is their recognition of our common humanity, and that whatever we cannot face in ourselves, we will have difficulty facing in others. Yet many mediators are reluctant to risk being deeply honest and empathetic. Why are we so willing to settle for superficial conversation when meaningful, heartfelt dialogue lies just beneath the surface? One reason is because we rarely receive permission to address underlying issues until the problems have become so serious there is little left to preserve. Even then, the parties want it over, and are rarely willing to examine the reasons they kept it going.

A more subtle yet powerful reason is that people will not explore deeper issues in their conflicts or take off their masks if their mediators are unwilling to do the same. Nor will we be able to think of the right questions to ask, or recognize underlying truths when they appear, if we have not been willing to ask the same questions and accept the same truths about ourselves.

It is difficult to see anything clearly until we see ourselves, until we see *who* it is that is seeing. But seeing the one who is seeing is like holding two mirrors together, creating a feedback loop, an infinite regress without any visible center. For this reason, we need not only insight, but perspective as well. We need not only intuition, but outside feedback that allows us to see ourselves and our actions more accurately. Since there is no such thing as neutral feedback, unless we regularly videotape ourselves, every perspective will emanate from someone who also needs to develop insight, who also requires feedback. While our capacity for honest, accurate insight and feedback are therefore limited, both are essential in moving conflicts beyond settlement to resolution, beyond resolution to personal and organizational transformation, and beyond transformation to transcendence.

Listening to the One Who is Listening

Our most profound and lasting ideas regarding conflict were forged in our families of origin. These painful lessons taught by parents were refined in early relationships with siblings, cousins, childhood friends, and teachers. Unfortunately, few of us experience family conflicts as positive examples of resolution, transformation, or transcendence.

The raw emotions and rough tensions that emerge during mediation call on us to be centered in our emotional experiences. We have a responsibility to search for completion of our family conflicts, so as to assist the parties in being centered and completing theirs. Childhood traumas such as incomplete grieving over the loss of family members, unresolved pain from incest or abuse, fears resulting from dangerous incidents, or anger over divorce and unfilled needs can easily prevent mediators from exploring similar conflicts in the parties.

Everyone experiences at least three primary forms of conflict in early childhood. These include conflicts with parents, in which we learn how to respond to superior power and authority; conflicts with siblings and peers, in which we learn how to respond to competition and differences; and conflicts within ourselves, in which we learn how to manage our inner lives.

In parental conflicts, we seek to satisfy our needs and desires, yet often receive more or less than what we need or want. The following table (5.1), based on work by psychologist Ruthellen Josellson, lists some of the needs we commonly have as children and continue to have in our adult lives. Next to these needs are examples of feelings we experience when the response to our

Table 5.1. Getting Too Much and Too Little

Example of Need	Insufficient	Excessive
love	neediness	distancing
holding	falling	suffocation
attachment	loss	clingy, dependent
gratification	deprivation	satiation
validation	rejection	egotism
support	distrust	gullibility
idealization	disillusionment	worship
passion	numbness	obsession
identification	alienation	loss of self
resonance	dissonance	duplication
belonging	disconnection	conformity
self-awareness	withdrawal	narcissism
caring	indifference	compulsivity
mutuality	loneliness	merger
teamwork	isolation	loss of individuality

needs is insufficient and we do not get enough of what we want. In the last column are feelings we experience when the response is excessive and we get more than we need.

How many of these needs and feelings are you carrying with you? How do you typically respond to people in mediation whose childhood needs and feelings were opposite to yours? How do you respond to people whose responses were similar? What do you need to do to let go of the past and take responsibility for expressing and satisfying your own needs and desires?

Every mediator sooner or later encounters a party whose problems reflect her own incomplete issues from the past, issues that require resolution in order for her to feel whole, either in work or personal life. These moments are *gifts* that provide unique opportunities to learn, grow, and resolve issues from the past. Just as we encourage parties in mediation to use their conflicts as openings for transformation, mediators need to pursue their own transformations through completion of the past.

Poor Self-Esteem

Resolution of one's own issues often requires grappling with self-confidence, self-image, and self-esteem. Everyone suffers from poor self-esteem at various moments in their lives. But when mediators lack self-confidence, it becomes far more difficult to assist parties who suffer from similar feelings. We cannot recognize a problem in others when we are blind to it in ourselves.

Being in conflict *automatically* lowers people's self-esteem, partly because they are bound in relationship with someone they do not like, or who does not like them; and partly because no one behaves very well when they are in conflict. Nearly everyone gets angry, treats others disrespectfully, and feels guilty or ashamed of what they felt, thought, said, or did to each other.

Parties who secretly feel ashamed of themselves are prone to find fault with others, as well as with the mediation process. They often complain that the mediator did not stand up for them or argue strongly enough for what they wanted. They transform their own inability to speak out into someone else's fault, even when they did not say a word themselves, and actively agreed to what was suggested. As a result, they often feel disinclined afterwards to honor the agreements they reached, or disparage the mediator and sabotage the process.

I was once asked to assist a team in conflict. At the center was a young woman, Marcia, who had a physical disability. With the assistance of special equipment, she could participate in team meetings, but felt a lack of acceptance from other members of the team. She had extremely poor self-esteem, starting with names she had been called as a child because of her disability, and was still trying to gain acceptance and attention from the "other kids."

In private conversation, she told my comediator and I that she felt useless, that her only way of earning attention or respect was disagreeing with fellow team members and blocking their meetings. She felt trapped in a pattern of forcing the team to talk about her issues and include her in their agenda. The team leader, who might have understood this and played the role of mediator, had her own self-esteem issues and was unable to help.

Marcia bounced back and forth between placating and blaming. Her hidden assumptions were that they were at fault or she was no good. We met with her and the team, and asked her to share her feelings. We asked dangerous questions about her feelings of self-esteem growing out of her disability, including: "How does your disability affect the way you feel about yourself?" She had a hard time answering, but responded with a deep level of vulnerability and honesty. Other team members experienced a profound empathy with her and adopted a similar level of truth-telling.

One team member said: "I hate to say this to you, Marcia, but I don't trust you because you're always hiding behind your disability." Her willingness to be honest and Marcia's willingness to be vulnerable created a breakthrough. Marcia cried and talked about her history of feeling rejected, and described her decision to reject them before they could reject her. The team members apologized for not reaching out to her and made supportive comments about what she had contributed to the team.

The team leader admitted her unresolved self-esteem issues had aggravated the conflict, and she apologized to the group for her lack of leadership. They had the same issues, but chose different ways of manifesting them. Later, they elected Marcia to represent them on a coordinating body of all the teams in the organization. Marcia's self and worth soared and she became less abrasive and more productive, and the conflicts on the team evolved to a higher level.

A word of caution. The flip side of poor self-esteem for mediators is wanting to be the hero, rescuer, or helper, who needs to do the right thing always, everywhere, and for everyone. This ideal, egoistic image of the self is equally destructive, partly because it is a mask, cover, and restraint for less than ideal feelings. As novelist D. H. Lawrence observed in himself:

> The ideal self! Oh, but I have a strange and fugitive self shut out and howling like a wolf or a coyote under the ideal windows. See the red eyes? This is the self which is coming into his own.

Positive self-esteem means allowing our "strange and fugitive selves" to live and flourish alongside our ideal selves, until they merge and lose meaning. Self-esteem is grounded in authenticity, knowing who we really are, not suppressing parts of ourselves, and fully expressing our innermost natures.

Questions for People With Poor Self-Esteem

It is difficult to convince people with poor self-esteem of their innate self-worth. Sometimes this is because the mediator has never faced or resolved his own self-esteem issues. Sometimes it is because what needs to be said could be perceived as the mediator taking sides. Sometimes it is because it feels like surrendering to one's opponent.

For those who suffer from low self-esteem or are in conflict with someone who acts out of a sense of shame or doubt, mediators can simply become curious. Nonjudgmental inquiry allows people to reveal themselves without shame, and become confident of their own inner qualities. Asking dangerous questions can alter the way people think about themselves and can shift their feelings from shame and doubt to authenticity and pride. Most of these questions are rhetorical and some are hard-hitting, so make sure you have permission before asking them.

- What is it specifically you don't like about yourself?
- By what standard are you measuring yourself?
- Who set or created that standard? Why did they create it?

- Who lives up to that standard? What price do they pay for doing so?
- Who in your family planted the idea that you were inadequate? Who planted it in them?
- What benefits do you get from poor self-esteem? Can you get these benefits any other way?
- What price are you paying for poor self-esteem? What price have others paid?
- What might you learn from the parts of yourself you see as deficient?
- For each of your defects, what is a corresponding strength?
- For each of the strengths you admire in others, what is a corresponding defect?
- Who do you think cares whether you think badly about yourself? Why do they care? Is it because of who you are, or because of their own insecurities? Why do you care?
- What would happen if you felt good about yourself? What would you gain or lose? What would others gain or lose?
- How much of your life are you prepared to waste feeling badly about yourself?

The Pose of Professionalism

When self-esteem suffers, people overcompensate and give an appearance of self-assurance, arrogance, or professionalism. When mediators adopt a pose of professionalism in order to make themselves appear superior to the parties, they are not being authentic or honest. They appear false, untrustworthy, or unfeeling to others, act like officials, and behave as though they are following a script. It is almost as though they are not really present at all, or responsible for their actions or relationships with others.

The "Professional Mediator" requires parties to follow the process logically, in a step-by-step fashion. This gives an appearance that there is "no one home," or that the mediator is unwilling to truly listening to what the parties need to say. There is a positive aspect to acting professionally, in the sense of knowing technique and applying it skillfully. The negative aspect is that mediators may distance themselves from others because they cannot allow themselves to be vulnerable.

As mediators, it is possible to be touched deeply without losing professional competency. We can be moved, stimulated, and affected by people, by their anger and angst, shame and betrayal, and at the same time work skillfully to resolve their conflicts. We can be in touch at every moment with our authenticity, emotions, and inner sense of honesty and empathy, and still mediate professionally.

Professionalism describes itself as neutral, suggesting distance from the parties and suppression of subjectivity. Yet to resolve disputes, we need to bridge subjective distance, acknowledge and affirm our subjectivity, become aware of and drop our poses, and mediate as though the conflict were ours.

Professionalism historically proceeds through a number of stages, starting with the discovery of useful techniques, creative development, and systematization of skills. Next come professional self-consciousness, the search for legitimacy, and the beginning of territoriality and proprietary behaviors. This is followed by a codification of rules and ethics, escalation of fees, formalization by attorneys, legislators, and judges, and formal certification. Finally comes dismissal of the impecunious, grandfathering of the unqualified, marginalization of the unorthodox, and promotion of the mediocre.

While these problems are not widespread in mediation today, they are tendencies to be watched. Many mediators in corporate and litigation settings, for example, are expected by their clients to behave neutrally, mediate safely, and avoid probing beneath the surface of masks or poses. These expectations are a common response to fear of conflict. This automatic, idealized, inauthentic behavior, and sterile, bureaucratic professionalism are described by psychologist Erich Fromm:

> Today we come across an individual who behaves like an automaton, who does not know or understand himself, and the only person that he knows is the person that he is supposed to be, whose meaningless chatter has replaced communicative speech, whose synthetic smile has replaced genuine laughter, and whose sense of dull despair has taken the place of genuine pain.

Maintaining our access to internal emotional, subjective truths revitalizes us and allows us to keep our focus and energy alive for the parties. For the most part we do this through empathy, placing ourselves in both parties' shoes, by asking and answering deeply honest, *dangerous* questions about ourselves, which can be extended to the expectations we bring to mediation itself.

Evaluating Expectations

It is invaluable to periodically evaluate our expectations and observe how they mold our realities. These evaluations can be used to dangerously reveal the mediators' or the parties' expectations regarding the process. For example, *before* beginning a session, consider asking the parties the following questions, and to rate their expectations regarding their own participation on a scale of 1 to 10, 10 being highest:

- How valuable a mediation do you plan to have today?
- How participative and engaged do you plan to be?
- How much risk do you plan to take?
- How open, honest, and constructive do you plan to be?
- How willing are you to listen nondefensively and nonjudgmentally?
- How willing are you to accept critical feedback about what you have contributed to the conflict?
- How willing are you to feel empathy or compassion for the other side?
- How responsible do you feel for finding solutions that work for the other side?
- How committed are you to actually implementing whatever you decide today?
- How willing are you to let go of the conflict and improve your relationship with the other side?

After each person answers these questions, ask them to reveal their ratings, and explain why they assigned the scores they did. With some modification, the same questions can be asked of mediators, to assess their expectations regarding their own performance. As with any dangerous technique, it is important to use it cautiously and only when appropriate. The purpose is to reveal hidden expectations that can undermine the process and increase self-awareness. This becomes especially important when we mediate conflicts that involve deep levels of fear, apathy, insanity, and dishonesty.

Chapter Six

Mediating Fear, Apathy, Insanity, and Dishonesty

*We will convince them that they can never be free because
they are weak, vicious, worthless and rebellious . . . In the
end they will lay their freedom at our feet and say we don't
mind being your slaves as long as you feed us.*
FYODOR DOSTOYEVSKY

Mediating dangerously produces fear, not merely in parties, but in
mediators as well. These fears are easily rationalized, because damage can be done by anything that is dangerous. We need to find
ways of encouraging parties and mediators to overcome their fears,
not only in relation to honesty and empathy, but other dangers as
well. Unfortunately, our efforts to counteract fear or force it into
submission often result in it digging in and refusing to budge.

Anger is often an expression of fear of danger. As an illustration, consider how most parents react when they see their child do
something dangerous. The first response is usually anger, which is
designed to cause minor pain to the child to stop her from getting
hurt in the future. Yet if we probe deeper, we discover that immediately before the expression of anger came a feeling of fear. And
if we probe deeper and ask what frightened the parents, beneath
their fear is an anticipation of pain. If we go deeper still, and ask
why the parents might feel pain, it is because they love their child.
In other words, beneath anger lies fear, beneath fear lies pain, and
beneath pain lies love.

Notice that these are four entirely different conversations. Anger states: "Don't you ever do that again." Fear states: "That scared the hell out of me." Pain states: "It would hurt me terribly if anything bad happened to you." Love states: "I love you so much I wouldn't want anything bad to happen to you." In response, anger stimulates pain and fear in the listener, yet these can become excessive and paralyzing. Fear stimulates excessive caution and withdrawal, and pain stimulates guilt and aversion, but love only stimulates love. Honesty and empathy allow us to move along this scale of responses until we come to love, which is the ground state and deepest truth of this conflict. The same shift to deeper conversations can take place in any conflict.

How to Mediate Fear

When mediators encounter any fear, including a fear of honesty or empathy, several responses are possible. We can recognize fear as a signal of sensitivity or anxiety in relation to possible pain, and we can explore the pain rather than the fear. Or we can approach it as we would any other fear, using a variety of methods and techniques, such as inviting parties to:

- Name their fear.
- Relax and breathe slowly into it.
- Take it out into the light and look at it closely.
- Try to understand more deeply where it came from.
- Speak to it, but not in anger or in pain.
- Invite it in and accept it as a teacher.
- Refocus on what is positive, what they are not afraid of.
- Set it aside for a while and face it when they are ready.
- Imagine in detail how they will overcome it.
- Take baby steps to confront it.
- Laugh at it.
- Assume the worst has already occurred.

In the end, the real danger lies not in honesty but superficiality, and the refusal to learn the deeper truths of our conflicts. As Gertrude Stein wrote, "Considering how dangerous everything is, nothing is frightening."

Fear of Freedom

At a deep level, parties in conflict are frightened by freedom and death. The first is a fear of the loss of externally imposed limits, of crumbling internal walls, or of identity with the oppressor. All oppressive relationships give birth to and depend on a fear of freedom, which is the source of fascism, as psychologist Erich Fromm has pointed out. For one to dominate, another must submit.

This dynamic also arises in families, corporations, nations, and social relationships. It pops up whenever we would rather be told what to do than figure it out ourselves; whenever we refuse to take responsibility for making important decisions in our lives, or allow others to make them for us; whenever we refuse to face up to the need for honesty in our relationships and conflicts. Instead of being free and responsible, we act out of fear, hoping our problems will fix themselves.

I comediated a dispute between teachers and a principal at an elementary school. We asked the faculty, with the principal's agreement, to create a plan for school reform and solve problems at their site. Several faculty refused to participate out of fear that the principal would retaliate against them. We created overlapping anonymous processes, including written responses to us, random small groups, and meetings without the principal. We tried to reduce their fear, but to no avail. Instead of working together to improve their conditions, which they saw as risky, their fear kept them powerless and indecisive. This forced us to mediate dangerously, and ask them whether they thought it would be easier to prevent retaliation by not caring about their school, or by uniting and standing up for each other if retaliation occurred.

People raised in authoritarian families by oppressive parents often end up embracing authoritarianism and becoming oppressive themselves, or they continue to live in fear of it. There is a third path, however—that of confronting their fear and embracing their freedom. This is the most difficult, dangerous path to choose, causing those who fear freedom to search for someone who will deny it, thereby reinforcing and replicating their fear.

The prospect of release, freedom from an oppressive relationship, and resolution of their conflict is often more than parties can stand. Indeed, there is a direct connection between resistance to resolution and a fear of freedom. They are frightened of being alone, or of being fired and being unable to find another job, or even of discovering that they might succeed, or are not as terrible as they think. Sometimes it is a fear that they are more terrible than they think, and that they will always be isolated and unloved. Sometimes it is a fear that without conflict they will be forced to look more closely at themselves, or lose the sympathy or attention they need, or be blamed for mistakes or failures.

The fundamental, unambiguous meaning of freedom is that we are all responsible for our choices, actions, values, and lives. Freedom means we create ourselves, our characters, and our experiences. It means we have no one to blame for our unhappiness and failures other than ourselves. Yet at the same time, no one is completely free. We live in specific times and places that limit even what we can imagine. Freedom then consists, as the German philosopher Hegel argued, in the recognition of necessity, including the necessity of release from fear.

Our most powerful fears represent our greatest desires. The freedom we fear most is the possibility of transformation, because it necessitates change, releases us from ego, and asks us to discover who we really are. Alongside that fear is another, its flip side: that we will fail in the process; that in transforming we will die; or that we will discover we are unworthy of being loved.

This formulation leads to freedom. We are free of the fear of being alone to the extent that we embrace solitude and discover in it a capacity to accept ourselves. We are free of the fear of loss to the extent that we recognize it as a new beginning. We are free of the fear of failure to the extent that we identify it as a form of learning. We are free of the fear of death to the extent that we accept its inevitability, and the possibility of transformation. Buddhist monk Ta Hui wrote in response to a man who was afraid of dying: "What are you afraid of, you're already as good as dead," or as Franklin Delano Roosevelt put it: "We have nothing to fear but fear itself."

Fear of Death

The fear of freedom can also translate into a fear of death, or the desire for release from fear through death. The combination of fear and desire attract frightened, insecure, uncertain people to fascistic and authoritarian leaders. There is a clear, direct relationship between how we feel about death and how freely we live our lives. A fear of death translates into a fear of living, and if we are not ready to die, we are not really ready to live. Antoine de Saint-Exupéry wrote: "Man imagines that it is death he fears; but what he fears is the unforeseen, the explosion. What man fears is himself."

Much of human civilization and conflict can be seen as a product of this fear in all its varied forms—of the knowledge that death is certain, combined with not knowing when it will occur. It is this duality that feeds much of the dread, denial, and diversion that fills our cultural lives—movies and operas, newspapers and novels, jokes and entertainment. As Ernst Becker wrote in *The Denial of Death:*

> [T]he fear of death must be present behind all our normal functioning in order for the organism to be armed toward self-preservation. But the fear of death cannot be present constantly in one's mental functioning, else the organism could not function. And so we can understand what seems like an impossible paradox: the ever-present fear of death in the normal biological functioning of our instinct of self-preservation, as well as our utter obliviousness to this fear in our conscious life. . . . The irony of man's condition is that the deepest need is to be free of the anxiety of death and annihilation; but it is life itself which awakens it, and so we must shrink from being fully alive.

We live much of our lives focusing on the past or preparing for the future, rather than experiencing the present as a point where anything can happen, including death. As a result, we live our lives in parts, rather than as a whole. Yet death reminds us harshly of the *whole* of our lives, teaching us to return to what really matters.

Death, Change, and Conflict

Death, change, and conflict require us to relinquish the illusion of our importance and immortality, our wish to be in control. Indeed, every loss of control, every unanticipated change from divorce to downsizing, can be interpreted as a metaphor for death.

Because we are afraid of death, we shun not only those who are dying, but those who agitate for change and those are embroiled in conflict for fear that we may lose control. We do not know what to say or how to act with people who are dying. We debate whether to tell the person or their spouse or relatives of their impending death. We make decisions for dying people without asking their opinions, and in opposition to their express wishes. We try to preserve life through technical support and extraordinary medical feats, all of which fail to recognize or satisfy the emotional and spiritual needs of the dying person.

We are afraid of the look of death. We lie to children about it or keep it a secret, as though we are ashamed of it. We tend not to celebrate people or their accomplishments until they die. Then we forget the problems they created and remember only their good points. We publicly glorify those who die in combat, but briefly and romantically, encouraging others to do the same. We are angry at people for dying, but cannot express it, except as exaggerated grief or insensitivity. We are secretly glad we are not the ones who died.

Similar ideas occur to people who see others in conflict. Every effort to promote resolution or transformation through mediation implies a loss, which subconsciously reminds people of death. The ending of relationships, the loss of positions, the surrender of control over outcomes, the reaching of closure—all are terminations that intimate the terminus of death. Parties in mediation often grapple indirectly with their fear of death, which they express through resistance to change, unwillingness to surrender illusions, or continued false expectations.

As we make peace with the inevitability of death and loss, we become more available to live in the present, and every moment becomes more open and alive. Yet unresolved fears of death and unprocessed grief and loss lie at the core of many conflicts. Much of the anger expressed by divorcing couples is a guise for unprocessed grief, as is the pain and rage expressed in organizations undergoing mergers, downsizing, and dramatic change, all of which require grieving.

Unprocessed grief is often shifted to those who are closest, triggering highly emotional conflicts over who will get grandmother's gold earrings, or which spouse will have custody of the children on

Christmas Day, or how a manager communicated a termination. Though the trigger may be small, the aftermath can be enormous and last for years.

Mediating Grief

When we mediate with people who are frightened or in denial, or crying, or feeling angry, or guilty, or ashamed of death, we need to accept their responses and the fear of death that triggered them. These are the tortured responses of the living. We need to create opportunities to grieve and process their loss.

Grief and pain are often masked by anger, as fear of loss is masked by denial. This makes it necessary to search beneath the surface of these volatile emotions for a deeper truth. As mediators, we venture into dangerous territory when we attempt to lance wounds of unprocessed grief, at the frontiers of emotional intervention. Yet it is often necessary for mediators to assist conflicting parties in releasing their pain, acknowledging their loss, and overcoming their fear of death to fully resolve a conflict. We do this by:

- Facilitating the communication of uncomfortable emotions.
- Soothing, consoling, and acknowledging pain.
- Validating, listening, sharing, and verbalizing loss.
- Ventilating anger.
- Normalizing grief and fear.
- Relieving guilt.
- Creating rituals of acceptance or relinquishment.
- Supporting recovery.
- Releasing expectations.
- Mentoring parties in moving on with their lives.

We encourage parties to *use* their loss as a lever to overcome their fear of death or freedom, fuel their honesty, deepen their empathy and compassion, resolve their disputes, and transform their lives. We ask dangerous questions about what they learned from their fear or grief, how their lives may have improved as a result of their loss, what was the worst thing anyone said to them during their grief, whether there is anything they will miss about their suffering, what they need to say or do in order to let go of it, and what will happen if they do.

From Fear to Apathy

One response to fear is apathy, which dramatically limits our ability to resolve conflicts or learn from them. Fear gives mediators something to work with, a toehold, a small space to identify what needs to be changed. Apathy is a more powerful form of resistance, because there is nothing to grasp, no clues to a deeper self.

Apathy is the deadening of emotion, vitality, spirit, and engagement. When intimate connection and deep caring are perceived as threatening, or when the fear of loss is great, parties may numb themselves and adopt a pose of apathy. It allows them to feel protected from the vicissitudes of life, and gives them an illusion of escape from fear and pain. Unfortunately, they do not realize that they cannot diminish their capacity for suffering without reducing their capacity for pleasure and for life.

As mediators, we search for the sensitive places where people connect to life, feel more authentic, and learn from their pain and suffering. We work intuitively, often guessing at the sources of discomfort, searching for tiny openings. To the apathetic, caring is dangerous. As a small example, in mediating between an apathetic son and his mother, I spent nearly an hour asking questions, all of which he answered with, "I don't know." I then initiated the following dialogue:

Mediator:	[To the son] "What is one thing your mother could do that would make your life easier?"
Son:	"I don't know." [Long, uncomfortable silence] "Give me a million dollars, I guess." [Giggles]
Mediator:	[To the mother] "Would you do that?"
Mother:	"What?"
Mediator:	"Give him a million dollars."
Mother:	[Confused] "Of course not."
Mediator:	[To the son] "Would you like to ask for a smaller sum?"
Son:	[Confused] "I don't know. How about $100 a day?" [Giggles again]
Mediator:	[To the son] "What about $15 a week?"
Son:	[More seriously] "O.K."
Mediator:	[To the mother] "Would you be willing to pay him

$15 a week?"

Mother: "For what? I might pay him $5 a week if he washed the dishes at night and cleaned his room."

Mediator: [To the son] "How much would you want your mother to pay you to wash the dishes every night and clean your room once a week?"

Son: [Feeling trapped] "I don't know."

Mediator: "How about $10?"

Son: [Getting into the spirit of it] "O.K." [To his mother] "How about $10?"

Mother: [To her son] "How about $5."

Mediator: [To the son] "Ask for $7.50."

Son: [To the mother] "How about $7.50?"

Mother: [Pleased, but uncomfortable] "O.K." [Son and mother smile at each other]

Mediator: [To both] "Congratulations. O.K., now what just happened? [Silence] [To the son] "You started off asking for a million dollars, thinking probably that this whole conversation was pretty dumb, and ended up with $7.50 a week. Not bad. How did that happen? How did you get the $7.50?"

Both sides were able to identify what they did that led to a successful negotiation and what the other side did that allowed them to respond. The mother recognized that her son's withdrawal and apathy were defenses against her controlling and nagging. Instead of giving orders, she needed to negotiate in ways that allowed him to get what he needed, and her to get what she needed. The son knew his apathy drove his mother crazy. He said he did it because it was the only way he could gain any power over his life. They saw that apathy produces control, and control produces apathy.

They recognized that hidden within their conflict over household chores were deeper, typical parent/adolescent debates over responsibility versus autonomy, control versus freedom, acceptability versus peer approval, safety versus adventure, and discipline versus self-discipline. They understood that each had an interest in the other achieving what they wanted; that life was a series of negotiations that could be conducted in ways that allowed both of them to win; and that only by asking for what they really wanted could they forge authentic relationships with each other.

This mediation was successful because the son's willingness to be "flip" or sarcastic was stronger than his desire to be apathetic, and because he and his mother genuinely loved and cared for each other, however difficult it may have been for them to reveal it. Underlying apathy is a desire so powerful it generates a fear that what is desired isn't possible or won't come to pass. These hopes are papered over with apathy, because they are too painful to accept.

Intuition and empathy allow us to imagine what might matter to us if we were in the other person's shoes and hiding behind apathy, and they allow us to probe for openings that reveal these deeper truths. For example, after hearing a series of cynical, negative, apathetic remarks by a high school principal, my co-mediator said, "It sounds like you care a lot about the kids in your school." The man burst into tears. His apathy was simply a defense against his own passionate caring.

The Significance of Silence

Apathy usually takes the form of silence, but there are honest and dishonest, empty and full silences. Novelist Salman Rushdie wrote of two people in conflict: "Silence grew around them like an accusation." Silence in the presence of evil, silence when speech really matters, silence that refuses to discuss what is real are forms of dishonesty or fear.

Our most difficult experiences in mediation have come from people who smother rage in a seething, furious silence that is so loud it is deafening. If a person will not honestly say what is bothering them, there is little we can do to help. Nonetheless, it is a mistake to equate silence with apathy. Silence in mediation is a complex state with many possible explanations. Here are some:

- Silence can mean one has turned inward, and been brought face to face with oneself.
- Silence can mean condonation or acquiescence in wrongdoing, or be a mask for blind obedience.
- Silence can be a sign of consensus, unanimity, or quiet determination.

- Silence can be an indication of injured feelings, or a search for anonymity in response to fear.
- Silence can be a sign of meditation or reflection, of stepping back from escalation.
- Silence can suggest an appreciation of ambiguity and paradox, or a deep question, and a search for answers.
- Silence can mean one has returned to natural momentum and internal rhythms.
- Silence can represent a vacuum in which anything can occur.
- Silence can be what precedes the storm or what signals transformation.
- Silence can mean one lacks the skill to handle what is happening.
- Silence can be what is left when one lets go and feels complete.
- Silence can be a refusal even to help oneself.

There are, in other words, creative and destructive, positive and negative forms of silence. As mediators, our role is to deepen the creative and diminish the destructive silences, and to know one from the other. Mediating dangerously means inviting parties to abandon their silences and increase their honesty and empathy. Thus, we draw them into more centered, complex, subtle understanding of the sources of their conflict.

Invest Action with Meaning

Sometimes, apathy is a cover for boredom and the assumption that nothing is ever going to change. Conflict resolution can seem pointless and impotent if it is not linked to some new action, or genuine change in behavior. These changes can be designed and brought into existence through the mediation process, by reaching and signing agreements, creating rituals of release and forgiveness, and taking actions that are invested with meaning.

Mediators invest actions with meaning in the same way religious officials invest ceremonies with meaning, by making the context and significance explicit. Insight, feedback, and ritual are ways of making the unspoken outspoken and clear. Otherwise, the meaning of any action will be defined differently, based on each person's own unexamined prior experiences.

We invest actions with meaning by making process transparent—for example, by agreeing to a protocol for future communication. We may ask a series of questions, such as:

- How would you like to be told there is a problem in the future?
- What would it mean to you if he used those words?
- If he tells you in that way, what will you say in response?
- Why would you respond that way, as opposed to the way you responded before?
- Would that work for you?
- What makes it work for you?
- How would you like her to respond instead? Why?
- If she does, what will you say in return?
- Would you be willing to try that conversation right now?
- That was great. What could you have said or done that could make it even better?
- Why would that make it better for you?
- Would you be willing to try it again?
- What might keep you from being able to talk that way to each other in the future?
- Why might that get in your way?
- Are you both willing to agree to use these methods in your next conversation?
- What will you do if you slip or forget?
- Can the other person give you feedback?
- If you were the one receiving the feedback, how would you like it delivered? Why?
- What did you learn from what we just did?

These questions allow parties to understand the meaning of their behaviors and negotiate them. There are deeper, more dangerous questions as well. These often appear as follow-up questions based on answers given to the first set of questions that are directed at the deeper "why's"—"Why is it upsetting to you when she says things like that?" "What does that trigger inside you?" "Has that happen to you before?" "When?" "Why do you let yourself be spoken to that way without responding?" "What is it about his response that pushes your buttons?" "Why is that a button for you?"

The more dangerous the question, the less apathetic the response, and the deeper the dialogue.

Mediating Insanity

The capacity to comprehend what the conflict is about is essential to conflict resolution. Most of us, when we are in conflict, are gripped by powerful emotions, such as rage, shame, or fear, and behave in ways that seem crazy to others. How, then, do we distinguish the "ordinary," petty insanities that are typical of everyone in conflict from the profound dementia that limits the capacity even to understand what the dispute is about? What is the difference between thinking paranoid thoughts and being paranoid?

One difference lies in the parties' capacity for self-awareness and critical observation, subsequent reflection and correction, honesty and empathy. The potential for transformation must be there; or at least for listening, problem solving, negotiation, dialogue, and closure. In short, certain elementary thinking and communication skills are required for people to resolve their conflicts.

Insanity becomes a frontier in conflict resolution when either party is not just situationally, but innately unable to hear or understand what is said by the mediator and the other side. This can indicate a difficulty escaping the emotional consequences of conflict, which can cause people to spiral out of control into delusion, depression, or paranoia. This disintegration can happen to anyone who suffers repeated traumas or conflicts that cause them to lose touch with their inner sense of balance and capacity for reasoned dialogue. Their illusions become so powerful they finally overwhelm all sense of reality. This is where conflict resolution truly ends and psychotherapy begins.

Having said this, there is a clear difference between people who are insane and those who are "crazy like a fox." Most of the parties we encounter only appear insane to their opponents and are using demented behaviors to gain strategic or tactical advantage. Their manipulation is successful in producing the results they seek, such as gaining everyone's attention, or getting what they want.

I mediated a dispute involving a man who was five minutes late to work every day and who had been absent due to illness 116 days in one year. He exhibited numerous behavioral problems at work. Because no one could figure out why, they assumed he was crazy and sent him to a psychologist, who sent him back to work saying he was perfectly sane. The company fired him, then realized it had fired him for a legally insupportable reason, and agreed to mediation.

I met with him in caucus to find out the reasons for his behavior. It turned out he had been promoted to his own maximum level of incompetence. He was certain his manager knew of his inadequacy, so he created a series of smoke screens and diversions to keep her from acting. Once he revealed his secret, I was able to arrange a transfer to work at which he excelled. I then negotiated a set of unambiguous expectations regarding tardiness, attendance, and behavior, with serious consequences for nonperformance that he suggested.

The difficulty is that the line separating insanity from irrational behavior is neither solid nor well-defined. An example is addiction, in which irrational or insane behaviors make listening nearly impossible. Addictions can be mild, as with addiction to coffee or sweets or a favorite chair, or more serious, as with tobacco, alcohol, or tranquilizers; and extremely serious, as with crack or heroin. In between are a series of conventional addictions, such as to soap operas, sex, or overeating, or even to phrases or rituals. So where can the line be drawn?

One source of insanity is conflict itself, in the form of two opposing ideas, emotions, facts, and so on that appear contradictory or draw people in opposite directions at the same time. Combining opposites in a single act or sentence creates a double bind, leading to behaviors that appear irrational. Yet life is complex, and filled with paradox, or what appear to be conflicting ideas, emotions, or realities. For example, everyone needs to express grief, and at the same time find a way to overcome it. So how much grief is too much? How long should mourning last before it becomes irrational? Everyone needs to express anger, and at the same time find a way to release it; to survive; and at the same time, take risks. When is it too much, or not enough? Who decides these things? How?

All emotions and expressions of feeling naturally exist in opposite forms, so it is not unusual to experience contradictory sensations such as love and hate, pride and shame, or fear and courage at the same time. It is the combination and simultaneous expression of these opposing feelings that makes us appear irrational or insane, even to ourselves.

In this way, what is labeled insanity in others may simply reflect the labeler's own fear of responding in an insane way to other people's behavior. The labels we use to describe others distance us from their behavior and defend us against slipping into insane assumptions. For example, when we label someone a "control freak," we may actually be expressing our own vulnerability to being controlled, since we might use different words to say the same thing, such as "perfectionist," "careful," "detailed," or "precise." Our choice reflects our own difficulties.

Dishonesty in Conflict

A different set of issues arises when individuals or organizations are able to lie without detection. This is not to say that subjective truths do not differ profoundly, or that every conflict story is not in some way false. Most people, however, do not intentionally and consciously mislead each other over important subjects that cannot or will not be corrected through honest, open dialogue and mutual exploration of the truth.

Often, the problem is not simply with their dishonesty, but with *our* desire to believe their story because we want it to be true. Is the alcoholic lying when he promises never to drink? Probably. But are we not equally dishonest when we believe him because we want it to be true? The artful liar is one who engages the listener, by telling a lie he desperately wants to believe in: a lie that tells him he can get rich quick, that everything will be okay, that someone loves him.

Everyone in conflict lies in the sense of failing to tell the whole truth, and leaving out the disagreeable parts. Everyone rationalizes, justifies, fabricates, diverts attention, changes the subject, becomes defensive, counterattacks, minimizes, and grandstands in order to gain advantage. What is of greater concern are the untestable assertions, the intentional half-truths, the fictions on which critical reliance must be placed. As the English political philosopher John Stuart Mill wrote: "It is not the violent conflict between parts of the truth, but the quiet suppression of half of it that is the formidable evil."

In nearly every conflict, trust is broken, forcing conflicting parties to corroborate the validity of possible misrepresentations, perhaps by using witnesses, documents, outside experts, attorneys, or investigators. But where fundamental, pervasive dishonesties are not apparent and cannot be detected, where the lies are so thorough and believable they have the perfect shape of truth, neither conflict resolution nor litigation can produce a fair result.

Lies come in many shades, and it is often difficult to distinguish a convenient untruth from a deliberate fraud. We lack a failsafe method for distinguishing truth from falsehood, or an easy classification scheme that separates the "white lies" of the well-intentioned from the manipulative fabrications of the sociopath or con artist.

Yet it is not the intention of the liar, but the damage that results from reliance that is our greatest concern. For example, even a simple lie about the weather may seem harmless, until it is told to the skipper of a small craft heading out to sea. Mediations are filled with these "innocent" lies, any of which can create a counterfeit outcome.

The difficulty is that it is not possible for us to ascertain the truth by independent investigation without substantially altering our role, and objective truth cannot be determined by consensus. For this reason, conflict resolution is less concerned with defining a single objective—quantifiable, impersonal Truth. Instead, it seeks to surface a multitude of subjective, qualitative, deeply personal truths, because these are more important for resolution than a careful dissection of the facts.

Someone defined a novel as "a lie in search of the truth." Similarly, the stories people tell about their conflicts usually reveal the metaphoric truths they have hidden within their lies. Dangerous mediation consists not of confronting the lie, but of treating it as a metaphor and an excuse to ask deeply honest questions. We can, for example, treat someone's lie about a successful career as an honest statement of shame and fear of failure. To understand more about conflict stories, see *Resolving Personal and Organizational Conflict: Stories of Transformation and Forgiveness* (Jossey-Bass, 2000), coauthored with Joan Goldsmith.

Mediating Dishonesty

Reliance on subjective truth in mediation does not make the search for scientific validity useless. Disagreements about facts can often be resolved by scientific methods. Yet the purpose of the search for truth in conflict resolution is twofold: first, to help the parties achieve a substantively fair result; and second, to help them *feel* a result is fair, allowing their wounds to heal. While the second purpose is not always achieved, it cannot take place without a level of personal honesty that is hard to fake, particularly when each side believes they have been treated unfairly. Genuine sociopathic behavior is difficult to mediate, mostly because the false appears authentic, and the lies are not even metaphors.

As mediators, we often propose a ground rule that the parties agree to fully and honestly tell the truth. We surface concerns over trust and accuracy, and press disputing parties to resolve their doubts by objective means, such as documents, experts, criteria, witnesses, or whatever proves satisfactory to them. We caucus with each side to explore the veracity of critical information whenever we suspect intentional dishonesty. We press parties to reconsider outcomes that do not seem fair to both of them, or at least equally unfair. We directly confront dishonesty with curiosity about what made the person do it, and why. Beyond this, we have to accept that whatever agreements the parties reach belong to them. It is, after all, *their* sense of what is fair that matters, not ours. At the same time, to be able to own the results of the process, they need to have a sense that the truth has been told.

It is not uncommon for one party to assume he or she has borne the brunt of the sacrifice, or relied on a falsehood, or cannot prove the other person's dishonesty, particularly in divorce mediations, where this becomes a way of ending the relationship as a victim. Often, the complaint is a disguised form of grief, which rationalizes the act of leaving by finding fault with the other person's lack of integrity. Yet it also is a subtle form of dishonesty, albeit one that is personal, that cheats the one being dishonest out of truths that only emerge by working through the pain and grief of loss.

For example, if a husband has an affair, his wife may rage and call him names. But it is also useful for her to ask herself: "Were there other, earlier instances of dishonesty that I did not confront?" "How soon after meeting him did I first realize he might lie to me, or betray me?" "In what way was this marriage not intimate or satisfying for me?" "Why didn't I do something to save it at the first sign of trouble?" "What did I contribute to its demise?" These lead to learning, growth, change, and preparation for a different kind of relationship, while the first response does not.

Dishonesty in nondivorce conflicts similarly limits the parties' capacity to resolve their disputes. It creates a continuing sense of unfairness and inequity that prevents healing, which is aided by emotional catharsis and truth-telling. Dishonesty rekindles false expectations and builds relationships on sand, rather than cement, leading to eventual structural collapse and future conflict rather than closure.

I comediated a sexual harassment dispute involving two women who had kept a diary over a period of several years chronicling every obscene comment, lewd gesture, and sexual suggestion their supervisor had made. The evidence seemed extremely damaging. The supervisor, however, denied everything and insisted they had made it all up. One of the attorneys representing the company, in finding out who was telling the truth, ordered a scientific analysis of the diary. The tests revealed that the pen used to make entries for 1993 was not manufactured until 1995. The claim was dropped when the lie was exposed in mediation, but without the test, no one would have believed the supervisor.

As conflict resolvers, mediating dangerously means encouraging people not to agree when they think information is dishonest or outcomes are unfair, and taking steps to verify the accuracy of assertions that might be untrue. Only in this way can everyone be satisfied with their agreements and surrender their desire for revenge.

Chapter Seven

Dismantling the Desire for Revenge

TAMORA: . . . *I am Revenge, sent from th' infernal*
kingdom
To ease the gnawing vulture of thy mind
By working wreakful vengeance on thy foes.
Come down and welcome me to this world's light;
Confer with me of murder and death.
TITUS: . . . *O sweet Revenge, now do I come to thee . . .*
Long have I been forlorn, and all for thee.
Welcome, dread Fury, to my woeful house.
Rapine and Murder, you are welcome too . . . .
SHAKESPEARE, *TITUS ANDRONICUS*

At some point in our lives, we all experience a desire for revenge. This desire is often a cover for a deeper desire to communicate our pain and humiliation to the person we think caused it. Sometimes it reflects a longing not to be hurt any more by that person, or a desire that the conflict be over, or a thirst for fairness, or an urge to escape our own fear, guilt, or shame. These deeper needs are diminished, discouraged, forgotten, and denied in the search for revenge.

When someone seriously seeks revenge, mediation becomes dangerous, if not impossible. It is common for people in conflict to detest and abhor their adversaries, and even desire their immediate, painful annihilation. Many people fantasize secretly about revenge. Few actually carry it out. Most hire lawyers instead.

A desire for revenge is present in miniature in every conflict, though it is more significant in divorce, sexual harassment, wrongful termination, discrimination, victim and offender, and neighborhood disputes. In any conflict involving boundary violations, or where shame and humiliation are significant, the desire for revenge can become profound and resolute. Yet in form and substance, the desire for revenge is the same in major and minor disputes. It is a matter of degree.

What is Revenge?

Revenge can be defined as a willingness to hurt *oneself* in order to cause pain to others. Like anger, it is double-edged and injures, often in subtle ways, those who wield it. While a desire for revenge can make mediation ineffective, it can also open a path to forgiveness, leading directly to the heart of the perpetrator. The alchemy of dangerous mediation often transmutes leaden revenge into golden forgiveness.

Every search for revenge can be seen as a desire to communicate how it felt to be treated unfairly. Communication creates an opening for learning, transformation, and transcendence of whatever led to the desire for revenge in the first place. But transformation implies an orientation to the future, and a letting go—not of the act, but of rage at the person who committed it. Revenge and forgiveness are thus distinguished by the degree to which one focuses on the person or the problem, the past or the future.

All conflicts, no matter how serious or justifiable, carry within them the seeds of revenge and forgiveness. Every dispute causes suffering that calls out for punishment of those who initiated it. Pain easily turns into anger, which naturally asserts itself against the rights and interests of the "enemy." Shakespeare described it best, in *Othello:*

O that the slave had forty thousand lives!

One is too poor, too weak for my revenge.

And again in *Measure for Measure:*

The very mercy of the law cries out

Most audible, even from his proper tongue,

'An Angelo for Claudio, death for death!'

Empathizing with the Desire for Revenge

To mediate the desire for revenge, we need to cultivate a *dangerous* form of empathy that allows us to locate the urge to violence and destruction within ourselves. Exploring our own desire for revenge is dangerous because it raises feelings and thoughts we may prefer to leave unexamined. As mediators, we are reluctant to admit feeling rage, hatred, or desire for revenge. Indeed, we may have chosen mediation as a profession precisely because these thoughts are uncomfortable for us, or in hopes that professionalism will dampen them.

As mediators, we can support revengeful parties in communicating the extent of their pain, fear, guilt, and shame. We can caucus with each side to defuse their anger. We can encourage the parties to get on with their lives, or ask them what they want in their future. We can articulate a choice between revenge and some attractive or compelling alternative, such as a child's emotional well-being. We can even ask a party to envision an ideal revenge, describe it in detail, then imagine moving beyond it and letting it go. We might ask them to consider a *worse* revenge, help them find one they would reject, find out why, and apply those reasons to the revenge they are considering, though this is risky. We can also help parties channel their desire for revenge and redirect it toward some acceptable or socially beneficial form, such as supporting people who have been similarly injured.

Everyone has the power, if not the right, to choose suffering and to refuse to heal. They may need their pain in order to feel alive or defined. It may create a negative energy that keeps them feeling tied to each other. It may be so poignant they want others to experience it also. It may lead them to litigation, as a civilized form of revenge. As we risk confronting revenge in ourselves and others, we learn creative ways of articulating why revenge, other than as a symbol of release from suffering, is in no one's best interest. Spiritual writer Carlos Warter has powerfully described the nature of revenge and hatred, pointing out that it takes place inside us, dominating and poisoning our souls. He writes:

> The one you hate is the one you have assembled, constructed in your mind—therefore the one you hate is in you, and your hate becomes a vibration that inhabits and affects you.

Hatred freezes and simplifies our opponents, while forgiveness makes them fluid, complex, and changeable. When we are able to surface and respond to the deeper reasons for hatred, when we reveal its effects on people's lives, revenge becomes less attractive as an option. Nonetheless, those who seek revenge are often unable to surrender their desire, and by wasting valuable time, money, and emotional energy, can face ruin before they are ready to give it up.

A Brief History of Revenge

It is helpful for mediators to develop a sense of emotional history. Knowing how we have handled revenge in the past can help us understand its dynamics in the present. Our principal ideas about revenge and how to respond to it emerge from our history, yet are alive and active today, even in disputes where the desire for revenge is minimal.

A large part of the history of the world can be written as a search for revenge. The desire for revenge is ancient and universal. To "get back," "even the score," or "return the favor" is simultaneously to seek compensation and punishment. While in modern civil and criminal law punishment and compensation are separated, in the ancient world they were one. It took the intervention of the state to separate restitution, or payment of money to the victim, from incarceration or punishment of the offender. Yet the intervention of the state makes revenge bureaucratic rather than personal, slow rather than swift, indirect rather than direct, and intellectual rather than emotional.

The ancient vision of a vengeful god or goddess who punished criminals and rewarded their victims is a myth, which, like all compensatory myths, reflects the failure of society to reward the victim. The desire for fairness, which held little attraction for the absolutist slave states of the ancient middle east, found expression in a higher calculus. "Vengeance is mine, said the Lord" halted the vendetta, allowing victims to be compensated with righteousness and the moral superiority of forgiveness.

The famous "law of the talon," cited in Exodus 21 of the Bible, called for "life for life, eye for eye, tooth for tooth, hand for hand, foot for foot, burning for burning, wound for wound, stripe for stripe." In this view, retaliation and restitution were linked. Restitution was positive because it gave back to the victim what was taken away. Retaliation, on the other hand, was negative because it striped the perpetrator, at least symbolically, of whatever power or respect they had gained and the victim had lost. Compensation was not merely quantitative, but qualitative, and the penalty had to fit not only the amount, but the kind of damage done.

According to the ancient Hittite Code, for example, a man who killed another was required to provide the family of the deceased with one or more substitute workers. In Hammurabi's Code, if a man killed another man's daughter, the father was authorized to kill not the murderer, but the murderer's daughter.

Created to inhibit the blood feud, this ancient right centered attention on the victim as opposed to the criminal or the state. It provided an emotional release for pent-up feelings of hostility and anger, even against animals and inanimate objects. Thus, if one tripped over a neighbor's rock, the rock might be flung off a cliff, or if injury was incurred by falling from a neighbor's tree, one's relatives might come and chop it down.

The "eye for an eye," or "law of the talon," not only limited the use of private vengeance and established an Aristotelian "due proportion" between crime and punishment, it made everyone equal before the law—not in their crime, which remained unique and subjective, but in their *punishment*. All injuries were now valued, in theory, according to a single standard of reciprocity.

It was the purpose of this early law to make the perpetrator experience the crime in reverse and destroy the objectification of the victim that preceded it, thereby rendering victimization subjective and personal. This forced criminals to internalize what they had previously externalized through crime, and confront their antisocial actions. It negated the crime by turning it inside out within its creator, forcing a rude equality between the victim and the perpetrator.

The Pythagoreans believed in equal good for good and equal bad for bad. The punishment had to equal the crime quantitatively. It was not until the age of Socrates and Plato that justice became an ethical principle, an attribute of individual "virtue." What made the law of the talon "just," therefore, was not simply its focus on the victim, but its victimization of the wrongdoer, and its forceful placement of the criminal in the shoes of the victim. Two elements coexisted: one was psychological and rehabilitative; the other physical and punitive, with both based on an equality of right between the victim and the criminal.

To whatever extent the wrongdoer recognized and accepted the perspective of the victim, it was less likely that future wrong would be done, and society was served. Yet in ancient Greek and Roman class-divided societies, this kind of resolution became impossible. In these societies, the master could not accept that the slave was capable of understanding him, or that they should be treated as equals.

The main difficulty with the law of the talon was addressed by Socrates in the following terms: if we concede that the central purpose of justice is to improve society, we must ask whether a dog is improved by beating it, whether a plow is improved by twisting it, or a person by punishing him. If the answer is no, then punishment itself is unjust, because society is forced to play the role of criminal and continues to be victimized by future crimes, while the criminal is turned into a victim and justified in committing future crimes by the ill treatment received from society.

If we make the further assumption that the criminal is *already* a victim in the sense of being oppressed or a slave or "have not," the crime is compounded. The law of the talon, which developed without regard to class, station, gender, or rank, was thus one-sided and subject to hierarchical prerogative. All this perceived unfairness added a social element to the use of revenge.

The law of the talon later resulted in a kind of *social guilt,* because the state substituted itself for the victim in replicating the criminal act, but without any desire for gain or reason for anger. Consequently, it responded in stiff, impersonal, bureaucratic ways, which encouraged punishment because of frustration, embarassment, defensiveness, or guilt. There was no genuine interest in rehabilitation or reintegration, even after punishment was complete.

The evolving role of the state in punishment reverberated throughout ancient myth and literature. Before leaving for the Trojan War, Agamemnon sacrificed his daughter Iphigenia to the gods in exchange for wind to fill his sails. On his return, he was murdered, partly for this crime, by his wife Clytemnestra and her lover Aegisthus, who were in turn murdered by her son, Orestes.

In the play *The Eumenides* by Aeschylus, the Furies, who were ancient goddesses of revenge, pursue Orestes to the statue of Athena where he begs her intercession. The Furies are incarnations of revenge, or "Spirits invoked for evil," who argue that Orestes should be punished by them or the world of mortals will become reconciled to sin. Orestes counters that his mother killed his father and deserved to die. Athena answers by shifting the right of revenge from the family or spirit of the victim to the state:

> Hear now my institution, ye Attic people, on holding this first trial for bloodshed. And for future time also this court . . . shall ever remain in force . . . , a court held in respect by the citizens, a fear allied with awe shall restrain them from injustice . . .

On this first jury, Athena, who was born full grown from the ear of Zeus, chairs and casts the deciding vote for Orestes, declaring:

> . . . there is no mother who gave me birth, and I approve of the male side . . . in all respects with my whole heart, and am entirely in favor of the father's cause. Thus I shall not pay undue regard to the death of a wife who slew her husband, the manager of her house . . .

The Furies threaten to pollute the land for overriding their ancient right of revenge, and are only placated when Athena places them in charge of "family felicity" and makes them "keepers of the hearth" for all time, in "a victory that brings no disaster."

What is most fascinating in this drama is the simultaneous shift from private revenge to public trial, from matriarchal right to patriarchal privilege, from ancient action to official adjudication, from emotional to rational, from female fury to family felicity. The spirit of revenge in Greek mythology was female, older even than the gods, irrational, and based in blood, kinship, and the law of the talon. The spirit of the law was male, young, rational, and based in logic, procedure, and technicality.

In place of the "eye for an eye" there was a win/lose verdict, trial by jury, an end to the blood feud, and civil order based on coercion by the state. With patriarchal power came the overthrow of ancient female rights, and their replacement with domesticity, harmony, an adjudicated compromise, and a bribe that brought no disaster, yet settled disputes without resolving them.

Why Revenge?

In order to mediate issues of revenge, it is necessary to understand why people choose it, to place ourselves as fully as possible in the position of those who are prepared to harm others and themselves at the same time. We do so not to sound preachy, superior, or distant about issues that have intense meaning in their lives, but to take them apart and understand from the inside why they ultimately fail.

Revenge begins quite simply when anger slips into rage. Anger is a path of least resistance taken by shame between rage and passivity. The ability to express anger is healthy, even when its actual expression is not. Encouraging people to express anger in mediation can be extremely dangerous, because it can quickly escalate into physical action. Nonetheless, everyone needs to learn how to express anger constructively. Worse things happen when we have no safety valve, and what is felt becomes a barrier to communication, relationship, and learning on both sides. What is better than expressing anger is understanding the reasons that created it and transcending them through dialogue.

In mediation, anger is a map leading us to the source of the conflict. It releases the self-restraint parties use to silence or suppress what they actually feel. It is the flip side of vulnerability. For that reason, it is also a step in vulnerability's direction. All couples know there is something worse than anger, which is indifference. Yet when anger turns into rage, revenge rather than understanding becomes the goal. Boundaries are blurred, and the other person is falsely identified as responsible for ruining an otherwise peaceful, satisfying life. When this takes place, action in the form of revenge seems more potent than inaction, letting go, and moving on.

In short, anger can be constructive or destructive; it can clear the air or pollute it. It is a mistake for mediators to forbid or prohibit the expression of anger. Expressing, hearing, and acknowledging anger allows parties to have a *complete* experience of it, in preparation for releasing it. Revenge, on the other hand, is always destructive and cannot be encouraged or engaged in without negative consequence. That, indeed, is its very purpose.

Some Valid Reasons for Revenge

There are many sound reasons for revenge. The most compelling is that revenge promises a return to the ancient justice of the eye for an eye—that evil will be struck down and virtue rewarded. Revenge promises a release from rage through activity or ritual, a remedy for shame through arrogant action. Revenge allows the victim to communicate to the perpetrator what it actually felt like to be victimized. It makes the crime understandable to the criminal by repeating it in reverse. It tears off the masks on both sides, revealing a deeper layer of feelings, thereby creating equality between the victim and the perpetrator—in power, pain, humiliation, and sacrifice. Revenge allows the victim to commit a criminal act legitimately, cause harm to another, and experience the ecstasy and sensuality of violence. More profoundly, revenge satisfies the perpetrator's secret desire—and, as the German philosopher Hegel argued—their *right* to be punished.

While many of these reasons for revenge are extremely powerful and seem convincing, on closer examination there are problems with each one that will inevitably lead even a person overflowing with rage to question whether revenge is the best way to respond to their victimization.

How to Mediate Revenge

The desire for revenge is often a product of multiple, possibly conflicting justifications, each of which may need to be addressed separately. For mediators who want to tackle revengeful desires, the best place to begin is by listening deeply and trying to pinpoint the origin of the desire. Listening to the issues will not suffice. It is necessary to locate the thing that induced the shame, humiliation, or sense of powerlessness that triggered the compensatory desire for arrogant action.

It is critical that mediators not be judgmental regarding the desire for revenge, but empathize and encourage its full expression. This is dangerous, because it appears to justify taking action. Our intent, however, is to locate the source of the desire for vengeful action and channel it in a constructive direction. One way of doing so is to first broaden the desire for revenge to include destroying the dysfunctional system that gave rise to it, or helping all the victims who have suffered in the past, or halting all the perpetrators who may exist in the future.

Another approach is to broaden culpability to include not just paltry, individual opponents, but all their allies and supporters, the system that permitted it to happen, the people who knew about it and did nothing, and the people who should have known about it and didn't. Czech novelist Ivan Klima wrote, following the "velvet revolution" that ended Soviet control of Czechoslovakia, about the serious difficulties with systemic revenge, even when an entire nation recognizes its complicity and guilt:

> . . . who can establish a borderline between guilt and innocence, when that borderline runs somewhere right down the middle of each and every person? . . . What was justice? Justice was revenge wrapping itself in a cloak of high principle.

Shifting parties to higher principles is actually a powerful mediation technique in response to the desire for revenge, since it allows parties to hold onto their outrage without causing harm to an actual person. Transferring revenge to a higher plane *ennobles* the harm, rather than trivializing it.

Why Revenge Doesn't Work

An extremely useful technique is to involve the victim in a dialogue about the likely impact of their proposed actions, so they can see what is actually involved and decide against it. The mediator can point out, for example, that the act of revenge makes it difficult for the victim to achieve satisfaction for a variety of reasons:

- It strips the person using it of the title "victim," and removes the mantle of respect due by sympathy to the one who is acted upon.
- It is a confession of powerlessness, even when it is powerful.
- It transforms the victim into a perpetrator, no different from the one against whom the victim seeks revenge.
- It is humiliating and degrading even when it is satisfying.
- It encourages the victim to identify with the aggressor, and to justify acts of aggression.
- It cuts both ways and, like all violence, wounds the victim along with the perpetrator.
- It is easily overdone and ignores the humanity of the victim, leading to guilt and remorse.
- It is inhuman, impersonal, bureaucratic, and cruel when accomplished by the state.
- It supports and sustains a culture of violence.
- It is socially divisive and self-replicating, even over generations.
- It refuses to acknowledge the prior victimization of the perpetrator or focus on the system that presented, encouraged, or created it.
- It focuses on the past, stasis, and punishing the person, thereby diverting attention from the future, change, and solving the problem.

Mediators can help parties discover these difficulties with revenge through dialogue over how to respond to the brutality of others. It is easy to make the point that when we act brutally against another, even in response to brutal action against ourselves, our very act of revenge ensures that brutality continues into the future. In the poignant words of Jane Stanton Hitchcock, revenge is a "violent act that pierces the atmosphere, leaving a hole through which the cold, damp draft of its memory blows forever."

Dangerous mediation means helping victims recognize that revenge, while understandable as a response to brutalization, sustains suffering by proactively passing it on and opposes brutality with an equal or greater brutality. Dangerous mediation means making it possible for those who have been brutalized to *embrace* their suffering and find courage and strength, even in their victimization. It means helping them transcend their brutalization by exposing it with techniques that are not brutal. A deep understanding of what motivates people to do harm needs to be combined with ownership by the victim of the harm that was done, and a commitment not to let it go forward.

This is difficult to do and is dangerous because it can sound like blaming the victim. It is, rather, an effort to ennoble isolated, potentially destructive, individual victims by transforming them into connected, potentially creative social reformers, empathetic students of brutality, and teachers with genuine experiences to share with their perpetrators, whose insensitivity calls out for correction.

If the aim of revenge is to teach the perpetrator what it feels like to be victimized, mediators can point out that there are ways of doing so that do not condone violence by repeating it. Certainly, if the only choice is between the outward strength of the brute and the inner weakness of the victim, transformation is impossible. A third alternative is to enable parties to combine outward gentleness and empathy for others with inner strength and a collaborative resolve to satisfy each other's interests. Mahatma Gandhi expressed this well when he wrote: "We will not submit to this injustice—not merely because it is destroying us, but because it is destroying you as well."

Alternatives to Revenge

Most of the world's religions preach against private revenge, while offering substitutes in the form of divine punishment after death, spiritual punishment in this life, karma, or visitation by the modern emotional Furies of guilt and remorse. Yet these have proven inadequate to solve the problem and are of little use in mediation.

Consider the difficulties of mediating revenge with victims of violent crime. As the state has grown increasingly impersonal and bureaucratic, and religion has become more and more institutionalized, revenge has lost much of its original meaning. The criminal justice system offers a kind of official revenge that is no substitute for the real thing, leaving victims feeling cheated and criminals feeling not punished, but harassed and disregarded.

For these reasons, urban communities are increasingly using victim and offender mediation programs to process minor crimes. These victim and offender restitution or reconciliation programs (VORPs) mediate between victims and offenders without the intervention of the state, often successfully securing restitution for the victim and reconciliation for the offender, helping victims communicate the pain of victimization without resort to revenge. VORPs have been shown in studies to reduce the rate of recidivism substantially, increase grades in school, and improve family relationships.

In a typical case, a woman was driving her car on the freeway when her windshield shattered and she almost collided with cars in front of and behind her. Two young boys shooting a BB gun near the freeway were arrested, and the case was referred to mediation by the district attorney. At the mediation, the woman turned to the two young boys and yelled angrily at them, "You little sons of bitches, you almost killed me!" They realized for the first time that their actions had caused real harm to a real human being, and they began to cry. As they cried and apologized, she realized for the first time that they were not "criminals," but children who had genuinely begun to understand what they had done.

Since they had no money to pay for her windshield, they agreed to come to her house and wash her car once a month for six months. She was nervous at first, but when they showed up and worked hard (symbolically washing away their guilt), she felt compassion for them and served them milk and cookies. She began to enjoy having them around, so she hired them to continue coming on weekends to mow the lawn and take out the garbage. Their relationship deepened, and when the oldest child decided, with her encouragement, to go to college, she paid his tuition.

No criminal court could have produced a result even remotely close to this, yet it is quite common in victim-offender mediation programs for victims to surrender their desire for revenge in response to genuine remorse and restitution. If it were only possible to produce it once, the expenditure, in my mind, would have been worth it. In fact, it is possible in every criminal case, no matter how violent the crime or how old the criminal.

Sooner or later we all learn, as novelist James Baldwin has written, that: "It is a terrible, an inexorable law that one cannot deny the humanity of another without diminishing one's own; in the face of one's victim, one sees oneself." This fundamental truth is available to both sides through a dangerous form of mediation, in which the parties tell the truth and use dialogue to reach resolution. The mediation process used in this example can be applied, with minor modifications, to any conflict in which there is a desire for revenge. To learn how, it is necessary to explore the equally dangerous magic of forgiveness, which is the most powerful force available for mediating revenge.

Chapter Eight

The Magic of Forgiveness

I imagine forgiveness comes to us like a far-off song, and
when your body is seized by that distant music, you can't
fight it; your hips begin moving, then the rest of you, even
if you can't really hear the damn melody, don't recognize
the tune . . . What I mean to say is: I want to forgive my
ex-husband. I don't want to die hating, or even resenting
him. We will never make love, never even kiss again.
Never. So where is that song of forgiveness, reputed to be
so sweet?
GENE ZEIGER

It is difficult and dangerous for a mediator, or anyone outside a conflict, to suggest to those inside it that they should forgive what was done to them. The mediator may be thought to be advocating capitulation or surrender, or favoring the other side. It is possible, however, to approach the possibility of forgiveness subtly, powerfully, and steadfastly, once the primary issues have been resolved. Like revenge, forgiveness is possible in every conflict, no matter how painful or serious.

The reasons for forgiveness can be more emotional than rational, and have nothing to do with "forgiving and forgetting." On the contrary, for forgiveness to occur, both sides need to examine the reasons for their emotions and *not* forget what was done to them. Only by acknowledging the crime can we consciously choose forgiveness and avoid the appearance of cowardice in the face of evil. This seeming contradiction makes mediating forgiveness dangerous.

The Option of Forgiveness

When parties have been deeply injured by their opponents and tried every escape they can think of to no avail, when they are stuck in fantasies of revenge that are sapping their energy, when they have settled their conflicts, but are still angry and stewing with injured feelings, there are only three alternatives available to them.

First, they can choose to hold onto their anger, and convert it into an icon or obsession, feeding and stoking it into a white heat of rage. Being victims all their lives is neither fun nor interesting. Sympathy and love are not dispensed to "professional victims" in perpetuity. Instead, people increasingly turn away, leaving the victim isolated and alone. At this point, the victim may decide to act on his anger and seek revenge, thereby launching a new round of conflict in response, but leaving the underlying reasons for the conflict untouched.

Second, parties can slip into amnesia and denial, containing their anger, suppressing their desire for revenge, and trying to forget what happened to them. Yet even in denial, they do not easily forget their victimization, or the shame and humiliation that always accompanies it. They then replay, obsess over, and return to the conflict throughout their lives, often in dreams where they relive its horror. Suppression and denial are not effective in the long run. They create a distorted perception of oneself and others that often leads to poor self-esteem, hypersensitivity, selective blindness, illness, addiction, and death.

Third, parties can engage in a process of forgiveness, releasing themselves from the conflict by working through their anger against the other person. The value of forgiveness for the "victim" is that it cleanses the wound and allows it to heal. It erases the humiliation that was suffered, replacing it with pride and positive self-esteem. It encourages the expression of love, even love for the "perpetrator." It allows parties to see each other as human, and therefore as fellow victims. It permits empathy for the suffering of others. It allows each to hear the other's pain nondefensively. It defuses the incident that triggered the anger, allowing it to be released without being forgotten. It encourages the "perpetrator" to recognize the error, apologize, and take responsibility for their actions by doing whatever is necessary to compensate for the damage they caused. Forgiveness supports the victim morally and emotionally, with less cost to both sides, and society as well.

Transmuting Rage into Acceptance

We have all encountered people whose anger has become a force more powerful than their own self-interest or capacity to control it. They have locked their hatred so firmly inside themselves that it has become inextricable from their identity. These people are unable to resolve or accept the cessation of their conflicts once their interests have been satisfied, and they resist when it is in their direct interest to release.

The following story is extremely painful to relate, because it identifies the terrible price we pay for unresolved anger, and how close we all are to unimaginable disaster. I once counseled a seemingly intelligent, mild-mannered law professor who was going through a difficult divorce. An attorney advised him to remain in the house with his estranged wife until all legal issues were resolved, but their anger was escalating rapidly. I urged him to move out immediately and resolve his issues through mediation.

The night before he was scheduled to move out, they had a verbal battle that became a physical fight, and he stabbed his wife to death. He is now imprisoned for life, his wife is dead, and their children lost to both. I wondered what I might have said to have made a difference, what signs I missed that pointed toward rapid escalation and violence. Mediators need to watch for triggers and flashpoints that mark the growing rage of conflicting parties. Mediators need to become better at protecting people from causing injury or being injured themselves.

There are many ways anger can be handled so that rage and hatred do not grow too powerful to control. Through a consistent, deep, and *dangerous* kind of empathy, we can help victims and offenders see each other as people not unlike themselves, to find someplace within themselves where they might have done something similar. At the same time, parties can learn to see themselves through each others' eyes and discover that there is a clear path to release from the prison of shame and blame, pain and punishment—that is, the path of forgiveness. Novelist Willa Cather described a chance occurrence that has happened to many of us, when someone lost in hate experiences a sudden awakening through empathy or compassion:

> Sometimes a neighbor whom we have disliked a lifetime for his arrogance and conceit lets fall a single commonplace remark that shows us another side, another man really; a man more uncertain and puzzled, and in the dark like ourselves.

A first step conflicting parties can take along this path is to own their hostile feelings and not blame them on others. They can try to discover the underlying reasons for their anger, which often originates in the distant past. Letting go of ancient grievances and releasing old, unfulfilled expectations helps parties return to the present where all genuine listening takes place, in order to build their relationship in the here and now. Writer Anne Lamott remarked that forgiveness means "giving up all hope of having a better past." It is also a concrete step toward creating a better present and future.

A second step on the path to forgiveness is for the parties to communicate their feelings before they become angry at *themselves* for having put up with painful or disrespectful treatment. They can share these difficult feelings and perceptions directly with the people whose actions triggered them, as soon after the event as possible. They can be clear about what they feel, and differentiate between being upset, irritated, angry, irate, furious, enraged, and murderous, or being dismissive, arrogant, pompous, derisive, condescending, and contemptuous. They can use nonjudgmental "I" statements, and ask questions to discover whether the other person intended to cause them pain or shame. They can communicate their intention not to respond in kind. They can focus on solving the problem, rather than blaming or shaming. They can search together for creative solutions that allow both sides to win. They can use empathy and honesty to discover hidden reasons for their behavior and where it came from. And they can relax, and forgive each other for their mistakes.

Shame, Rage, and Resistance to Forgiveness

There is great beauty and power in forgiveness, yet there is also great resistance to pursuing it. It often appears easier to remain stuck in a conflict than to give up our victim status, forgo our view of the other side as evil, surrender our most precious complaints, and forgive the person whose actions or behavior caused us pain.

Resistance occurs when parties get stuck in a cycle of shame and rage about what was done to them. This occurs more frequently when they experience multiple incidents of a similar nature. We have seen many lives ruined by a series of terrible incidents that cast them into a labyrinth or downward spiral of shame and rage. On entering, they became unable to recover or find their way out.

Professor Suzanne Retsinger at the University of California at Santa Barbara has videotaped parties in conflict and has observed their communications deteriorate into a "shame/rage spiral." My summary of her findings appears in Figure 8.1:

Figure 8.1.   The Shame/Rage Spiral.

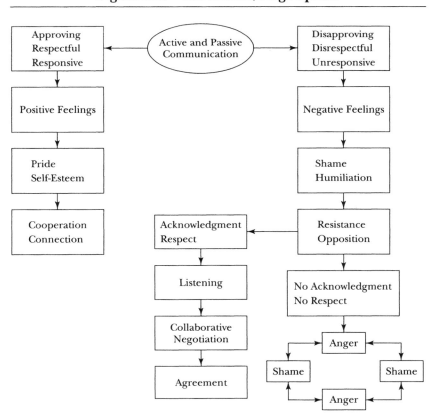

It is not just victims who are angry, but perpetrators as well. When we look deeper, we find people *need* their rage, sometimes as a substitute for affection, a diversion from self-blame and poor self-esteem, or as an expression of grief over the loss of precious, uncommunicated expectations.

I participated in an international conference on peacemaking. Among this group of highly committed professionals were two former partners who had not recovered from a painful partnership dissolution that had occurred five years earlier. One of the partners held onto his rage and paid a steep price in deteriorated health and self-doubt. He took the opportunity during a short break to explode with accusations, dump his anger publicly, and personally slander his former partner.

The partner silently withstood the attack, resulting in several sleepless nights and restless days. The inability of these "peacemakers" to express their feelings openly, own their contributions to the demise of the partnership, grieve its loss, forgive each other, and forgive themselves for tolerating abusive behavior kept their wounds open and exposed. Their unforgiving attitude poisoned their relationship. Two years later, one of the parties called the other, apologized, and asked for forgiveness, which was given.

Mediators can support parties in overcoming resistance to the idea of forgiveness by encouraging them to come to terms not only with their anger, but with their pain and suffering, their grief, and the loss of their expectations that life should have turned out differently. When parties focus on the evils their opponent did to them, forgiveness takes the appearance of capitulation, condonation, surrender in the face of evil, and implicit permission to engage in similar actions in the future. As novelist Jane Smiley wrote in *A Thousand Acres,* regarding her protagonist's memory of childhood incest:

> So all I have is the knowledge that I saw! That I saw without being afraid and without turning away, and that I didn't forgive the unforgivable. Forgiveness is a reflex for when you can't stand what you know. I resisted that reflex. That's my sole, solitary, lonely accomplishment.

Resistance to forgiveness is often based on the unexamined belief that people and their actions are one, that when an unforgivable act has taken place, the person who did it can never be forgiven. The principal difficulty with this idea is that while actions are a part of the past and never change, people live in the present and change all the time. When victims refuse forgiveness, they trap themselves in the past and become incapable of living fully in the present or planning for the future. Their past becomes their all.

In such cases, victims need to be asked *dangerous* questions that directly challenge the role of victim and reveal its hidden costs. Assuming everyone owns 100 percent of their life energy, victims need to be asked how much they are willing to subtract from their present and future to invest in a past that cannot be altered, no matter how much energy they invest in it. They need to be asked whether they want to remain connected through vendetta, investing energy in someone they do not want in their present or future.

Some resistance to forgiveness originates in the phrase "forgive and forget." Victims are correct not to forget what happened, or to forgive out of pain or weakness. The danger in forgiveness is that indignation will dissolve in sentimental confusion and surrender to weakness and fear, rather than result in strength and compassion. Victims need to remember precisely and in detail what happened to them, and then refuse permission for it to happen again. Only then can they separate what happened from who did it. When they do so, it becomes clear that forgiving the person is a *condition* for never forgiving what they did.

Our conflicts are profoundly transformed when we distinguish clearly between people and their actions or behaviors. When we confuse people with problems, we end up either trivializing their behaviors or demonizing their character. In a strange way, we let them off the hook by suggesting that they are bad people or implying that they had no choice in what they did, thereby diminishing their responsibility for changing their behavior.

When conflicting parties confuse people with problems, it becomes far more difficult to be relentless, unforgiving, and rigorous about solving the problem. If they define the problem as the person, instead of as their actions or behaviors, they are automatically drawn to attack the person and seek revenge, disarming their compassion so it will not get in the way. Yet in doing so, they slip into a personal revenge that only solves a superficial problem, while the real problem is systemic and remains untouched. For example, by attacking racists personally, rather than racist behaviors and the system of discrimination, victims may defeat some petty, deluded person who is only a cog in a much larger wheel, leaving larger issues untouched. This is not to suggest that victims should condone racist acts, or that people should not be held accountable for their behaviors. Rather, it is to say that it is possible to have a far more powerful impact by enacting legislation or repairing the lives of victims.

What is Forgiveness?

Forgiveness is not only a result, but a process of letting go of the past and opening to the future, of reclaiming energy from people and events we do not need in our lives, and of accepting ourselves more fully. It is a way of releasing ourselves from the past, from the burden of our own false expectations, and from the pain we have experienced at the hands of others. It is a release from judgment, including our judgments of ourselves.

Forgiveness does not mean we agree with what the other party did, or that what they did was right, or that we should excuse their actions. It means separating forgivable people from unforgivable actions. Forgiveness does not mean we can change what happened or erase what was done. What's done is done. All we can do is release ourselves from continuing to suffer for what happened in the past and dedicate ourselves to making sure that it does not happen in the future.

Forgiveness is not something we do for someone else, but to free *ourselves* from unhealthy pain, anger, and shame. Anger gives the appearance of being powerful, but leaves us feeling frustrated and powerless. Forgiveness appears weak, but leaves us feeling stronger and less vulnerable to others. Forgiveness is a gift to our own peace of mind, our self-esteem, our relationships with others, and our future. It frees us from entanglement in the past. It helps us reestablish control over our lives by letting go of unpleasant events and people, and by reconnecting us with healthier, more positive people and directions.

Forgiveness cannot be forced or coerced, but can only be given freely. Each of us has the power to do so independently of others. It is a choice, and it is within our control. Anger hurts not only those it is directed against, but those who wield it as well. By not forgiving the person who wronged us, we continue to inflict the pain they caused on ourselves.

Forgiveness is a personal choice that requires us to take responsibility for our actions and feelings. It requires us to be responsible to and for ourselves, even for our own continued pain and humiliation. It means being responsible for the choices we make, including anger and releasing ourselves from anger. It means taking back the responsibility and power we have given to someone else for our feelings.

Suffering is a gift, because it reminds us of our humanity and the need for compassion and forgiveness. It can also be a need and an addiction. Forgiveness requires that we let go of our need to be pitied, to be right, to feel an intense connection with our tormentor through rage. Anger links us through a negative bond with the person we cannot forgive. When we cannot forgive, the other person remains, haunting our thoughts. A single memory or sight of them can throw us off balance or spark an addictive response. By refusing to forgive them, we are as controlled by them as we would have been if we had never left their side. Forgiveness leads to release from being controlled negatively by the image of them that we have internalized.

We have not learned how to reach forgiveness, but we know intuitively that it begins in the heart. To start the process, all we need to do is *want* to be released from the past. While the other person need not even be physically present, it is better if they are. Forgiveness is learning to see the other person and ourselves without negativity or judgments.

Forgiveness means giving up old patterns, addictions, and obsessions, which is a loss. If our self-image is tied to being a victim, coming to peace with others can result in the loss of a familiar form of self-identification. If we have a fragile sense of self based on identification as a victim, we strengthen who we are by creating a positive identity through forgiveness.

It is possible for us to forgive each other as a way of releasing ourselves from conflict, yet still choose not to be friends or co-workers or see the other person frequently. Forgiveness in this sense means letting go of the conflict and the reasons for it, but does not necessarily mean being best friends.

Beyond forgiveness lies the possibility of reconciliation, which is the point at which the conflict comes full circle and is actually, completely ended. This last phase of the resolution process takes place after the fighting has ceased, the issues have been settled, and the other person has been forgiven. Reconciliation means being able to be in the other person's presence without a twinge of anger or discomfort.

Exploring the Limits of Forgiveness

While there is a danger of slipping into condonation every time we consider forgiveness, there is an equal danger of slipping into revenge, hatred, and ineffectiveness every time we do not. As an illustration, consider an extreme hypothetical: a decision to execute Adolph Hitler. To push your thinking about revenge and forgiveness to its limits, here are some questions to ponder before executing Hitler:

- Which is the greater evil, Hitler or the system of fascism he fostered?
- By executing Hitler, do we in any way let fascism off the hook?
- Could you do it yourself—not by pulling a switch, but with your bare hands?
- What would happen to *you* if you did? Would that be worth it? Who, or what, would have won?
- What about all of Hitler's administrators, supporters, and assistants who made him possible? Would you execute them as well? Where would you draw the line? Does not the line separating guilt from innocence run through the entire nation, the entire world?
- Could you imagine a fate worse than death for Hitler?
- What would you design as a form of poetic justice for him?
- Why give him the lesser punishment and let him off the hook by executing him, when you could make it worse?
- Who does his life belong to—the families of his victims or the state?
- If you gave the families of Hitler's victims a choice between personally executing him and having him work for the rest of his life to pay them back and do their bidding, which would they choose?

My point in asking these questions is not to suggest that Hitler go free. It is not even to suggest that he not be executed, assassinated, or subjected to some merciless revenge. But if the United States and other allied powers were partly responsibility for Hitler's rise to power, beginning with the Treaty of Versailles, the lack of military support for the Spanish Republic, corporations that invested in the Third Reich, and a host of other actions, what should *our* punishment be?

Many would be willing to pay the cost and pull the switch, while others would advocate doing both. What is most important is to see that by executing Hitler we do not execute the system of fascism of which he was the nominal head. Others who were responsible for making fascism succeed have been allowed to go free, including ourselves, partly because it is difficult to draw an accurate line separating guilt from innocence.

I picked a painful case to reveal a painful truth that has validity even in smaller, less onerous situations. In ordinary conflicts, the same questions can be asked. It is clear that execution, or any revenge, makes one an executioner, and that execution thereby wins. It is also clear that victims are not served by executions, which can be a substitute for restorative justice. What is needed are reparations and dedication to eradicating the conditions that caused the victimization. This leads us to focus not simply on Hitler, but on the needs of his victims. We need to recognize the fertile soil of mindless obedience in which his ideas thrived and continue to thrive long after his death.

What is needed is an objective, a principled target, a focus for the pain and hatred that is not personal, but oriented to solving the problem. This idea has been beautifully and profoundly expressed by author Olive Moore:

> Be careful with hatred. Handle hatred with respect. Hatred is too noble an emotion to be frittered away in little personal animosities. Whereas love is of itself a reward and an object worth striving for, personal hatred has no triumphs that are not trivial, secondary and human. Therefore love as foolishly as you may. But hate only after long and ardent deliberation. Hatred is a passion requiring one hundred times the energy of love. Keep it for a cause, not an individual. Keep it for intolerance, injustice, stupidity. For hatred is the strength of the sensitive. Its power and its greatness depend on the selflessness of its use.

The ideas of selflessness in the exercise of hatred, of keeping it for a cause rather than an individual, of the costly energy required to maintain it brilliantly highlight the negative power of hatred. The optimal outcome is to forgive the person while never forgiving their actions, but translating them into commitment and a *real* revenge, which makes sure it will never happen again.

Who is Responsible for Conflict?

One reason it is difficult to mediate forgiveness is that doing so forces parties to take responsibility for their actions and inactions, to recognize that they contributed to the problem or allowed it to continue. Yet most parties duck responsibility to avoid being blamed, or shift blame onto others. They tell others only what they want them to hear or think they ought to know. They are silent or lie when they ought to tell the truth. They minimize the seriousness of the problem or their involvement with it. They say "yes" without meaning it, or say they didn't mean it, or accuse others of misunderstanding, while denying their own miscommunications. They generalize to the point of absurdity. They procrastinate or say they simply forgot. They put others on the defensive by attacking them. They claim they were too busy or had more important things to do.

All these efforts at denying responsibility ignore the fact that responsibility is a precondition for learning, growth, change, and transformation. Without responsibility, we cannot address the systems that generate many of our conflicts. Without responsibility, there is no community, no relationship, no society, no survival.

We need to acknowledge that responsibility extends not simply to those who acted and should not have, but to those who did *not* act and *should* have. Responsibility, in the example of fascism, extends not only to those who did it, but those who ordered it done, those who proposed it, those who profited from it, those who supported it, those who justified or applauded it, those who defended it, those who obscured it, denied it, or covered it up, those who knew about it and did nothing to stop it, and those who ought to have known but chose to disregard it. In short, responsibility extends to everyone within reach of the problem.

This is not meant to let anyone off the hook, but to put everyone on it. In doing so, we discover that the parties are not wholly innocent of the victimizations they complain about, and they bear responsibility—not blame—even for what they did not do to stop it. For this reason, we need to consider forgiveness differently.

Five Fundamental Steps to Forgiveness

Assuming that forgiveness is desired by the parties, it is no easy matter for mediators to achieve it. There is a "magic" to it. Some of this magic flows from simple conflict resolution techniques that require moving through the usual stages of the mediation process, settling outstanding issues, then letting go of them. Some of what happens is beyond technique.

Personal forgiveness can be seen as taking place in five fundamental steps that are sometimes experienced in joint session, sometimes in caucus, and sometimes by people on their own. These are:

1. Ask the least powerful person to remember in detail what happened and how it made her feel.
2. Ask the more powerful person what happened and how it made him feel.
3. Ask each to identify all the reasons that prevent them from reaching forgiveness, and all their expectations of how they would have liked the other person to have acted.
4. Ask each to choose to accept responsibility for their past, present, and future life, release themselves from their false expectations, and explain why they need to let go of each of the reasons that have prevented them from forgiving.
5. Ask each person to design a ritual act of release, letting go, completion, and forgiveness—for example, by shaking hands or burning lists of things the other person did to them.

Additional Techniques to Deepen Forgiveness

Forgiveness involves more than simply ending the conflict, settling it, or even resolving the underlying reasons that fueled it. It can become extremely complex, and involve a number of diverse techniques that build on the five listed above. These are most effective when introduced by a mediator in the presence of both parties, but can also be experienced alone, or with a friend. They are most effective when spoken, but can be completed through writing, ritual, and gesture:

- State what you think forgiveness means.
- Indicate what, with hindsight, you would have done differently, what you contributed to the conflict, or what you plan to do differently in the future.
- Identify what would change in your life if you were able to reach forgiveness, what keeps you from achieving it, and how to create a path that leads there step by step.
- State honestly what you need to say or hear for the conflict to be over.
- Express your feelings, including anger, guilt, and desire for revenge.
- Recognize that beneath your anger is pain, and speak from your pain.
- Reframe each other's descriptions of the conflict or insults in neutral or positive terms.
- Write down a list of metaphors, insults, or phrases that describe what you like least about your opponent, and next to each word or phrase, write the name of the member of your family who comes closest to fitting that description.
- Say how you separate the person from their actions or behavior.
- Say how you would like the other person to have acted or said.
- Acknowledge that the other person did not act or say what you wanted, and explain why.
- Identify the other person's legitimate interests, good intentions, and humane motives.
- List what you have in common.
- Create a mutually acceptable, integrated story about what happened, without demonization or victimization.
- Apologize for whatever you did or felt that was not 100 percent what you think you ought to have done or felt.
- Rate your apologies on a scale of 1 to 10, then improve them until you receive a perfect 10.
- Say why you have chosen to forgive the other person.

- Identify anything for which you need to forgive yourself.
- Affirm that by forgiving each other you are taking responsibility for your own actions and feelings, and reclaiming the rest of your life.
- Say what you admire or appreciate in your opponent and what you admire or appreciate in yourself.
- Say what you wish or hope for your opponent and what you wish or hope for yourself.
- Brainstorm ways of reducing distrust over time—for example, by meeting for breakfast once a month to talk about your present, future, or distant past, but not about the conflict until you can do so without recreating it.
- Agree to engage in some symbolic act that ends the conflict for you, and celebrate your decision with friends or by yourself.
- If you are unable to reach forgiveness, congratulate yourself on your efforts and keep trying.

As a mediator, remember not to pressure anyone into forgiveness. It is not your relationship, and the choice belongs to them. Also, there is no technique for producing magic in every case—the human mind is far too subtle for that. It is more a question of listening with the heart, reaching for the painful honesty that lies at the center of the conflict, and recognizing that holding on will not help them get on with the rest of their lives.

Methods for Difficult Cases

There are several methods that work well in difficult cases, such as those involving date rape, sexual harassment, or termination of employment, where shame or humiliation runs deep. In these cases, mediators can:

- Help the victim create a "virtual revenge" that allows her to release her rage without actually causing the perpetrator to suffer, or herself to experience guilt. For example, ask the victim to say what her favorite revenge would be, and make it humorous—even ask her to act it out with the mediator as a stand in, or use a doll or symbol instead. Afterwards, debrief, encourage her to release her anger, and point out the reasons for not taking revenge.

- Elicit from the perpetrator the words the injured person most wants to hear, like "I'm sorry," or "What I did was unforgivable."
- If the perpetrator is unable to say these words, say them yourself, as in: "Perhaps what she should have said was, 'I'm sorry,' or 'What I did was unforgivable'" and watch body language for signs that the listener is relaxing or releasing anger.
- Ask whether the perpetrator has ever felt victimized, and if so, when and by whom, revealing the origins of victimization in the perpetrator's distant past. Point out that revenge causes revenge, which causes revenge, down through generations, and that perpetration and revenge are simply ways of being proactive in the face of one's own victimization.
- Reveal that revenge is a form of victimization, by asking the victim questions that expose the prejudices, stereotypes, demonizations, and objectifications common to both. For example, ask both parties to list the words that describe the other person, then comment on their similarities in tone and metaphoric content.
- Encourage them to hold on to their grievances and mistrust, and jointly brainstorm ways of doing so, or ask what they will do next, then assess the costs of doing so.
- Explore the self-interest of the victim in preventing future victimizations.
- Ask the victim to imagine how forgiveness and revenge will feel in the long run, and ask which they would rather experience.
- Focus on the spiritual strength of nonviolent solutions and not demeaning or reducing oneself to the other person's level.
- Suggest that revenge may be exactly what the other person wants, and that refusing it may be a higher form of revenge.

Forgiveness is the natural state of grace before the fall of victimization, the heavenly end after the death of hatred. It usually benefits the victim far more than it does the perpetrator, because it breaks the cycle of rage and shame that is without end. Ironically, forgiveness is also the highest form of revenge. For this reason, Oscar Wilde wrote, "Always forgive your enemies—nothing infuriates them so."

Creating Rituals and Ceremonies of Forgiveness

The only thing more powerful than being stuck in a rut is creating a ritual. In order to actually forgive another person or give up the desire for revenge, it is helpful to engage in a ritual of release as a way of letting go of the conflict. Rituals like marriage are powerful ways of changing attitudes, and mediators can help parties design them for maximum effect.

To design a ritual that will help someone release their anger and reach forgiveness, or any ritual for that matter, take the following steps:

- Ask the party to specify the desired change.
- Symbolize it in the form of a specific action.
- Chose a time and place where it will take place.
- Embody their intention in action.
- Affirm their commitment publicly.
- Celebrate their transition.

I often work with parties in conflict to design rituals for forgiveness and reconciliation and try to create a unique design for each situation. Here are some alternatives to help parties design their own rituals:

- Ask them to draw a picture of the conflict, create a dance, or write a song or poem about it. Repeat the exercise with forgiveness or reconciliation as the theme.
- Ask them to create a sculpture, using themselves or whatever materials come to mind, to represent the conflict, then ask them to change it so it reflects forgiveness.
- Using role reversal, ask each person to become the other person in the conflict and say what they think the other person feels. Ask the first person if this is correct, and trace the incorrectness to perceptions and communication problems.

- Ask each person to describe how they met or what their relationship was like before the conflict, or what each one especially values in the other.
- Ask them to role-play meeting for the first time, and find out about each other as though they had never met.
- Ask each person to bring a gift for each other to the next session that represents what they see in the other person that they don't see or value in themselves.
- Set an empty chair in front of one of the parties. Ask them to imagine that the other person has died, and that their spirit is in the chair. Ask them to say whatever they want to the other person's spirit, then answer.
- Create a joint task for them, perhaps in friendly competition with each other. For example, ask them to come up with ideas for what their relationship should be like in the future.
- Ask them to go out to lunch together, talk about what they most deeply want in their lives, and focus on listening and solving their problems.
- Ask them to write down their secret expectations of each other.
- Ask them to come to the next session in their favorite costume or disguise, or dressed as they see the other person, then roleplay a dialogue in which they put forth their ideas and reach forgiveness.
- Give them one minute to brainstorm all the words or expressions they can imagine to communicate the feeling of forgiveness (such as, "wow!"). Then ask them to do the same for the feeling of not reaching forgiveness (for example, "awful"). Ask which set of words would they prefer to use in describing their future relationship.
- Ask each person to role-play being unwilling to forgive or reconcile, then describe how it felt.
- Ask them to face each other or imagine the other person in front of them, and complete the following phrases:
  "I fondly remember when we. . . ."
  "I am sorry for . . . or that we were unable to . . ."
  "I wish you . . ."
- Ask them to thank each other for something they learned or experienced from their relationship.

- Ask them to design a ceremony of forgiveness that reverses the meaning their conflict had for them.
- Suggest they celebrate and go out to dinner or have a party, and invite others who are important in their lives. If they are co-workers, have them ask to be put on the agenda for the next staff meeting to say what they each learned from the conflict.

Stages in Reconciliation

After forgiveness comes reconciliation, which is the ability to be in the presence of one's opponent without feeling angry, ashamed, or vulnerable. Reconciliation is the highest point of healing, short of transcendence. It is the conflict coming full circle and returning to the harmony from which it sprang.

Parties commonly go through a number of stages in reaching reconciliation that are not linear or sequential, but overlap and shift back and forth. These start with confusion, in which trust and distrust coexist alongside each other. There are shifting emotions without clarity of purpose, and a tendency towards continued blaming and forgiveness, along with a confused, sometimes suppressed desire for increased contact with the other person.

Next, there is increasing vulnerability and openness toward each other. The parties speak openly about the causes of their conflict and gradually come to accept a more neutral story of its origins. There is increasing willingness to share feelings about the future, the present, and the past. Through listening and empathy there is a deeper understanding of what the other person experienced. The parties begin to understand their "system," to see the "self-as-other" and the "other-as-self."

Gradually, there is increasing honesty, both with each other and with themselves. The parties become more authentic as they say what they really think and feel. With honesty, there is a discovery of new bases for trust arising out of communication or agreement, either about the future or the present but not necessarily the past. They learn to break old patterns and share responsibility for their past behaviors.

Next, there is completion, in which the conflict is over and there is a feeling in both parties of having moved to a different place. The parties can then release their need to continue feeling angry with the other person, though not necessarily with what they did. They release themselves through rituals of forgiveness and symbolically surrender past grievances. Finally, they create a new basis for their relationship by renewing their connection or friendship, and sharing present problems and future hopes. They openly express affection for each other, with nothing left over from the past.

Forgiving Oneself

In the middle of a forgiveness activity in a workshop I cofacilitated for mental health professionals, a woman began to sob. We waited for an opportunity to ask her about the source of her pain. As her tears subsided, she told us she had been unwilling to forgive her sister who had inflicted a lifetime of pain on her. As we helped her look more closely, she realized it was herself she had not forgiven, for provoking her sister's aggression and destroying their relationship. She knew she had to apologize for what she had done, and forgive herself in order to be complete.

Many reconciliations have broken down because while people are prepared to forgive, they are not ready to be forgiven. Forgiving the other person is not the last step in the process. Everyone in conflict needs to forgive themselves. This may sound a little like pop psychology, but we often find people who are deeply angry at others are also angry that they tolerated disrespectful or painful behavior, so they turn their anger against themselves. For conflict to be transcended, it must be let go of at both ends, and in the middle as well.

Even when forgiveness and reconciliation occur, they need to be reinforced and supported by others, and by the culture of the workplace, school, organization, family, or relationship. Conflict and anger always appear easier, stronger, and more dramatic than forgiveness and reconciliation. Even small shifts in a positive direction can accumulate over time and produce long-term changes in the most entrenched combatants.

In an ancient story, a man came to see the Buddha in a rage and spat in his face. The Buddha smiled, but his supporters were extremely upset and wanted to punish the man. The next day, the man returned to ask for forgiveness. The Buddha said, "No. I cannot forgive you. Whoever you spat on is no longer here. And the person who spat is also no longer here. You are not the man who did that. Today there is fresh water in the river. It is not yesterday's water. But do not worry, if I ever meet that man, I will tell him to forgive you."

We are never the same once we have been harmed or injured, and we are never the same once we have reached forgiveness and reconciliation. Part of what makes forgiveness dangerous is that when we understand our enemies, and the parts of ourselves that shame us, we are forced to surrender our identity as victims, as well as our desire for revenge. In their place, we find identity as people who have transcended hatred and the conditions that created it. Fundamentally, all the difficulties with revenge and reasons for forgiveness boil down to one: spiritual growth. To grow spiritually as mediators, we need to learn how to work with spirit and approach each conflict as a spiritual path.

Chapter Nine

The Significance of Spirit

To learn the Way, you must be sharp yet inconspicuous. When you are sharp, you are not confused by people. When you are not confused by people, you are inconspicuous. When you are inconspicuous, you do not argue with people. Not being confused by people, you are empty and spiritual. Not arguing with people, you are serene and subtle.
LIAO-AN

Conflict is not only an extraordinarily powerful emotional, intellectual, and physical experience, but a profoundly spiritual one as well. Indeed, our experience has been that conflict is *overridingly* spiritual, because every conflict presents us with a life choice, an opportunity for transformation, and an invitation to transcendence.

In addition, each resolution is a kind of minor miracle, in which parties move from impasse to solutions, antagonism to collaboration, revenge to forgiveness, isolation to community. How this happens has more to do with spirit than with logic, emotion, or physical sensation. To understand why and how this makes mediation dangerous, we need to understand what spirit is and how it impacts people in conflict.

The Difficulty of Writing about Spirit

It is difficult to write clearly about spirit, or what *actually* shifts when people resolve their conflicts, transmute revenge into forgiveness, or achieve transformation or transcendence. Indeed, it is difficult to write about anything deeply important without potentially cheapening it, even when we do so with understanding.

Moreover, when we write about spirit, we are writing about the very thing that is writing. For this reason, the search for spirit is sometimes described as "riding an ox in search of an ox," because there is no external vantage point from which we can see our seeing or understand our understanding. While the mind knows by analysis, the spirit knows by experience. In the words of Zen, the sound of the rain needs no translation.

It is also difficult to write about spirit because people confuse it with religion, or belief in God, or "New Age" ideas. I consider it a form of energy everyone possesses regardless of religion, belief in God or New Age thinking. It is neither occult nor mysterious, but a quality of ordinary, everyday life; it is not outside, but inside; not beyond but within. The Chinese word *chi*, referring to "life energy," may be a more accurate expression.

As with energy, spirit is wavelike, in constant flux, impossible to fix, isolate, or freeze. Who we are consists of two parts—one inborn, internal, and unchanging, the other relational, environmentally impacted, and in constant motion. One is a deep, melodic strain or recurrent theme, while the other is a variation played out by events that pluck, blow, and drum us. As every human life is an evolving, unique journey along uncharted paths, no one's life is a complete guide for any other. Thus, when we search for spirit, we cannot provide packaged answers or generic solutions—only constantly moving questions, options, and possibilities.

Nonetheless, seeking answers is important because the opportunity to achieve profound personal and organizational transformation through conflict depends less on thinking than on spirit. To guide parties toward this opportunity means learning to mediate not merely with ideas, feelings, and body sensations, but with spirit as well.

Mediating conflict spiritually is dangerous, not only because of the inherent imprecision and unknowability of spirit, but because of its confusion with orthodoxy and religion, its infinite depth, and the limitless vulnerability it requires. Mediating spiritually is dangerous because it is the ground on which every conflict and every resolution rests, beneath which there is nothing.

What is Spirit?

In spite of countless efforts over centuries, there is no rigorous definition of spirit, nor is it likely one is possible. Defining spirit means defining the essence of life. The more specific we become in trying to define it, the less we understand it. This is because any effort to define a whole reduces it to a mere sum of its parts. Among these parts, it is impossible to identify anything that looks like it could have a holistic or synergistic effect. No organ in the human body contains life, or suggests the possibility of artistic imagination, scientific curiosity, or romantic love.

Moreover, the act of definition collapses and freezes what it seeks to define. Spirit exists *only* in flux, in being rather than in thought, feeling, or sensation. It is domiciled nowhere, yet dwells everywhere. It is expressed physically, intellectually, and emotionally, yet is reducible to none of them. It is present in genius and stupidity, good and evil, success and failure, love and hate. Defining spirit is often described in Zen as putting legs on a snake— something that is both duplicative and pointless.

In spite of these difficulties, it is important to clarify what spirit means in the context of conflict resolution. By striving to render spirit intelligible in mediation, we increase our fluency and capacity for directly communicating with it, recognizing when it is diseased, and leading it in the direction of resolution, transformation, and transcendence. What follows is less a definition of spirit than a search for ways of exploring it.

In Search of an Understanding of Spirit

Here is one way of understanding spirit: consciousness is fundamentally made up of two parts—one that feels and thinks, and another that is *aware* of what is being felt and thought. The second part knows what is felt, yet does not itself experience feeling. It understands what is thought, yet does not itself think. This deep level of awareness can be thought of as spirit. In this sense, spirit means focused attention, awareness, and concentration, resulting in a form of implicit learning we call wisdom. Lack of focused attention and failure of wisdom can cause conflict, and increased awareness and insight can produce resolution.

Spirit can also be understood as essence, the life force, the energy that flows through our bodies, the animating principle. It can be read in the simple self-awareness of babies and the radiant disengagement of those who are dying. It can be sensed in acts of self-sacrifice, in the faces of the suffering, and in works of artistic inspiration. Opposing this flow of energy can cause conflict, and releasing it can trigger resolution.

Spirit can be understood as an expression of the essential oneness of all people, the interconnection of all living things. Conflict denies this oneness and interconnection. Reconnecting people and reminding them of what they have in common results in resolution.

Spirit can be thought of as a hologram, each part of which contains the whole, just as each piece of a holographic plate contains an entire image. Spirit cannot be reduced to thoughts, emotions, or senses, or to what *prompts* thoughts, emotions, or senses, or even to the average of all thoughts, emotions, and senses over our entire lives. Conflict is also a hologram, in which each separate issue reflects the whole. Revealing in each issue the deeper hologram that created it can generate resolution.

Spirit, then, is what makes each of us distinct and separate, and at the same time united and inseparable. In a commonly used metaphor, every wave in the ocean is distinct and separate, yet part of the same ocean. Whenever a wave is created in one location, its impact is felt in the ocean as a whole. Similarly, whatever we do in conflict is something that happens to the entire human race, because we are not separable from it, but expressions of the whole.

Locating Spirit

The first step to take in mediating spirit is to locate it. Science locates things by separating, reducing, and isolating wholes into their divisible parts. This makes it difficult to locate spirit. One way to locate your sense of spirit is through meditation. When you allow your actions, thoughts, emotions, and bodily sensations to become still and silent, what is left is spirit, or the direct experience of awareness.

Spirit is the ground state of sentience, without separations or distinctions. Getting there consists simply of removing the clutter, eliminating everything that is not direct experience, and identifying self with other until they merge. Spirit can be located in any activity or reflection in which self merges with other, disintegrating the idea that there is a subject experiencing awareness separate from the object of awareness. The Chinese poet Li Po described this beautifully:

> We sat together, the forest and I
>
> Merging into silence
>
> Until only the forest remained.

Spirit can be understood mathematically as an expression of zero or infinity within a finite world. Certain simple mathematical equations regularly produce infinite results. For example, it is not possible to describe a circle without reference to *pi,* an infinite number. If the self can be likened to a circle, *pi* would represent spirit. Conflict also touches something infinite within us—not only infinite feelings like rage, but infinite possibilities for learning, growth, and transcendence, each producing a locatable change in spirit.

Spirit can be located in what we feel when we unite or collaborate, or when we act as one. These moments occur accidentally, without planning, sometimes in emergencies and crises, sometimes in the midst of extraordinary natural beauty, sometimes in moments of intense love. They also occur when we discover common ground in mediation, feel deeply connected through honesty, empathy, and compassion, resolve conflicts, and reach forgiveness.

Spirit can be located in collective energy. It is what makes a house different from a home, a block from a neighborhood, a city from a community, or a committee from a team. The latter possess a *collective* energy that is absent in the former. Similarly, there are discernibly different energies in conflict and resolution, sympathy and empathy, denial and honesty, revenge and forgiveness, that can be sensed in mediation.

Spirit can be located at the boundaries between people. When mediating, try shifting the distance between yourself and the parties, by moving slightly closer or farther apart. You should be able to feel differences in intimacy, depth of communication, degree of permission to ask dangerous questions, and ease in being deeply honest and empathetic.

Spiritual energy can be positive or negative, directed outward or inward. In conflict, people direct negative energy outward against others or inward against themselves, which drains their positive energy and confuses ego with spirit. They judge others and resist vulnerability, because they are afraid or ashamed of what they will find when they look deeply inside.

It is the seamless combination, the unification and integration of positive and negative, outward and inward, that reflects true spirit. Wholeness means there is no systemic difference between polar opposites. It means we can resolve conflicts by redirecting positive energy outward through acknowledgment and feedback, and inward through authenticity and ownership of the conflict. This is perhaps what Zen monk Ta Hui meant when he wrote: "When a person is confused, he sees east as west. When he is enlightened, west itself is east."

Spirit in conflict can be located in quality of intention; or rather, every quality of intention reflects a different spirit or kind of energy. Spirit is contained in everything said and done, and in everything neither said nor done. Many people believe spirit is love, but there is also spirit in hatred and in every living connection. The energy of revenge is very different from the energy of forgiveness, yet energy itself is neither good nor evil, this nor that. It is beyond categories, and therefore *simultaneously* each, both, neither, and beyond. In conflict resolution, both can be found in each, and each in both.

The best way of locating spirit is simply by feeling the energy of the conflict as it moves from one person to the other, from one vibratory quality to the next, and watch as everything external manifests itself internally. Spirit can be thought of as a bandwidth, only a small part of which is audible or visible, like sound and light. Perhaps the greatest lesson I have learned in resolving conflict is that all energies operate in both directions at the same time. Anger toward others is always accompanied by angry feelings within ourselves, just as love of ourselves inevitably allows us to experience greater love toward others.

Spirit in Mediation

Mediators have been trained to recognize and respond to conflict within emotional, intellectual, and physical parameters, but know little about the spiritual side of conflict. Few people in organizations, workplaces, law offices, communities, or families have much awareness or skill in responding to spiritual needs or crises, or in communicating at a spiritual level. Yet spirit is at the very core of every human process.

Most mediations commence with formalities, such as setting ground rules, discussing confidentiality, explaining process, and completing forms. After each party recounts their version of the facts, mediators identify issues, facilitate problem solving, write agreements, and solidify commitments. During this time, the spirits of the parties are largely ignored, concealed, or excluded from the process.

Without directly addressing the spirits of the parties, it is far more difficult to reach resolution, let alone forgiveness, reconciliation, transformation, or transcendence, all of which are fundamentally spiritual in nature. Mediators are then left to settle a range of relatively superficial, legalistic, petty issues that lack engagement, depth, or the energy of authentic possibility.

We know that both conflict and resolution take place in ways that can be described physically, intellectually, and emotionally. As mediators, we watch body language and eye contact, acknowledge emotions and hidden feelings, listen to ideas, and analyze proposed solutions. Each improves our understanding of the conflict and directly influences our choice of effective resolution techniques and procedures. Why not consider spiritual information as well?

Most Native American cultures open and close mediations not with intellect, emotion, or body language, but spirit. This is expressed in Figure 9.1, depicting the medicine wheel, which actually points in six directions, including up and down, or external and internal, that are not shown. The first movement is always toward spirit.

The suffering people experience during conflict is manifested physically, emotionally, intellectually, and spiritually. Parties often become physically ill, emotionally angry, and intellectually

Figure 9.1.   Native American Medicine Wheel.

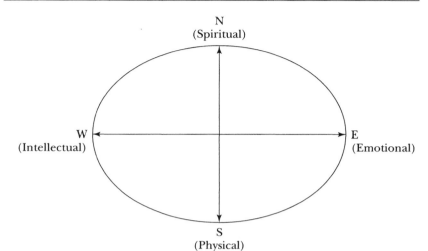

confused. In addition, they feel off-center, drained, low on energy, disconnected, disheartened, untrusting, or lonely. Each quality of suffering influences others, and when they heal in one area, it reduces suffering in others. In this sense, there is no clear boundary between spirit, mind, emotion, and physicality. They are all parts of a whole, a circle, and cannot be dissected without doing damage to the whole.

Using spirit in mediation means discovering what the conflict means at a deep level, exploring what lies beneath its surface. It means using dangerous forms of empathy and honesty, listening and acknowledgment, apology and ownership. It means turning inwards, letting go, and discovering what it feels like to be on the other side. It means acting on values and integrity, finding common ground, resolving the reasons that led to the dispute, and reaching forgiveness and reconciliation. It means authenticity and the possibility of transformation and transcendence.

Spirit is simply awareness of a deeper reality that bridges the distance between self and others. It is located at a ninety-degree angle from accusations, justifications, attachments, and defenses. For this reason, it appears dangerous, nonexistent, otherworldly, and impractical.

Spiritual Choices in Response to Conflict

Spiritually, mediation is an effort to escape false dichotomies between self and others that are reflected in the seemingly endless game of victory and defeat, praise and blame, gain and loss, pleasure and pain that characterize chronic conflicts. There are four fundamental spiritual choices in response to conflict, each with its own distinct qualities:

1. Shutting down and retreating out of fear, avoidance, or capitulation.
2. Tightening up and fighting out of anger, aggression, or greed.
3. Suppressing and surrendering out of shame, accommodation, or guilt.
4. Opening up and exploring out of love, collaboration, or curiosity.

Most people adopt one of the first three options and respond to conflict out of fear, anger, or shame. They become frightened that something terrible will happen if they drop their defenses and invite their conflicts in. Yet doing so frees them of fear, releases their anger, and makes them unashamed. They discover, in the wonderful words of a Zen poem:

> Now that my house has fallen down
>
> I have a much better view of the moon.

The spiritual message of mediation is that house and moon are both inside us. If we are willing to topple the house of victimization and demonization, with its elaborate self-justifications and rationalizations, we can glimpse the moon of authenticity and collaboration. Every conflict shakes the house of our assumptions and reveals the moon of transformation. Yet transformation requires a *dangerous* exposure, exploration, and curiosity. In the process, we discover that conflict is simply the pain we experience giving birth to a new self, the pain of transcendence.

Conflict and the Journey of the Spirit

Most conflicts result from misperceptions and miscommunications that vanish when we see them in a new light. Where, then, did they come from, and where did they go? Conflicting parties are often described as being miles apart, yet they are also inseparable. How is it possible for them to be both? When we act with integrity, honesty, compassion, and generosity toward others, we feel better. Why do we have this feeling, where does it come from, and why is it so hard to maintain when we are in conflict?

We operate under a mistaken assumption that what we *do* when we are in conflict is more important than who we *are*. But we are not reducible to our actions any more than to our thoughts, emotions, and senses. Spirit tells us we are also observers of these parts, and that we are a whole that is greater than the sum of them. Changing who we are shifts what we do, just as changing what we do alters who we are.

Because outward orientation and inward contemplation are intertwined, because every external action creates an internal response, and every internal change alters our response to those around us, external conflicts and resolutions are reflected inwardly, just as internal conflicts and resolutions are projected outwards. Mahatma Gandhi expressed this well when he wrote:

> I believe that if one man gains spiritually the whole world gains with him, and if one man falls, the whole world falls to that extent. I do not help my opponents without at the same time helping myself and my coworkers.

The spiritual journey of conflict resolution starts when the parties disarm their immediate responses to conflict, and choose to watch, listen, and learn from their opponents. There is no room on this journey for illusions, for seeing themselves as victims and others as enemies, for fears that conflict will harm them. Losing their house of fear leaves them feeling open, naked, and unprotected, and able to spot the moon.

As mediators, we need to build physical, intellectual, emotional, and *spiritual* contact with parties, to support them in being open about their deepest needs and desires, and encourage them to risk direct, heart-to-heart communication with their adversaries. We need to search for ways of building spiritual solutions into mediation agreements and describing spiritual aspects or dimensions of the process.

We need to increase our capacity for spiritual intervention, including intuition, empathy, and subtle awareness. This does not mean imposing our spiritual practices on others. It means encouraging openness to forgiveness and reconciliation; creating results consistent with integrity; meeting deep human needs and desires rather than merely dividing property or cash; eliciting acknowledgment and respect; improving relationships; deepening communications; and developing authenticity and self-esteem. Doing so transforms mediation into a spiritual path.

Chapter Ten

Conflict as a Spiritual Path

> *In order to swim one takes off all one's clothes—in order to*
> *aspire to the truth one must undress in a far more inward*
> *sense, divest oneself of all one's inward clothes, of*
> *thoughts, conceptions, selfishness, etc., before one is*
> *sufficiently naked.*
> SØREN KIERKEGAARD

At issue in most mediations are not only money, power, position, and legal rights, but respect, honest and empathetic communication, trusting collaborative relationships, responsibility, forgiveness, and closure. While a knowledge of law, finance, psychology, negotiation, and organizational development are useful in resolving the first set of issues, an understanding of the spiritual dynamics of conflict is essential for resolving the second.

At a deep level, the issue in every dispute is ourselves, and our relationship not only with our adversaries, but with life itself. Every conflict provides us with unique opportunities to deepen our spiritual energy, our sense of wholeness, and our connection with life. When we are able to empathize with people we have feared or hated, we open hidden parts of ourselves and become more centered and authentic. This is the beginning of a spiritual transformation that extends not only to the parties, but to mediators as well.

The Zen of Mediation

Mediators do not always approach conflict resolution, or their own conflicts, as opportunities for learning or journeys of transformation. Yet *dangerous* mediation requires us to do so. Accepting mediation as a spiritual path means continuously cultivating awareness, empathy, honesty, authenticity, forgiveness, and reconciliation within ourselves. Doing so means practicing what we call "The Zen of Mediation," which includes:

- Being as empathetic with both parties as possible, without losing ourselves.
- Being as honest with both parties as possible, without being judgmental.
- Being as committed as possible to revealing choices involving resolution and transformation, without caring one bit what either party chooses.

When we are empathetic without being honest, neither side hears what they need in order to learn or grow from their conflict. When we are honest without being empathic, either side may feel judged and resist or respond defensively. When we are invested in other people's choices, we cheat them out of being responsible for important decisions and violate the boundary that separates them from us.

Spirit is suppressed not only by dishonesty, insensitivity, and boundary violations, but by formality, inauthenticity, and professional distancing. Mediating spiritually is dangerous because it means stepping away from professional language, definitions, and expertise. The real work of mediation cannot be learned through PhDs, law degrees, or traditional forms of certification. Honesty, empathy, awareness, community building, and equanimity are not taught in universities, but learned throughout our lives.

Locating Opportunities for Transformation

Those who wish to experience conflict as a spiritual path will find it useful to identify the nodes of spiritual contact within mediation. If we adopt the metaphor of acupuncture and think of conflict as a body, we need to locate the "meridians" of energy and points where it can be tapped. We want to know when and how the possibility of transformation arises in conflict and what mediators can do to point parties in the right direction.

We can start by encouraging parties to disengage their "fight or flight" responses, clear their minds of everything they think they know about the conflict and each other, and listen responsively and empathetically to what each other is saying. The only way to learn from conflict on a spiritual level is by listening with spirit and heart to what the conflict is trying to teach them.

All conflict behaviors can be thought of as requests for spiritual engagement, for relationship, and for authentic communication. In order to listen at a spiritual level, parties need to learn how to listen for metaphors. They need to recognize that the stories they tell about their conflict, while framed as a description of their suffering or the other side's wrongdoing, actually consist of a request for more collaborative, open-hearted relationship.

Spiritual issues lie beneath the surface in conflict, waiting to be released so that transformation can take place. Every search for the source of conflict takes us to its spiritual center, to the authentic person behind the mask. Every hidden issue impedes spirit by preventing the free flow of energy. We encourage spirit by asking dangerous, heartfelt questions. Here are some that help identify transformational possibilities:

- What is the crossroads at which you are standing at this moment in your life or in this conflict?
- What is preventing you from moving forward?
- What have you done or not done that has contributed to or sustained the conflict?
- What price are you paying for this conflict? How long do you intend to continue paying it?
- Is there anything in this conflict you wish you had done better?
- Is there anything for which you would like to apologize?
- What kind of relationship would you like to have with each other? What is stopping you from having it? How could you help or support each other in creating it?
- What is one thing for which you would like to be acknowledged? What is one thing for which you would like to acknowledge the other person?

- If this were your last conversation, and you were never to see each other again, what is the last thing you would want to say to each other? On what note would you like to end?
- What does your heart tell you to do? Speak directly to the other person from your heart right now.

Mediating Spiritually

As mediators, we assist parties by separating people from problems, future from past, and positions from interests. Most people in conflict assume the other person is the problem, their past is their future, and the only solution is theirs. Opportunities for spiritual connection arise when we separate people from problems, focus on the future, and transform debate over positions into dialogue over interests. Positions, past, and debate are traps that narrow thinking, perceptions, and the range of imaginable outcomes. Interests, future, and dialogue broaden them and introduce a spiritual element by asking who people are, rather than what they want.

We can ask parties to jointly brainstorm problems and solutions, create visions, and agree on shared values. Working on common projects diverts attention from superficial issues and permits positive spiritual interactions to take place beneath the surface while completing these tasks. Using a collaborative negotiation process to agree on shared values and standards allows anger to transition into problem solving and discovery of common ground.

We can encourage people to surrender their judgments about each other, focus on improving their skills at handling difficult behaviors, let go, forgive themselves and others, and move on with their lives. Judgments are simply admissions of a lack of skill at responding to difficult behaviors. They keep people trapped in the past, and unable to imagine a different future.

We can encourage people not to surrender so the conflict will go away. Spirit is not served by capitulation or conflict suppression, but by transforming conflicts into opportunities for collaboration and learning. When people surrender, they cheat themselves and their opponents out of confronting what the conflict was trying to teach them, and condemn themselves to experiencing it repeatedly, until they learn its lessons. When they give up on principles, their spirits are sapped, they lose self-respect, and they grow angry at their own resignation.

We can help people recognize that larger societal issues express themselves through conflict, and that acceptance of social responsibility contributes to the creation of a more peaceful, spiritually sensitive world. We are not islands unto ourselves. As society becomes increasingly complex, problematic, and riddled with conflict, we can help people recognize that conflicts reflect larger societal problems, yet are *experienced* as personal.

Unexpected Obstacles on the Path to Resolution

Parties are often blocked in resolving conflicts by four simple, powerful, yet frequently unrecognized obstacles that are deeply spiritual in nature. These obstacles reflect a failure to see conflicts as opportunities, or journeys of transformation and transcendence.

1. *Conflicts are not resolved because the solutions are too close to recognize.* People become so embroiled in their conflicts they are unable to separate themselves from them or see their way out. Yet the solutions are already contained in their conflict. Through honest, empathetic dialogue, they create enough distance from the conflict to see it and themselves more clearly and discover solutions waiting to be revealed. For example, I mediated a dispute between a supervisor and an employee in which I asked about family background. It turned out they both came from families of thirteen children. The supervisor was first-born and the employee last. Once they saw how close the problem was, the solution became obvious.

2. *Conflicts are not resolved because the possibility of resolution is too profound to accept.* When people are stuck in conflict, they have no idea how to escape it. Yet they know intuitively that resolution could result in collaboration, forgiveness, and reconciliation. The possibility that their suffering could actually be over and they could create a close relationship with their opponent is too profound to accept. Collaboration, forgiveness, and reconciliation are difficult steps; yet once taken, people feel suddenly relieved of pain and stress. I mediated a divorce in which a husband made a generous settlement offer to his wife.

I asked her to respond, and she said she couldn't. I asked why, and after several minutes of silence she said that if she agreed, their relationship would be over. I helped her clarify that what she wanted was a friendship, and we mediated the terms of a new relationship.

3. *Conflicts are not resolved because resolution is too easy to think possible.* People think that if their conflicts were really that easy to end, they would have been able to resolve them earlier. After they invest enormous amounts of time, energy, money, and emotion in battle, they don't want to accept the possibility that they could have easily come to an agreement. They are stuck needing to justify their investment, yet all that is required to end most disputes is to search for solutions. I mediated a dispute between a homeowner who put a metal guard over his fireplace to keep rain out and his neighbor whose was kept awake all night by the sound of rain pounding on metal. They raged and screamed at each other, but it was not until mediation that it occurred to them to place a piece of rubber over the metal to muffle the sound.

4. *Conflicts are not resolved because the possibility of resolution is too beautiful to accept.* The enormous pleasure that comes from resolution, forgiveness, and release from anger is so great that parties reject it because they want it too much. They can't believe it is possible or that they deserve it. I mediated a dispute in which a teacher was being fired for cursing at other teachers in front of children, shortly following her retirement as union chairperson for twenty years. She grew increasingly angry and defensive, so I asked: "Has anyone ever thanked you for what you have done for this school?" She burst into tears and apologized profusely. I asked the other teachers who had come to complain to say one thing she had contributed to the school. Her anger disappeared. While she was prepared for criticism, she was *defenseless* against compliment. The idea that she would be acknowledged was too beautiful to imagine.

The effort to resolve conflict in these ways automatically creates a possibility of transformation, of overcoming superficial polarization through deep, collaborative action. Transformation signifies a profound level of learning that can lead to transcendence, in which a particular kind of conflict ceases to be of interest. Transcendence implies overcoming obstacles, freedom from false assumptions, and spiritual release. As Milton Glaser remarked:

> [A]ll life is about transcendence. If you're ugly you have to transcend your ugliness; if you're beautiful you have to transcend your beauty; if you're poor you have to transcend your poverty; if you're rich you have to transcend your wealth. . . .You get nothing at birth except things to transcend.

Every conflict and every resolution has a spiritual dimension, an energy that can be read and responded to by spiritually attuned mediators. To address spiritual issues in mediation, it is necessary to become aware of and cultivate spiritual experience within ourselves, which means pursuing mediation as a spiritual path. This is difficult, not only for the reasons we have explored, but because there is little support in our society for nonreligious spiritual development.

Having examined a number of inner frontiers in conflict resolution, we can now turn our attention to the outer frontiers where we consider the challenges posed to mediators by fascism and oppressive relationships, power contests, adversarial litigation, systemic dysfunction, electoral politics, destructive ways of fighting, and transnational disputes.

Part Two

The Outer Frontiers

Chapter Eleven

Mediating Fascism and Oppressive Relationships

Human beings are so made that the ones who do the crushing feel nothing; it is the person crushed who feels what is happening. Unless one has placed oneself on the side of the oppressed, to feel with them, one cannot understand.
SIMONE WEIL

To thoroughly understand any technique, approach, or methodology, to master it and use it strategically, it is necessary to probe its limits. We need to push it to the point where it begins to break down, crumble, and snap. In its shattering, we discover something of its real inner nature that will prove useful, even when it does not reach its limits.

Socially destructive, conflict-inducing ideas and behaviors such as fascism and oppression impact conflict resolution, challenge us to track the tenets of mediation to their logical conclusions, and rethink fundamental assumptions about the nature of the resolution process. One tenet of mediation is that we should resolve our disputes peacefully rather than engage in destructive strife over things that do not really matter, and that we should communicate openly and honestly even with our worst enemies.

Yet in spite of extraordinary progress in developing mediation technique, it has been consistently difficult to resolve certain classes of conflict. Are there disputes for which the mediation process does not or cannot work, and if so, which and why? It is time we reexamine these disputes and search for underlying, interconnecting patterns.

Battering and Oppressive Relationships

Many of the examples cited to support the idea that mediation has limits do not represent its real natural limits. Rather, these examples reveal the paucity of our skills, the infancy of our understanding, and our fear of mediating dangerously. A commonly cited example is spousal battering, which poses extremely challenging, complex, confusing problems for mediators. Yet there is nothing intrinsic in spousal battering conflicts as a class of behaviors that indicates they cannot be mediated successfully. We must therefore ask, what is it about spousal battering conflicts that makes many of them dangerous to mediate?

Battering disputes pose a distinct set of problems, including the risk that by superficially resolving them, the mediator will actually initiate a new cycle of abuse that opens with the abuser's apology. In oppressive relationships, the apology rarely touches the oppression, but remains superficial—an invitation to ignore an inevitable betrayal. Understanding where and why mediation breaks down is critical if we are to recognize when dangerous techniques become foolhardy, impossible, or counterproductive. Before we intervene as mediators in relationships that rely on battering, oppression, humiliation, or degradation, we need to answer a number of questions, including:

- What is it in relationships of oppression that suggests a natural limit to the mediation process?
- What are the cognitive, behavioral, and psychological limits on listening and problem solving?
- Where *precisely* does the dialogue between spousal batterers or oppressors and their victims break down?
- In these moments, what is it possible for mediators to do?
- When is it necessary to revert to rights- or power-based processes, and encourage people to fight for what they believe is right?
- Is it possible for people to participate in such battles without destroying their capacity for honesty and empathy?

- How do we encourage people to fight fairly and justly without losing our own empathy and honesty?

Seeking answers to these partly unanswerable questions encourages us to rethink our fundamental personal, professional, social, political, and human values, as well as our willingness to confront brutal behaviors that threaten or contravene those values. One of the difficulties in finding answers comes from mislabeling the problem. If we define spousal battering as a husband or wife using physical violence to humiliate or suppress a spouse, we have defined the problem as a person, ignored other forms of battering, and targeted only part of the system that created the problem. This will predictably result in a cycle of blame, recrimination, and accusation, followed by apology, defense, and counteraccusation.

If we recognize that the batterer's apology is the first step in a new cycle of violence, it becomes clear that a precondition for the success of mediation is that the cycle be broken at or before the point of apology. Yet most mediators, on hearing an apology, are likely to encourage the other side to accept it as a positive step toward resolution when, in fact, acceptance merely allows the perpetrator to reveal their self-loathing and deny their contempt.

A more dangerous form of mediation would be to stop the apology before it is accepted and inquire into whether the apologizer has a pattern of apologizing that cycles into repeated battering. The mediator might ask: How is this apology different from previous ones? What punishment could the batterer name and the spouse accept, in the event of a repeat performance that would actually result in the battering not repeating? How would it feel to double it? How does apologizing let the batterer off the hook? What is wrong with apologizing? What would happen if the apology were not accepted, if there were no forgiveness? On a scale of one to ten, ten being highest, how would you rate the apology? Why?

The danger in these questions is that both sides may find honesty inconsistent with a continued relationship and, as a result, regard the mediator as biased or directive. But the real danger for the parties and the mediator comes from *not* doing so, thereby allowing the incident to be repeated. For us, the price of "peace at any price" is exacted from our spirit for having colluded in the continuation of potentially deadly oppressive behavior. To reveal another approach, it will be useful to understand the *ideological* justification for battering and oppression, which is fascism.

Mediation and Fascism

For those who live under fascism, oppression, or tyranny, or face a fierce, unprincipled adversary, or are afraid even to exercise their own freedom, it may become necessary to engage in conflict, resist oppression, reject settlement, and raise their voices against the silence of acquiescence. Consider an extreme example. If you had been asked to mediate the conflict before World War II between Hitler and the Allied powers, would it have been acceptable to sacrifice Czechoslovakia as a compromise in order to avoid war? France? Spain? Clearly the answer is "no." But what is the difference between these examples and the settlement of smaller, more personal conflicts, as between batterers and their wives? Or employers and employees who have been fired without just cause? Or rapists and their victims? Or slumlords and tenants who live with rats? Or abusive parents and molested children? Is peace always the highest priority?

I am not advocating that these conflicts continue indefinitely without resolution simply because they are brutal. Rather, I am suggesting that there are limits to the desirability of ending them *prematurely*, without a fair and honest examination of the underlying issues, and without the full participation of people whose lives will be irrevocably damaged by them.

The primary problem with the conflict resolution process that actually took place in Munich between England and Nazi Germany was *not* Neville Chamberlain's desire for peace. Rather, it was his willingness to compromise over matters of justice, his failure to include in the negotiations representatives of those who would suffer most if they failed, and his adoption of a conciliatory, peaceful approach to a deadly, bullying, implacable power.

England and Germany certainly could have negotiated their differences, but imagine what might have happened if Poland, France, or Czechoslovakia had been invited to the table? What would have changed if the chief rabbi, king of the gypsies, chairman of the communist party, or others whose death warrants had already been signed, were invited to the negotiating table or included in Allied councils?

Chamberlain, those in Vichy, and others who conciliated and compromised with fascism for "peace at any price" were labeled Nazi collaborators. Yet their approach to conflict was actually one of suppression, settlement, concession, and conciliation. Collaboration implies mutuality and partnership, and even compromise involves give and take, but fascism merely took, giving nothing in return.

The Limit of Fascism and Oppressive Relationships

With the resurgence of right-wing militias and neo-Nazi organizations worldwide, we are confronted with serious, *dangerous* questions—not only regarding our values as a profession, but our role in the rise of hatred and mean-spiritedness. In the process, we need to ask ourselves whether and how we might aid in resolving these disputes, without endorsing capitulation, conciliation, and compromise, or in-kind responses that simply multiply the hatred.

The spectre of fascism and genocide has continued to haunt us since World War II. It is not enough, however, to remember what happened. Ultimately, we have to consider how we would respond to fascism—not only on the large scale of Hitler, Mussolini, and Franco—but on a far smaller, more personal scale. Fascism is more than a national political ideology. It can also be found in the little cruelties, depravities, and petty prejudices we witness or experience in daily life. Fascism is alive and well, whether or not it assumes a political form, whenever we create or tolerate relationships based on inequality, prejudice, brutality, and oppression.

To begin with, we need to recall that fascism, like all forms of oppression, starts with a *tolerance* of intolerance, a peaceful attitude toward preparation for war, and a forgiveness not of people, but of revenge itself. In her novel *Stones from the River,* Ursula Hegi describes the easy complicity of ordinary citizens and how their silence contributed to the rise of fascism:

> It was like that with many other events, and it took courage for the few who would preserve the texture of the truth, not to let its fibers slip beneath the web of silence and collusion which people—often with the best of intentions—spun to sustain and protect one another.

This web of silence and collusion is not very different from those spun by oppressors and their victims, batterers and their spouses, addicts and their codependents, precisely in order to sustain and protect each other. As mediators, we are asked whether we can put a halt to these seemingly endless cycles of cruelty and appeasement, viciousness, and conciliation.

Oppressive relationships continually crop up, now in one nation, now in another, now in one family or organization, now in another. Mediating dangerously means asking a difficult set of questions and searching for answers that involve taking risks, for example:

- How do we, even in less dramatic cases of oppression, avoid becoming appeasers, suppressors, conciliators, or compromisers, as Neville Chamberlain did with Hitler in Munich?
- How do we respond when one party rejects or suppresses the other party's capacity to participate fully in dialogue? What do we do when one party accepts their own diminished rights? How do we participate in a conflict resolution process that accepts limits on full participation, even of a single person?
- How do we know when we have slipped into an oppressive set of assumptions, or a cycle of chronic violence that begins with an apology for the previous cycle? What do we do when we feel this may be happening?
- If we ultimately find these actions destructive and oppose their effects, how do we reconcile participating both in dialogue dedicated to peacemaking and in opposition to oppressive behaviors?
- How do we avoid turning into what we oppose, becoming part of the problem, or becoming oppressive ourselves, justifying our harmful behavior by the destructive behavior of others?

It is important to carefully consider our answers in light of the myriad minor, behavioral forms of fascism and oppression, which spark countless conflicts. There are no quick or easy answers to these questions. I share them with you because they are always with us. By observing them, we can improve our ability to mediate oppressive relationships.

Behavioral Definitions of Fascism

The issues in our daily lives seem simple compared with those raised by fascism, so why even consider it? How can our understanding of fascism or the bankruptcy of appeasement at Munich inform the way we resolve disputes between employees, teachers, and divorcing couples? What does it have to do with mediating dangerously?

We commonly define fascism by referring to large-scale economic and political policies adopted by right-wing political parties and governments before World War II. But we can also define it in ways that capture its personal and social character and that lead us to consider what it looks like at the level of individual behavior. These definitions allow us to see that fascism is simply the large-scale organization of small-scale, day-to-day, oppressive, brutal, chauvinistic relationships.

Behavioral expressions of fascism are useful because they allow us to reflect on the limits of mediation. By focusing on fascism, we expose the places where we become complicit and partly responsible for oppressive outcomes. Defining fascism in terms of everyday life challenges the comfortable thought that it belongs to the past. Instead of focusing on fascist leaders, nations, parties, or movements, we need to consider fascism a *tendency* that is present at all times in all nations and communities, as well as in every one of us. In doing so, I recognize that no behavioral definition can come close to describing the genocidal destruction brought about by Nazi Germany. The scale of evil is crucial in assessing how to respond to it.

The following list of core fascist beliefs and behaviors draws on theory, history, and fiction to illustrate its connection with oppressive relationships. In my mind, fascism consists of:

- Beliefs, attitudes, or behaviors that endorse the innate superiority of some over others, whether by race, gender, nationality, religion, culture, physical condition, or sexual orientation, or by personality, skill, education, position, or wealth.
- Hostility toward women, as expressed in policies of exclusion, marginalization, male superiority, and sexual repression; or in trivializing and justifying sexual brutality, harassment, and humiliation.

- The creation of alliances or "negative communities," based on fear of differences and hatred of others, especially Jews and people of color, but also based on appearance, wealth, and status.
- Physical violence directed toward gays and lesbians combining homoeroticism with homophobia.
- The worship of hierarchy and power, based on elitist submission to superiors, while regarding inferiors with contempt.
- Taking pleasure in punishment and punishing pleasure; censorship of art, combined with the art of censorship.
- Making evil banal and ordinary.
- Engaging in, encouraging, justifying, or refusing to apologize for brutality or cruelty, while silently tolerating hatred of others.
- Treating dissent and nonsupport as disloyalty or treason, and silencing those who disagree with intimidation, threats, and fear.
- Substituting external authority for internal responsibility and replacing self-discipline with discipline by others, thereby encouraging "escape from freedom," silence, apathy, and acquiescence.
- Appealing to the angry, violent instincts of frightened, frustrated, humiliated people; inciting the envious; encouraging the "revenge of the weak"; and promoting the escalation of conflict for the sake of conflict.
- Personalizing failure with shame and blame, while demonizing or scapegoating others as a substitute for constructive criticism.
- Sloganizing and simplifying language in ways that make complex, creative, critical thought impossible; rejecting enigma, paradox, contradiction, and nonduality as descriptive catagories.
- Creating a cult of pride and glory based on partial, ahistoric truths, and suppressing criticism of patriotic history.
- Undermining democracy as inefficient and an obstacle to power, while wielding public power as though it were private property.
- Behaving in irrational, hostile, and covert ways, while opposing reason, intelligence, kindness, and openness.

- Using prejudice as a club to seize the wealth and power of others.
- Obsession with conspiracies as an explanation for powerlessness, yet acting them out; creating a cult of heroism, death, and war leading to inevitable Armageddon.

It is difficult to read this list and not recognize many nonfascist organizations, families, and individuals whose behaviors carry the seed of fascism within them. Ultimately, fascism relies on the intimidation of weak individuals, forcing them to follow others out of fear and a desire to conform. Polish novelist Witold Gombrowicz wrote in his *Diaries:*

> Does man kill or torture because he has come to the conclusion that he has the right to do so? He kills because others kill. He tortures because others torture. . . [I]n concentration camps the road to death was so well trodden that the bourgeois incapable of killing a fly at home exterminated people with ease. . . . It follows from this that the spring of action is not housed in the human conscience but in the relationship that is formed between it and other people. . . [A] sin is inversely proportionate to the number of people who give themselves up to it. . . . [v. 1, p. 43 and v. 2, p. 78].

There are no easy remedies. Yet self-awareness, respect for diversity, and relationships based on integrity, empathy, honesty, and equality, which undermine fascist behaviors, are all encouraged in mediation. Hannah Arendt was correct in identifying fascism with banality, which increases the ease with which it is possible to slip from small acts of cruelty to genocidal reasoning. Through dangerous mediation, these small acts can be confronted, challenged, and overcome.

Mediating Sexual Harassment and Oppressive Relationships

Mediators face enormous problems in trying to mediate oppressive or fascistic relationships, which require high levels of skill. Here are some small ways mediators can reverse oppressive relationships. We can start by comediating in male and female, black and white, employer and employee teams. Before mediation, we can speak with both sides in caucus or by telephone to build trust for subsequent dangerous interventions. In tone, speed, and softness of voice, we can make sure both sides recognize the seriousness of the issues, and are prepared to respect each other's boundaries. No matter what the allegations, we can avoid being judgmental.

We can make sure there is adequate physical separation and security in arranging physical space. We can ask the accuser to speak first and make certain the accused is emotionally present. We can create safe spaces for both parties by asking them to speak to us initially, rather than to each other. We can allow the accuser to describe what happened in the presence of the accused. Most accusers are understandably reluctant to reexpose old wounds, yet those who do become stronger and heal the damage done by their own perceptions of complicity and powerlessness. Healing only happens when wounds are exposed, but without force.

As the accuser describes the incident, we can create a "tunnel" of intense, focused attention, so it feels as though there is no one else in the room, and take the accuser deeper into the pain and humiliation of the event in a respectful, healing manner. We can ask the accused to speak directly to the accuser if a respectful and productive dialogue is to ensue. If not, we can bring the accuser back to a safe level of discourse and ask the accused to acknowledge the pain experienced by the accuser. We can assist the accused in understanding that it is possible to be sorry for the *effects* of their behavior, without apologizing for *intending* harm. If the accused is unable to apologize, we can do so as "surrogate" apologists, saying to the accuser: "Perhaps what he should have said to you is, 'I'm very, *very* sorry for what I did, and I know that nothing I say can make up for what I've done," adding what we would want to hear if we were the accuser.

We can ask both parties to create a list of systemic problems that caused or aggravated their conflict, including lack of employee awareness of where to go for help, lack of training for managers, or inadequate internal remedies or support systems for accusers. We can encourage them to form common cause in the creation of institutional solutions, make sure something will be done so it does not happen again, and encourage forgiveness through their experience collaborating on solutions.

It is not uncommon for parties to metaphorically reenact their relationship during the negotiation process. We can look for opportunities to point this out and reframe their discourse in terms of healing, rather than victimization or denial. We can ask both sides what they learned from their experience, what is one thing they will do to make sure something like this never happens again, how they plan to put this behind them and get on with their lives, what the other party could do or say that would help them reach an agreement, and what it would take for them to forgive the other person and themselves.

The main difficulty in mediating sexual harassment and oppressive or fascistic relationships is finding adequate alternative targets for the deep residue of pain, shame, rage, and desire for revenge that are triggered by intimately oppressive behavior. This requires mediators to develop *dangerous* methods of shifting parties from power- and rights- to interest-based processes.

Chapter Twelve

Power, Rights, and Interests

The measure of a man is what he does with power.
PITTACHUS

While the inner frontiers of conflict resolution take us deeper into personal issues and the self, the outer frontiers take us deeper into social issues and the systems that generate them. These conflicts challenge a number of critical beliefs we hold regarding the nature of mediation. The main dangers we face mediating along the internal frontiers of self and spirit are suppressive, emotional, and personal. The dangers we face mediating along the external frontiers of social and systemic conflict are repressive, economic, and political.

A significant danger in mediating external conflicts arises when we confront parties who are committed to using power as a means of resolving disputes. Power is inherently adversarial and dangerous in conflict, not only because it is harmful to those it attacks, but because it is addictive and corrupting to those it protects. Dangerous mediation consists of opening a path from power to rights to interests.

Distinguishing Power, Rights, and Interests

Everyone chooses how to respond to conflict. Fundamentally, we can respond with aggression and suppression, accommodation and surrender, avoidance and apathy, compromise and conciliation, or collaboration and dialogue. Each of these options results in a qualitatively different form of *community* and a different approach to resolving conflict.

These responses have resulted in three fundamental, historical systems for resolving conflicts, discussed by William Ury, Stephen Goldberg, and Jeanne Brett in *Getting Disputes Resolved*. These are

1. Exercising *power* through aggression, accommodation and avoidance
2. Asserting *rights* through compromise and conciliation
3. Satisfying *interests,* through collaboration and dialogue

To make this distinction clear, assume for a moment that you are in an air-conditioned room with a number of people, some of whom want the air conditioning off and some of whom want it on. What are the fundamental ways of resolving this dispute? If we assume the air conditioning is either on or off, there are three primary methods of ending the conflict.

1. Power
First, we can resolve this dispute based on power, in which the side that is strongest, most heavily armed, wealthiest, most articulate, of highest status, or the best organizer wins and the air conditioning is on or off. Human beings have used power to resolve conflicts for millenia. There are multiple problems with power-based processes, however, including these:

- If one wins, the other loses, which is not conducive to ongoing relationships.
- If one wins repeatedly, they become corrupt, presumptuous, biased, and abusive, disrespecting others as "losers."
- Considerable damage is done, including loss of life, limb, and trusting relationships, making the cost of power often greater than the benefits it secures.
- Revolt, resistance, sabotage, apathy, cynicism, resentment, and passive-aggressive behavior are common responses to power. These do little to encourage creativity, collaboration, motivation, or effective relationships.

2. Rights

We can also resolve this controversy based on rights. We have primarily used rights to resolve disputes over the last several hundred years. Rights are limitations on the exercise of power. Yet rights are secured in power contests, as when power is shared or compromised to end chaos or bloodshed. The test of any right is its enforceability, which depends on power, through coercion or force.

Examples of rights-based processes include legal systems, voting, and negotiated agreements. Every word in the U.S. Constitution is a limitation on the power of an absolute monarchy or dictatorship. Every collective bargaining agreement is a limitation on the power of employers to fire employees without just cause and on the power of unions to strike.

Resolving the air-conditioning issue based on rights might involve voting or negotiating or litigating whether it will be on or off. Problems with rights-based approaches include:

- The one side still wins and the other loses. This feels fairer than the use of arbitrary power, but ongoing relationships are still not sustained.
- People are corrupted and habitual losers are still abused.
- There is less likelihood of loss of life or limb, but trust is broken, and the cost/benefit ratio is still weak.
- Resistance, apathy, cynicism, resentment, and passive-aggressive behavior still occur in rights-based processes, resulting in reduced creativity, collaboration, and motivation.
- Rights-based processes uniquely generate bureaucratic, apathetic, official responses that discourage emotional authenticity, honest dialogue, and transformation.

In our highly litigious, bureaucratic culture, an almost medieval form of rights-based combat prevails. Law firms representing "damsels in distress" engage in verbal battle with "dragons" represented by different firms. Both ignore the facts and laws advanced by the other side. Both crave victory, even when the facts are subjective and the law ambiguous.

3. Interests

A third alternative in resolving the air-conditioning dispute is through interests. Interests are not what we want, but the reasons we want it. If I ask *why* you want the air conditioning off, it may be because you are freezing. In that case, I can loan you a sweater, or a space heater can be brought in, or if you are sitting under an air-conditioning duct we can switch places. If the reason is that it is too loud, I can use a microphone, speak louder, or move closer. If I ask why you want the air-conditioning on, the answer may be that it is stuffy, and I can open a window, bring in a fan, or take a break.

In other words, when we shift to interest-based processes, options emerge that do not require winners and losers, do not result in corruption and abuse, and cost less than their benefits. The main cost in interest-based processes is the time it takes to ask questions and work through to solutions. These are nothing compared to the costs of *not* using an interest-based approach.

Interest-based processes are grounded in consensus, which dissipates resistance, resentment, and passive-aggressive behavior. They encourage creativity, collaboration, and morale, reduce bureaucracy, and encourage active, personal communications. They support emotional authenticity, improved relationships, and transformation.

The fundamental problem with power- and rights-based approaches is their failure to recognize that it is unnecessary for one person to be cold so another is not stuffy. A false dichotomy is created, resulting in a "zero sum game" that forces win/lose outcomes, when win/win, or even lose/lose options would be preferable.

As humans have evolved socially, we have shifted from the exercise of arbitrary power to the recognition of legal rights, and the affirmation of interests, as alternative methods of resolving conflict. This evolution of methods is an expression of a deeper transition from aggression to compromise to collaboration in relationships between diverse, socially interactive groups.

Parties in conflict have three sets of interests for which they seek satisfaction: *content* gains, *process* fairness, and *relationship* improvement. Think of these elements as balloons inside a larger circle of constraints. If one balloon expands, the others must shrink. For this reason, fighting hard for gains in content can make the process feel unfair or that the relationship is going downhill. All three need to be in balance or expand together.

When content is repeatedly secured by one side against another, or when people feel rejected, excluded, oppressed, or exploited, there is no reason not to return to power and rights to expand their options for redress, ultimately including violence. Yet we identify the violence of the victim as the problem, rather than the oppression or lack of response that left them no alternative other than surrender. In this sense, every satisfaction of interests represents an increase in justice, democracy, equality, and fairness; every mediation represents a small-scale social transformation and a step towards the long-term reduction of conflict. To better understand the logic of social transformation through interests, consider the intrinsic opposition between rights and power, paralleled in the opposition between justice and the law, democracy and the state.

Rights vs. Power, Justice vs. Law, Democracy vs. the State

It is commonly recognized that rights are a form of power, that law increases justice, and that the state is an instrument of democracy. It is harder to discern that with every creation of rights there is a loss of power, with every increase in law there is a decline in justice, and with every state, even a democratic one, there is a diminution in democracy.

In the earliest human societies, rights and power were indivisible. There was no law distinct from justice, and neither state nor democracy were yet created. In this period, social mores in family groups and clan societies were enforced by custom—by ostracism and acceptance, criticism and praise, punishment and reward.

When society grew in numbers, anonymity, diversity, complexity, and conflict, "objective," "neutral" institutions became necessary to resolve disputes. The rise of internal separations based on gender, class, caste, race, religion, geography, and clan affiliation impacted the distribution of wealth, work, status, and power. Diversity and uneven accumulation pitted "haves" against "have-nots." As a consequence of this rise in social antagonism, efforts were made to mask and ameliorate it, to preserve a larger social unity through the fiction of a "neutral," legal, rights-based state.

In the beginning, people battled for rights *as* power, law *as* justice, and democracy *as* the state. Yet as these battles were won, the ground shifted, and gaps appeared between those with rights and those with power, between law and justice, democracy and the state. These became weapons wielded by conflicting social groups in an invisible war between haves and have-nots.

In countless battles and revolts over centuries, the haves prevailed, in arms and economics, politics and society. In response, the have-nots sought concessions. If they could not share power they might nonetheless enjoy rights. If they could not obtain justice they might yet have laws. If they could not control the state, they might, through democratic pressure, strive to influence it.

This battle is still being fought on a global scale and will undoubtedly continue until the injustices, inequalities, and inequities that drive it are resolved. At stake is a vast quantity of accumulated wealth, the lives and destinies of billions, the coherence of human society, and on some level, the ecological survival of life itself. With this much at stake, mediating these issues becomes highly dangerous.

Difficulties with Rights, Justice, and Democracy

Strong, centralized, military and political institutions are thought necessary by haves to defend against internal and external competition, just as strong, centralized, socially protective institutions are thought necessary by have-nots to support extensions of rights. Both sides contribute to the expansion of state and bureaucracy, the continuation of coercion and injustice, and an increase in formally neutral rights and laws. Neither negotiates interests.

Those who hold power try to turn rights into tokens, unimportant concessions, or public icons that lack substance. The powerful understand that rights are methods by which the powerless gain power. Every significant right therefore represents a loss, a compromise with the opposition, a temporary treaty of peace in which hostile combatants decide to suspend their fighting and share some of their power. Yet power *cannot* be fixed permanently, so new competitions continually erupt.

When these competitions erupt, they assume the form of conflict. Mediators face dangerous choices in resolving disputes between those with power and those with rights. For example, I recently comediated a dispute between a faculty union and college administration following two years of bitter battle, including grievances, unfair labor practice charges, state mediation, government factfinding, and civil lawsuits. We asked them what ground rules they needed to rebuild trust, and the administration asked the union to call off public demonstrations and picketing. The problem was that this felt like a unilateral cease-fire and surrender of legal rights, because the administration had power and therefore did not need to picket or demonstrate. We asked the union to name something the administration could do that would represent a similar sacrifice, and they agreed to make the following joint public statement:

> We agree to a two-week bilateral moratorium on all divisive activities, including organizing public protests, issuing unilateral press releases and letters to the editor, and making disparaging remarks about each other and the process, and to request the support of others in this effort.

This agreement, like others, is a temporary truce, a declaration of rights, and a limitation on their exercise of power that will last only a few years before the entire process starts all over again, renewing distrust, sowing the seeds of enmity, and preparing for a fresh contest between rights and power. Every declaration of rights is therefore *simultaneously* the ending of a civil war and the beginning of a new one. It is the triumph of a revolution and the initiation of a counterrevolution. It is a momentary unity in the conflict between competing factions, and an expression of the highest political consciousness of a people, in perfect preparation for their ensuing apathy and division.

Every right represents the partial healing of a historic division between people based on differentials of power and a decision not to heal it completely. Every declaration of rights implicitly recognizes that if rights genuinely existed, there would be no need to declare them. They are official guarantees that, by their very declaration, suggest the desire to undermine them. Rights are thus a contradiction in terms, an expression of their transitional role in shifting people from power to interests.

With every extension of rights, there is a gradual diminution in hierarchical power, as well as a corresponding increase in the ability to satisfy interests. With every increase in justice, law becomes less necessary. With every expansion in democracy, the state declines in strength. At times, an oppressive division of wealth or power is itself placed in question. The battle for rights then *becomes* one for power, justice overtakes the law, and an increase in democracy transforms the state.

Every struggle for expansion of rights, justice, or democracy is therefore simultaneously a battle for and against power, law, and the state. It is *for* the state in its role as guarantor of the new status quo and *against* the state in its role as protector of the status quo ante. Democracy, justice, and rights are first won against those who oppose their power sharing consequences, then secured against encroachment by being written into stone.

Yet by being secured, they are compromised, bureaucratized, and made consistent with their substantive denial. They *become* the status quo ante and a limit on their own capacity for expansion, generalization, and extension to others. The rights of all then become a condition for the rights of each, just as the rights of each subsequently become a condition for the rights of all.

At certain points in the expansion of rights, justice, and democracy, it becomes clear that power must be shared for rights to be meaningful. There must be justice for there to be a rule of law, and there must be democracy for there to be a state. This is the beginning of transition to interest-based alternatives. Mediation is effective partly because it represents, in smaller venues and scales, precisely these principles of power sharing, primacy of justice, and democratic governance. It offers the promise of something beyond these principles, including community and the satisfaction of interests.

What makes mediation *dangerous* is its implicit, even explicit, request that everyone disarm, lay down their power, and surrender their rights in exchange for the satisfaction of their interests. Fundamentally, power and rights are based on fear and distrust of others, but these are not easily surrendered, even when people are happier doing so. One of the reasons has to do with the language of conflict.

The Language of Power, Rights, and Interests

There are fundamental differences between assertions of power, declarations of rights, and statements of interests. It is easy to distinguish metaphors of victory (power), entitlement (rights), and satisfaction (interests) in the words used by conflicting parties. This allows mediators to encourage a shift to interest-based processes simply by substituting metaphors of satisfaction for those of victory or entitlement. It also allows mediators to assist parties in becoming more aware of and responsible for their metaphors.

For example, what is the difference between being "lazy" and "relaxed," "responsible" and "micromanaging," "talking" and "gossiping," "meeting" and "conspiring," "criticizing" and "bad mouthing"? One places the speaker in a positive, equal, interest-based relationship with the person being described, while the other describes a negative, unequal, power- or rights-based relationship.

A deeper problem, however, concerns how language in conflict resolution confuses core differences, colors parts of reality, and disguises the social sources of dysfunction. Whenever reality is discriminatory, official language turns neutral as a way of promoting peace and stability through a combination of formality, constricted meaning, and social amnesia. Mexican novelist Octavio Paz wrote:

> When a society decays, it is language that is first to become gangrenous. . . . Although moralists are scandalized by the fortunes amassed by the revolutionaries [in Mexico] under the ruling party, they have failed to observe that this material flowering has a verbal parallel; oratory has become the favorite literary genre of the prosperous . . . and alongside oratory, with its plastic flowers, there is the barbarous syntax in many of our newspapers, the foolishness of language on loudspeakers and the radio, the loathsome vulgarities of advertising—all that asphyxiating rhetoric.

The language of law is formally neutral, yet at the same time based on principles of equality and fairness. Formally, logically, and theoretically, these propositions can both be correct, yet they assume there is such a thing as "neutral equality" or "equal fairness." Neutrality, equality, and fairness become internally real in law only to the extent that the external existence of bias, inequality, and unfairness are ignored. The law, for example, is neutral in conflicts between landlords and tenants. The law assumes landlords may charge rent, ignores the fact that wealthier landlords hire expensive attorneys and contribute to judicial campaigns, and refuses tenants the right to plead hardship as a defense to eviction.

Because the law is abstractly committed to principles of neutrality, equality, and fairness, the harsh reality of bias, inequality, and unfairness must be formally disregarded, neutrally rephrased, or denied. Thus, legal language becomes hypocritical, artificial, and trivial, transforming truths into falsehoods and reality into caricature or farce.

At a deeper level, the self-serving language of power, and the neutral yet adversarial language of rights, confuse and undermine the parties' common responsibility for outcomes. Both languages do this by permitting each side to assert only their own truths and reject real consideration of the truths of others. Only interest-based processes and language encourage them to do otherwise.

The problem for mediators is to forge a new language that allows problems to be described as belonging to both parties, that does not victimize or demonize, that empathizes and acknowledges emotions, that strengthens heart and spirit, that encourages responsibility for resolution and openness to transformation. Consider, for example, how responsibility for conflict can be articulated in relation to crime, disputes between labor and management, and education.

Rights vs. Interests and Responsibility for Crime

Human societies have been historically divided by power and balkanized by rights into distinct, isolated parts, into victims and criminals, management and labor, teachers and students, rich and poor. In consequence, each group recognizes only its own needs, is responsible only for its own actions, defends only itself.

This fragmentation results in each group defending its power, asserting its rights, and guarding its territory against others. Each group focuses only on its particular product, so that politicians produce laws, criminals produce crime, courts produce convictions, and prisons produce punishment. No one is responsible for the whole or concerned with the difficulties others face. The context created by this specialization is one of social divisiveness, chronic conflict, no-holds-barred competition, and loss of solutions that address the problem as a whole.

In this environment, the actual reasons for crime are of as little concern to judges as the rationale for judicial decisions are to criminals. Nor are the real reasons for crime of concern to citizens, whose goal is only to avoid becoming a victim. No one accepts direct personal or social responsibility, either for the crime or the process of rectifying it.

In this way, law enforcement becomes the exclusive task of police and the courts. Violations of law can therefore be perceived either as acts against society, which has no voice, or against the state, which speaks in its name. If the state is regarded as representing the rich, who write the laws and become the judges who punish violations, crime may appear justifiable to the poor.

Thus, criminals are condemned by one group for acting against society, and celebrated by another for acting against the unequal power of the state. Justice is thereby made dependent on social class, with the consequence that neither side is encouraged to accept responsibility for crime. Rather, their role is to evade and deny that responsibility and to resist the personal humiliation of restitution, rehabilitation, and reconciliation.

Our prisons are filled with people whose sole crime has been to nonviolently harm themselves, primarily through drugs. Of the nearly two million people in prison, 1.2 million are incarcerated for drug use and other victimless crimes. We have created a private prison-industrial complex to house, clothe, and feed them. At the same time, we have created massive, tax-funded, public employment for police, prosecutors, defense lawyers, judges, court reporters, bailiffs, prison guards, probation, and parole agents to put and keep criminals there.

Once caught, a criminal is subjected to trial—not by the victim or society, but by the state. The trial takes the form of a ritual combat waged by a prosecuting attorney representing law, order, decency, and a morally outraged public, versus a defense counsel representing the downtrodden, constitutional rights, reasonable doubt, mercy, and forgiveness. The judge in this drama represents objectivity, reason, and paternal discipline, while the jury embodies subjectivity, justice, and maternal compassion.

It is possible to see this as a game of opposites, in which the whole is somehow encompassed in the coming together of each disparate part. It can also be seen as an enormous opportunity for miscommunication and conflict. This happens because prosecuting attorneys cannot be deeply concerned with criminals as human beings, or someone else's victims, or their feelings, or with facts that tend to prove their innocence. Defense counsel cannot be concerned with the suffering of the victim, the safety of society, or with facts that tend to prove their client's guilt.

For the criminal, neither side's version of the crime is correct, even when combined. There is neither an opportunity for honest dialogue about what happened, nor any form of acknowledgment, learning, or responsibility, which are preconditions for forgiveness. This failure is not without consequence for the criminal, the victim, or society.

By encouraging each side to act only in accordance with its separate power or rights, we articulate a response to crime that wastes social wealth on a massive trial and imprisonment industry that guarantees its own continuity. The enormously complicated legal and bureaucratic rules required to support this industry actually *undermine* the interests, not only of criminals, but those of victims and society as well.

It is in part this failure of responsibility of, by, and for the criminal—a failure encouraged, perpetuated, and rewarded by power- and rights-based assumptions—that prevents a broader acceptance of responsibility for justice. Thus, social responsibility for crime is vested in a bureaucracy where no one, not even the judge, is completely accountable, and crime is allowed to continue.

The Interest-Based Alternative

The effort to reduce crime has resulted in the creation of a number of highly innovative interest-based victim-offender mediation programs. These programs bring criminals, often juveniles, face to face with their victims. The criminals are asked to listen as their victims speak honestly from direct experience about how it felt to be victimized, then given a chance to apologize, acknowledge the pain they caused, accept responsibility for their crimes, and agree to restitution for their victims.

Mediation encourages criminals to accept personal responsibility for the suffering of victims and repay the damage they caused to society, rather than deny that responsibility. It allows them to release unconscious feelings of guilt and self-punishment that accompany acts of personal aggression, resulting in greater empathy and compassion and less future crime.

Success depends on the willingness of the criminal to appreciate the crime from the point of view of the victim and to apologize for what was done. The purpose is not punishment or blame, but acknowledgment, restitution, transformation, and reconciliation. The criminal's return to social favor is conditioned on restitution to those who suffered and on forgiveness by the victim.

Mediation works even with adult and violent offenders, though it is more difficult and dangerous, and the process takes longer. Obviously, there are cases in which mediation will not succeed, but we have no idea how to even identify these cases. Since the cost of mediation is miniscule compared to the tens of thousands of dollars we spend annually to warehouse each prisoner, it is highly cost-effective to try mediation in every case.

Socrates asked rhetorically whether a plow is made better by twisting it, or an animal by beating it. Since the answer was no, how are human beings made better by punishment? It is one thing to protect society by ostracizing people who are uncontrollably violent, but it is something altogether different to treat them like brutes and to become brutish in the process. All punishment harms the one who inflicts it, and repeats the crime in reverse. It is an application of power, rather than a recognition of rights or a satisfaction of interests.

Mediation works because it accepts criminals as members of society, who are responsible for violating its rules. Yet, in rights-based processes, criminals are excluded from legal, political, economic, and social rehabilitation. They are discouraged from admitting their crimes or apologizing to their victims. In more ancient societies, criminals are often the first to pronounce their punishment. If this is done arrogantly, as Socrates did when he requested free meals for life, the answer will be death by hemlock. But when criminals select a more serious penalty than would otherwise be deserved, society can relax and offer mercy instead of vengeance. Real justice is not legal, but poetic. It consists, like revenge, of teaching the criminal what it feels like to be victimized. This lesson is possible in mediation, but not in law.

In mediation, criminals become *personally* responsible for making and enforcing the law. They are no longer objects or outsiders, as in court. The real causes of the crime can be examined *with* the criminal, and remedies can be tailored to match unique circumstances. These may include employment, community sentencing, peer confrontation, family counseling or mediation, group therapy, volunteer community labor, relocation, drug or alcohol rehabilitation, coaching, mentoring, and other remedies. The most effective punishments are those designed and agreed to by the criminal, who is the only person who can take genuine responsibility for rehabilitation, and by the victim, who is the only person who can judge whether the criminal is sincere.

If the criminal has accepted full responsibility for the crime and agreed to restitution, the victim can follow with an offer of forgiveness and society can offer reintegration. Yet these rarely take place in rights-based processes, as Oscar Wilde recognized, writing from prison:

> Society takes on itself the right to inflict appalling punishments on the individual, but it also has the supreme vice of shallowness, and fails to realize what it has done. When the man's punishment is over, it leaves him to himself: that is to say it abandons him at the very moment when its highest duty toward him begins. It is really ashamed of its own actions, and shuns those whom it has punished, as people shun a creditor whose debt they cannot pay, or one on whom they have inflicted an irreparable, an irredeemable wrong. I claim on my side that if I realize what I have suffered, Society should realize what it has inflicted on me: and that there should be no bitterness or hate on either side.

When criminals own the damage they caused, victims can release their rage and fear, which are partly intended to communicate these feelings to the criminal. In this way, the interests of both sides are satisfied, leading to better outcomes than would be possible in rights- or power-based processes. Both revenge and the law lock parties in the past, preventing direct, honest, empathetic communication, and permitting them to continue holding false ideas about each other and themselves.

Society can proactively prevent and minimize crime by supporting families and communities where crime is commonplace, expanding victim-offender mediation programs, and funding schools so children do not grow up in the midst of poverty, hopelessness, and crime, or live constricted lives due to economic inequality, political exclusion, or social prejudice. In this way we reduce the sources of crime that are *our* responsibility, rather than the criminal's.

Rights vs. Interests and Responsibility for Labor and Management Disputes

The problem of narrow self-interest, failure to take responsibility for the whole, and adversarial rights-based processes are not restricted to criminal law. In a similar way, managers in organizations see themselves as exclusively responsible for technological progress, productive efficiency, and fiscal prosperity. At the same time, unions see themselves as exclusively responsible for fair compensation, decent working conditions, and adequate health and welfare benefits.

Management believes it needs to discipline employees to maintain efficiency and productivity, while labor believes it needs to defend them to prevent companies from abusing their power. Yet labor is as directly affected by reduced productivity and efficiency as management is by unfair wages and working conditions. Management routinely restricts labor's participation in decision making, while labor routinely blames management for financial losses. It is accepted by both that management's primary job is to make a profit, while labor's job is to obtain as large a share of it as possible.

Management's role in power- and rights-based contests is therefore to be fiscally responsible (that is, greedy and insensitive in the eyes of labor), while labor's role is to be humanly responsible (that is, irresponsible and belligerent in the eyes of management). Yet each of these roles by itself contradicts the common general interests of both.

For labor to become whole, it must advance not only the narrow interests of employees, but of the organization as a whole, of labor *as* management. For management to become whole, it must become sensitive and responsive to the human needs of labor, of management *as* labor. In this interest-based paradigm, each becomes responsible for all, for the larger community, and for the satisfaction not only of their own interests, but of the other side's as well.

To shift each side's perceptions regarding their role in labor-management conflicts, it is necessary to end reliance on power-based processes such as strikes and lockouts and on rights-based processes such as arbitration and collective bargaining, in favor of interest-based processes such as mediation and collaborative negotiation.

In workplace mediations, labor and management come together to discuss, own, and solve problems, rather than blame them on each other. They are encouraged not to deny, belittle, or rationalize each other's issues, but accept responsibility without blame and engage in joint problem solving to design collaborative solutions that work without coercion.

In a mediation I conducted recently, a school administration and teachers' union had traded accusations and attributed blame for years, then denied, belittled, and rationalized what the other side said, without ever discussing the issues. I stopped their accusations mid-sentence and asked a dangerous question: "Have you contributed in any way to this problem?" When the answer was yes, I asked how and was given specific examples. I then asked: "Do you think the other side would agree with the answer you gave?" When they said they did not know, I asked: "Would you like to find out?" They said yes, so I said: "Why don't you ask them?" I repeated this process with the other side, and we transitioned into dialogue over the issues.

In interest-based, mutual gain, collaborative, or win/win negotiations, the qualities each side really cares about are not lost in the quantities each side is fighting to achieve. Instead of viewing financial success as a limited *quantity* to be divided in a win/lose fashion, it becomes an unlimited *quality* to be shared based on consensus and win/win goals.

The unstated assumption of interest-based processes such as mediation, collaborative negotiation, and teamwork is that sharing power and rights automatically increases participation, responsibility, competency, partnership, motivation, and effectiveness. The true goal of mediation, though often unstated, is to achieve these outcomes on an individual-by-individual, conflict-by-conflict basis.

Rights vs. Interests and Responsibility for Education

The same dynamic operates in the world of education. As long as teachers are exclusively responsible for students' education, or administrators for the operation of schools, there will be a division of labor in which the job of one is to coerce and direct, while the other chooses either to blindly obey or resist. When teachers share responsibility for designing educational experiences with students, and administrators share leadership and responsibility for schools with teachers, obedience and resistance dissolve because there is no longer anyone to blame.

Only interest-based processes encourage educators to practice what they preach, model empathic listening, build consensus and collaboration, and encourage learning. No one is allowed to simply lay the problem at someone else's feet. Everyone is encouraged to listen, respond directly to others, realize they cannot solve their problems alone, and negotiate mutually acceptable solutions. Indeed, the very process of revealing interests, negotiating collaboratively, and jointly solving problems transforms schools from disconnected individuals into learning organizations.

A large part of what is required for teachers and administrators to end adversarial strife and destructive power- and rights-based contests is for them to refuse to be each other's enemies and take responsibility for the *whole* of their problem. To create more collaborative, interest-based schools, administrators need to surrender their exclusive power to decide outcomes. At the same time, teachers and students need to take responsibility for creating solutions. Acting as a whole, they can negotiate joint responsibility for learning through site-based shared decision-making councils.

For society to overcome its antagonisms and hostile separations, each part needs to become fully responsible for itself, which means taking responsibility for the whole. Whites and men need to be responsible for the equality of blacks and women, and blacks and women for the acceptance of whites and men, if discrimination is to be ended and power to be shared.

As a small example, in crosscultural mediations I often ask whites and men what the consequences of racism or sexism are for them. I ask couples arguing over household responsibilities, "Whose dishes are these?" In mediations between teachers and administrators, I create joint teams responsible for assessing, brainstorming, prioritizing, reaching consensus, and implementing solutions. Interest-based processes remind us of our fundamental connectedness and wholeness, the collective responsibility of all for each and each for all. Society is diminished by its deafness to cries for help that go unanswered, its blindness to inequalities and unfairness, and its refusal to accept responsibility for what it has done. Instead, our challenge is to create responsible communities based on interests.

Chapter Thirteen

Creating Responsible Communities

> *Families and communities are the ground-level generators and preservers of values and ethical systems. No society can remain vital or even survive without a reasonable base of shared values—and such values are not established by edict from lofty levels of the society. They are generated chiefly in the family, school, church, and other intimate settings in which people deal with one another face to face. The ideals of justice and compassion are nurtured in communities.*
> JOHN W. GARDNER

As a society, we have grown dysfunctional with power and rights, antagonism and privilege. Politically, economically, and socially, we create daily divisions in our ranks that reproduce rancor, apathy, amorality, cynicism, corruption, rebellion, and resistance. Interest-based processes overcome these obstacles to build community on every level.

The tendency to blame others—to single out criminals as solely responsible for crime, labor for reduced profits, or teachers for poor grades—reflects mutual powerlessness and irresponsibility. If the goal is to blame someone for the problem, we will not search for solutions that bring us together. In the same way that criminals feel powerless to change their lives, workers feel powerless to affect decisions about production, and teachers feel powerless to design their schools.

Creating Responsibility and Empowerment

Responsibility is intimately related to the collaborative search for interest-based solutions, just as individuals are connected with society. Separation is a fiction and blame is counterproductive, because it does not matter in the long run whose end of the boat is sinking. Responsibility for the whole requires real power sharing, which means relinquishing the right to control outcomes for others.

Practically, this means a surrender of power and rights by people who fought long and hard to obtain them. It implies the transformation of social, economic, political, and cultural systems. It suggests the simultaneous transformation of managers into leaders, employees into self-managers, and irresponsible children into responsible adults.

There is an unstated assumption underlying social, economic, and political divisions into opposing camps of managing and managed, responsible and irresponsible, powerful and powerless, that competency is a requirement for, rather than a consequence of empowerment. It is assumed that society, corporations, and schools can only be effectively managed by restricting access to power and rights, thereby also restricting motivation and assumption of responsibility for whatever is not working.

Only interest-based approaches encourage parties to act jointly and responsibly. In this way, mediation, collaborative negotiation, consensus building, teamwork, and other interest-based processes create a more humane, value-based, constructively conflicted social order. The true danger in using these methods is doing so half-heartedly, not trusting the process, not really empowering people to participate fully in making decisions on the issues that affect their lives, not pushing mediation to its genuine transformational limits, and not applying it broadly enough to all forms of conflict.

Creating Responsibility Through Community

The word "community" is often used to describe groups of people who live in close physical proximity to one another and share something in common. But community also has an energetic or spiritual component. It is a feeling of connectedness, a process of engagement, a method of being together, a relationship of collaborative synergy, a whole that is greater than the sum of its parts, a knowledge that each is responsible for all and all for each.

Community is therefore a kind of intimacy—a communion of souls that expresses the indivisibility and interdependence of its members. It is a living, organic connection between people. It is consensual, fluid, accepting, informal, egalitarian, creative, democratic, caring, and celebratory. It brings diverse interests together into one. It is what we feel when the artificial barriers that separate us are removed. It is our awareness of interconnection, and it is the energy we share with others and the rest of the universe.

Most people regard freedom as an individual attribute. Yet without community, we are not free to fully develop into social beings. It is only in relation to others that we experience love or hate, acceptance or rejection, success or failure, resolution or impasse. Only in community do we *create* ourselves through connection with others or recognize others as extensions of ourselves.

Community cannot be defined without reference to diversity or conflict. Indeed, there are "communities of conflict" that manufacture enemies in order to draw people together. Communities arise when what binds people together is stronger than what separates them, when internal differences and conflicts are overcome, creating a larger whole. This can be done in two ways: through "negative community," or communities "against" others, and through "positive community," or communities "for" others.

Racist communities in the southern United States, Serb-hating Albanians, and Albanian-hating Serbs are among numerous examples of negative-conflict communities. Workplaces and families can also become negative communities, in which people form alliances against those they hate, as opposed to what they have in common or like about each other.

Every response to conflict results in a unique form of community. When we avoid conflict, we create isolated non-communities of one. When we accommodate conflict, we create superficial, pseudo-communities based on civility, which are inauthentic and tolerant, yet repressive against nonconformity. When we are aggressive and use power in conflict, we create negative, adversarial, phobic communities based on anger or fear of others. When we compromise or use rights-based processes, we create legal, negotiated, divided communities. It is only when we use collaboration and interest-based processes that we generate positive, diverse, synergistic communities. Each of these varieties of community exists on a small scale in families, relationships, and teams, and on a larger scale in neighborhoods, organizations, cultures, and politics.

It is not possible to create lasting, positive, or synergistic communities through the exercise of power, because it ultimately relies on force and coercion. Power creates communities of pain and resistance among those who are oppressed by it, and communities of fear, denial, or guilt among those who wield it. Mediation cannot thrive in power-based communities, except by suppressing or settling conflicts and trading justice for harmony. In these societies, every mediation assumes a dangerous form, because interest-based processes challenge the very existence of power.

Nor is it possible to create lasting, positive, or synergistic communities through rights, which foster manipulation, bureaucracy, and hierarchical control. Rights-based processes create communities of apathy and irresponsibility among those who work in them, and communities of arrogance and control among those who administer them. Every rights-based process includes an involuntary element that enters into the creation of community and distorts it, reducing respect for other people's boundaries and the possibility of genuine connection between diverse members. This reality makes mediation dangerous in rights-based communities.

What happens in power- and rights-based communities can be seen clearly by comparing family or community mediations with corporate or litigated mediations. In the latter, power and rights often overwhelm interests, preventing deep discussion, dialogue, and transformation. Mediators routinely use pressure tactics, caucuses, manipulation, and evaluation to achieve results, rather than engagement, dialogue, empowerment, and collective problem solving.

For this reason, power- and rights-based processes both result in and are a result of false, negative, partial communities. These create an illusion of irreconcilable interests, as between haves and have-nots. Every action directed against the self-interests of others leads to divided community, in which common goals are based on opposition rather than affinity. These become communities of "us" versus "them," rather than communities of "we."

Creating Positive Community

Communities are complete only when they combine respect for diversity with commonality of interests. Communities based on identical interests are strong, but lack adaptability. They easily reach agreement, but as easily slip into mindless conformity and rigid enforcement of similarity. Diverse communities experience greater conflict, yet produce greater acceptance, richness, and depth through collaboration.

Positive communities cannot be created by proclamation. They arise wherever diversity is overcome and commonality is understood. Commonality begins with the discovery of difference and ends with empathy and acceptance. It is based on understanding, even *celebrating* differences, and on enjoying what makes us different. Community consists of sharing, which requires a combination of difference and acceptance, honesty and empathy, individuality and collaboration.

Why is it so difficult to create feelings of community in moments of quiescence, and why does it emerge so naturally in disaster? Why does it disappear so easily, to be replaced by self-seeking, adversarial, conflicted relationships? Why do negative communities seem to outnumber positive ones? How do we transform one into the other?

These are questions without easy answers. We know we cannot answer them without abandoning power and rights, which cause us to lose sight of common interests. We also know, from history and disaster, that positive communities have been created; that they are hard to maintain; that in their absence all manner of harm has been done, from genocide to intolerance; that they begin with the commitment of individuals to treat each other equally, yet distinctly; and that they reside in common purpose and mutuality.

For these reasons, it *seems* easier to create communities based on obedience, fear, and antipathy to others than to create communities based on diversity, affection, and consensus. The latter require individuality, autonomy, responsibility, listening, and empowerment as *conditions* for authentic community. Paradoxically, the more negative and individualistic the community, the more individuals suppress their self-interests to satisfy those of the collective. Yet the more positive and interdependent the community, the more easily diversity and individual self-interests are accepted. Therefore, the more positive the community, the more conflict it can support without losing unity and focus.

To create more genuine, positive communities, inequalities in power and rights based on race, gender, class, culture, sexual preference, and physical incapacity have to be overcome. The elimination of these disparities is a necessary but by no means sufficient condition for the creation of a larger sense of our common interests as a species. What we require are methods that encourage a sense of diversity and wholeness.

Mediation is one such method. Yet mediation becomes dangerous when it asks parties to surrender their power, rights, or privileges, even when what they receive in exchange is far more satisfying. In small, subtle ways, dangerous mediation dismantles negative communities based on power or rights and creates positive ones in their place.

When we elicit deep levels of empathy and honesty, overcome the desire for revenge, facilitate forgiveness, stimulate genuine listening, promote open dialogue and collaborative negotiation, achieve consensus, penetrate below the surface to discover real issues, and reach genuine resolution, we create small transformations that shift us from power or rights to interests and encourage positive community. In this way, each sequential degree of mediating dangerously creates a degree of freedom, that is reflected in a deeper degree of community.

Community is a commonality of spirit, sense, intellect, and emotion. Whatever reveals our essential interconnectedness creates community. *Dangerous* interest-based processes encourage us to risk being open, join with others in trust-building activities, and resist the lure of petty, negative, power- or rights-based efforts to unite some of us against the rest of us. These destructive alliances deny our larger community and rest on conformity and unresolved conflict. Interest-based communities are enemy-less, relying on diversity and sharing to bring us together and make us unique.

Taking Responsibility for Creating Community

To support a larger, global shift from power and rights to interests, it is important to consider what we can do as mediators, citizens, and members of society. A number of actions can be taken to achieve broad, institutional support for interest-based processes and positive communities. We can:

- Encourage every organization to create bridging or mediating structures and processes, whose goals and purposes are mutually defined by consensus and respect for diverse interests.
- Expand opportunities everywhere for people in conflict to participate in creating, selecting, and implementing solutions.
- Invite important decisions to be made on the basis of inclusion, openness, collaboration, prior consultation, consensus, and collaborative negotiation.
- Jointly establish uniform and fair procedures, regardless of potential outcome.
- Probe beneath the surface of power and rights language to reveal hidden causes and interests.
- Share power, responsibility, and decisional ownership with everyone affected by the problem.
- Share responsibility for results through collaborative negotiation and team process.
- Develop as great a concern for satisfying other people's needs and interests as for satisfying one's own.
- Take responsibility for changing the nature of relationships, improving process, solving problems and building trust, instead of blaming others.
- Collaboratively design conflict resolution systems to better prevent, manage, and resolve future disputes.
- Create expanded opportunities for spiritual communication, transformation, forgiveness, and reconciliation.

There is no institution in society that could not benefit from increased community, or that could not increase its level of openness, honesty, trust, participation, responsibility, empowerment, democracy, teamwork, collaboration, negotiation, and mediation. Unfortunately, few are as committed to these tasks as to multiplying their power or expanding their rights. To understand why, we need to examine in greater detail the rights-based institutions of the law and consider how to improve the way we fight based on interests. More important, as mediators we need to understand how to transform debate, which results in adversarial community, into dialogue that unites people in a collaborative search for truth.

Chapter Fourteen

What's Better Than the Rule of Law

*Take time to listen to what is said without words, to obey
the law too subtle to be written, to worship the unnameable
and to embrace the unformed.*
LAO-TZU

Most people today reject power-based contests as either damaging
or illegal and opt for the use of law instead. For this reason,
we need to understand in greater detail exactly what is wrong with
the law as a system for resolving disputes and what might actually
be *better* than the rule of law.

If the purpose of mediating dangerously is to allow parties to
discover the important lessons and positive outcomes that flow
directly from their conflicts, we need to recognize not only that
power-based conflict suppression and control are counterproductive, but that litigation, debate, adversarial negotiation, and other
rights-based processes also deprive us of their benefits.

While the rule of law has been effective in blocking dictatorship
and tyranny, it is not the last answer or the best one for a democratic society. The cost in human and financial terms, delay and dishonesty, resistance and bitterness, unworkable results and ruinous
relationships, has been too great not to question the belief that our
legal system represents the best of all possible alternatives.

Resolving conflicts through law actively encourages people to
form hostile, dismissive, adversarial judgments about each other.

Yet, as Honoré de Balzac observed: "The more one judges, the less one loves." Indeed, the very use of adversarial legal methods for resolving conflict encourages parties to:

- Demonize their enemies and victimize themselves.
- Argue over positions and ignore their interests.
- Assert correctness and deny responsibility.
- Confuse people with problems.
- Focus on the past rather than the present or the future.
- Concentrate on trivia and ignore deeper truths.
- Become lost in a maze of contradictory, ultimately unprovable judgments about who is right or wrong.
- Refuse to engage in dialogue, actually listen, or seriously come to grips with an opponent's interests.

Mediators can help convert these destructive, adversarial battles into constructive engagements that transcend the rule of law, for example, by:

- Supporting conflicting parties in shifting from power- and rights- to interest-based languages, processes, and solutions.
- Understanding how rights-based processes such as law operate, and discern how they can be used less adversarially.
- Aiding conflicting parties in avoiding the downward spiral of assumptions that support hostility, demonization of others, and victimization of themselves.
- Exploring ways of transforming debates over positions into dialogues over interests.
- Satisfying interests so the parties no longer care about their positions.
- Encouraging responsibility without blaming.
- Separating people from problems.
- Focusing on the present or future rather than the past.
- Skipping trivia and going for deeper truths.
- Revealing through deep honesty, empathy, and dialogue the pointlessness of judgments about who was right or wrong.
- Encouraging them to improve the way they fight.

What's Wrong with the Law from A to Z

It is frequently stated that while there are limitations and problems with the law, it is the best system available. Indeed, for centuries the rule of law has symbolized progress and been an effective bulwark against tyranny. It has expressed an ideal by which rulers and ruled are judged according to uniform standards and encouraged "equal justice under the law." Yet the law has a number of inherent defects and tragic flaws that limit its potential effectiveness as an instrument of conflict resolution, positive community, and collaborative social change. Here are some, from A to Z:

A. It takes too long.
B. It costs too much.
C. It often misses the point.
D. It is too dependent on definitions.
E. The process is too formal.
F. Results tend to be punitive rather than equitable.
G. It always creates a winner and a loser.
H. It focuses on the past rather than the future.
I. Outcomes are often unpredictable.
J. Unworkable results are difficult to correct.
K. It is not preventative or proactive.
L. Differences between judges permit unequal justice.
M. Relationships cannot be discussed or corrected.
N. Communication problems cannot be resolved.
O. It cannot act if the dispute falls outside legal definition.
P. The process is adversarial rather than conciliatory.
Q. A limited number of remedies are possible, with no provision for brainstorming.
R. Results tend to affirm the status quo.
S. Judges sometimes tilt their decisions in order to be reelected.
T. There is no opportunity for dialogue between the parties.
U. People are encouraged to be self-interested rather than collaborative.
V. Information is not exchanged early or used to prevent problems.
W. Witnesses are cross-examined rather than conversed with.
X. The process is controlled by judges and lawyers, not by parties.

Y. Questions are close-ended, rather than open-ended.
Z. Results are based on fault, not on resolving the underlying issues.

In addition, laws are enacted, interpreted, and enforced by governments, which are run by the very people they are supposed to restrain. For this reason, law is nearly always consistent with the demands and experiences of the actual, subjective persons who possess political, economic, and social power, and who guide the state. This makes respect for the rights of the powerless a matter of expediency, votes, or competing forms of power.

Because the wealthy constitute most of the legislators who make the rules, executives who enforce them, and judges who uphold them, law reinforces the dominant rights of haves over have-nots. Petronius Arbiter recites a popular song from the time of the Roman emperor, Nero:

> What good are the laws where Money is king,
> where the poor are always wrong,
> and even the mockers who scoff at the times
> will sell the truth for a song?
> The courts are an auction where justice is sold;
> the judge who presides bangs a gavel of gold.

No one would contend that fascist laws authorizing genocide were fair or just. Yet, in form, they were no different from other laws. All laws speak the language of rights, but ultimately act on the basis of power. When power is challenged, as during the U.S. Civil War, legal rights are suspended or compromised to suppress the threat of disorder, as often occurs with militant strikes and public demonstrations. The law itself permits this suspension, for example, through the idea that free speech can be suppressed whenever there is a "clear and present danger."

The law both limits and establishes the state, which limits and establishes the law. The state proclaims rights, and at the same time authorizes their suppression. It declares liberties, and simultaneously creates the coercive authority to do away with them. Why does it do this? How can the law fail to recognize the rule, when it so carefully carves out the exception?

How Legal Conflicts Get Resolved

Legal conflicts are resolved *bureaucratically*, by creating obstacles so tedious and enervating that all but the most die-hard tempers choose to quit. They are resolved *politically*, through changes in personnel or policies. They are resolved *psychologically*, by the illusion or assumption of superior power, by deference or obedience to hierarchical command, by guilt, fear, and shame. In difficult cases, they are resolved *coercively*, by bailiffs, marshals, and police, who are authorized to arrest people and forcibly seize or transfer property. Beneath talk of rights lies the reality of power.

In form, the law is coercive rather than consensual, hierarchical rather than heterarchical, autocratic rather than democratic, predetermined rather than flexible, neutral rather than omnipartial, limited rather than expansive, focused on the past rather than the future. Legal processes provide little or no help in improving communication or relationships, collaboratively solving problems, surfacing emotional issues, or informally resolving conflicts.

The inherently adversarial win/lose process of adjudication encourages lawyers to manipulate, tell half-truths, deny responsibility, and withhold crucial information in the interest of their clients, without regard to fairness. It requires judges and juries to pronounce judgment based on inadequate, untested, disguised, twisted, and defective information. It picks winners, based on technicalities rather than substance; and it picks losers, whose lives, motivation, loyalty, participation, and responsibility are damaged beyond reason or repair.

In the process, the victors also emerge defeated, and justice lies with the conquered. Franz Kafka described justice as "a fugitive from the winning camp," and Lenny Bruce quipped that "the only justice in the halls of justice is in the halls." If, in victory, one loses compassion, integrity, generosity, honesty, and humility, who or what has won? While it feels satisfying to take revenge on one's enemies, it is far more satisfying to turn enemies into friends. There is nothing in the law to support such a result. The law is designed to contain and control conflict, not resolve or transform it; to terminate disagreements, not learn from them; to suppress emotions, not complete them; to settle cases, not search for underlying issues; to announce third-party decisions, not facilitate consensus.

Legal decisions forge a temporary, artificial peace based on the fiction of judicial objectivity. In the process, subjective information is blurred or ignored, and consensus, closure, transformation, and forgiveness become unattainable. The results of legal objectivity include suppressed feelings, blind obedience, and silent dissent. Law regards emotions and subjective experiences as biased, disruptive, and irrelevant, while perceiving lack of caring, toughness, and objectivity as neutral or positive. For example, the "reasonable man" standard used in civil cases measures negligence against a highly patriarchal, ignoble form of logic, leaving little scope for everyday human emotion. Courts regard themselves as superior to the human beings they judge, finding them wrong, weak, and wanting. They see themselves as more rational, evenhanded, and just than ordinary mortals. This is reflected in the idea that governments should be "of laws, not of men."

There is no place within the rule of law for hurt feelings. There is no comprehension of paradox, enigma, or mystery. There is no room for different cultures or values or competing systems of thought. And worst of all, the law pretends this is not so. It argues, but it doesn't really listen. It pontificates, but it really doesn't care. It judges, but it lacks wisdom. It reasons, but it lacks a heart.

In content and in process, the law is old rather than young, masculine rather than feminine, white rather than black, rich rather than poor. It often behaves like a sterile, uncultured, unfeeling brute, with no music in its soul or art in its eye. It is not childlike or playful or affectionate or funny. It can't dance or sing or laugh, even at itself.

What's Better Than the Rule of Law?

Is there anything better than the rule of law? Is there a realistic alternative to the legal system? I believe there is. It is one in which results are obtained voluntarily, and decisions are made by consensus; where parties design the form and content of their negotiations; where there is informality and infinite capacity for creative results. It is one in which there are no rules of evidence, because there are no facts to find. It is one where emotions are expressed, acknowledged, and respected; where greater concern is shown for the future than the past; where third parties facilitate without deciding, and are empathetic rather than neutral. It is one in which people are encouraged to act honestly, empathetically, collaboratively, humbly, and creatively; where forgiveness and reconciliation are encouraged; where people are allowed to be human, direct, and open; where anyone can understand what is happening and participate fully without professional jargon. It is one without coercion, that encourages collaboration and permits both sides to win. It is mediation.

Mediation is justice coming full circle, a return to ancient tribal principles of wisdom, compassion, honesty, self-revelation, healing, and forgiveness. We need to move beyond the idea that mediation is "bargaining in the shadow of the law," or an "alternative" form of dispute resolution secondary to litigation. Mediation is also bargaining in the shadow of justice, ethics, emotions, values, and community, and a more "appropriate" form of dispute resolution in most cases than litigation. Mediation encourages people to be responsible for their acts. It is healing, because it cleanses old wounds and repairs emotional rifts that otherwise might continue unabated. It facilitates acceptance and refusal based on an expanded idea of self-interest, one that *includes* the self-interest of the other side.

Rather than try to fit round objects into square holes as legal definitions do, mediation examines what is unique in each case for each person and helps them design unique solutions. It is the only form of dispute resolution that lies outside the state, speaks the truth, equally empowers the participants, is preventative and healing, and arrives at voluntary agreements through noncoercive means.

Having said this, I do not expect the legal system to be replaced by mediation overnight. There will undoubtedly be many disputes that cannot be resolved in mediation, for which litigation in some form will be appropriate. These might include civil cases in which abstract principles are at issue, criminal cases in which defendants have lost the capacity for compassion, or spousal battering disputes in which neither side is willing to break the cycle. Yet there is nothing inherent, even in murder, battering, or crimes of violence, that makes mediation impossible. Even in these cases, mediation should be pursued initially and throughout the process, right up to the point of decision. But in cases where litigation is necessary, we can define new roles for attorneys and judges that partially address these limitations in the legal system.

Some New Roles for Attorneys

To transcend purely legal reasoning, attorneys and judges have to step outside the law and redefine the narrow roles they have been assigned. They may then discover that there are a number of ways they can help conflicted parties engage in dialogue with each another, give up trying to impose their will on others, and surrender their desire for victory and risk of defeat.

Attorneys and judges can begin by requiring mediation as the initial step in every civil suit and criminal proceeding. They can refer difficult cases to arbitration, as a less costly and time-consuming alternative to litigation that still produces final results. They can simplify and improve the litigation process, for example, by eliminating costly defenses against discovery, simplifying procedures, abbreviating motions and appeals, and establishing codes of conduct that preclude the worst adversarial behaviors.

They can also redefine the role of attorneys. Most attorneys define their role through the lens of the adversarial process, encouraging an assumption that the other side is evil, corrupt, or lying, and that whatever advantage they can gain is fair and equitable. This exclusively adversarial role of attorneys tends to preclude other possible roles that are more positive, for example:

- *Attorney as Consultant:* Parties need attorneys not only to engage in hand-to-hand combat with the opposition, but to help prevent future disputes. This means going beyond drafting legal documents to consulting on ways of proactively decreasing the amount and level of conflict their clients are experiencing.
- *Attorney as Teacher:* Every conflict presents both sides with the possibility of learning from their mistakes. But as long as the emphasis is on blaming others, the deeper lessons of the conflict cannot be appreciated. It is possible for attorneys to teach clients in greater detail not only what the law requires, but what they might have done to avoid the dispute, as well as similar disputes in the future.

- *Attorney as Coach:* As long as attorneys are champions and advocates, it is difficult for them also to be critics or coaches who bring "tough love" to the relationship *between* their clients. It is possible, though dangerous, for attorneys to tell their clients honestly, in front of each other, what they did wrong and could do better next time.

- *Attorney as Informal Problem Solver:* Rather than writing nasty, arrogant, self-serving letters to opposing counsel or searching for formal, large-scale solutions, attorneys can focus on creating constructive, informal conversations that are oriented to solving problems and give up trying to shift the blame.

- *Attorney as Systems Thinker:* Rather than thinking about their clients' conflicts as single, isolated, fragmented transactions, attorneys can help analyze the systemic sources of their conflicts, and suggest interventions and changes that break up destructive family, business, and organizational systems.

- *Attorney as Ombudsman:* Attorneys can serve as advisors and external change agents regarding organizational problems and the redrafting of rules, policies, and procedures that help people and organizations learn and change.

- *Attorney as Mediator:* Attorneys can act as mediators in many disputes, and even where they cannot do so, they can bring a degree of civility to their disagreements with one another, along with a less hostile, personalizing approach to their arguments.

- *Attorney as Promoter of Empathy with the Other Side:* Attorneys, even in criminal cases, can encourage empathy or compassion with those on the other side of the dispute. They could even ask their clients what they think it would feel like to be on the other side of their anger.

- *Attorney as Reconciler:* Attorneys can encourage parties who settle their disputes to reach beyond narrow victories and losses to seek full resolution, to offer and request forgiveness, and to pursue transformation.

- *Attorney as Conscience:* Attorneys can remind their clients to examine their own ethics, values, beliefs, and moral principles. They can call on those they represent to do the right thing, even when it means taking less or surrendering their claims.

- *Attorney as Moral Model:* Attorneys can act as role models and promote moral behavior, even when it comes to surrendering fees that have not been earned or that depend on legal mistakes or unnecessary adversarial posturing.

These new roles break the paradigm of law and return us to its original purpose, which was to resolve conflicts. A well-known attorney, Mahatma Gandhi, described this well, in terms equally applicable today:

> I learned the true practice of law. I learned to find out the better side of human nature and to enter men's hearts. I realized that the true function of a lawyer was to unite parties riven asunder.

By *dangerously* questioning the role of law and lawyers, we make possible new, interest-based forms of resolution that shift us from debate to dialogue.

Chapter Fifteen

Shifting from Debate to Dialogue

We ask only that men think it over carefully and then decide whether they will add to the misery of the world to achieve vague and distant goals, and whether they will accept a world crowded with weapons where brother kills brother; or whether, on the contrary, they will avoid as much bloodshed as possible in order to give future generations—who will be even better armed than ourselves—a chance for survival. . . . What we must fight is fear and silence, and with them the spiritual isolation they involve. What we must defend is dialogue and the universal communication of men. Slavery, injustice, and lies are the plagues that destroy this dialogue and forbid this communication, and that is why we must reject them.
ALBERT CAMUS

As a result of numerous problems with both power- and rights-based conflict resolution processes, we need to consider how to build interest-based alternatives. We can do so by turning debate into dialogue and improving the way people fight, thereby bringing people together in a collaborative search for resolution and learning.

One of the inherent defects in all legal systems is that they end conflicts prematurely, before the lessons they embody have been learned. We learn the most from conflicts when we do not resolve them quickly, but remain with them as their lessons unfold. What we require are interest-based dispute resolution processes that support curiosity, honest feedback, self-examination, open-ended questions, and complex answers that include paradoxes, enigmas, and contradictions. We require processes that do *not* settle significant issues, but leave them open to discussion, mutation, and learning. Dialogue is one such method.

The progression from power- to rights-based processes is paralleled in the shift from notification to debate. Notification is the form of communication appropriate to autocracy. In debate, communication becomes more democratic, since competing voices are allowed to be heard. A similar transition takes place in the progression from rights- to interest-based processes, paralleled in the shift from debate to dialogue. In dialogue, communication becomes collaborative and acutely democratic.

Just as power is an announcement that manufactures despots and rebels, haves and have-nots, rights is a debate that manufactures winners and losers, truths and falsehoods, those who are virtuous and those who are villainous. Few human conflicts are like this. Even in extreme cases, there is some truth and falsehood on both sides, and it is often difficult to tell virtuous from villainous behavior.

What is Dialogue?

Physicist David Bohm defined dialogue as "a stream of meaning flowing among, through and between us." This stream consists of all the ideas that have ever been expressed, from which we can draw or add to a sense of shared meaning. Dialogue is *thinking together,* a kind of "participatory consciousness," in which thought behaves like an organism whose disparate parts are coordinated to produce a single entity, a whole. Dialogue generates connection, community, teamwork, group learning, and trust. Ultimately, it is how every conflict gets resolved.

Debate is a circular process, in which the parties argue and disagree with each other and are usually more interested in convincing the other side they are right than in discovering the truth. Dialogue is different from debate in that truth emerges not from one side winning and the other losing, but from both discovering the *meaning* of their disagreement, explaining their perspectives, and searching for answers that address their different meanings and underlying interests.

In dialogue, one listens to discover. In debate, one listens to find flaws or develop counterarguments. Dialogue acknowledges feelings and builds relationships. Debate ignores feelings and relationships. Dialogue focuses on the problem as an "it" or a "we." Debate focuses on the problem as a "you." Dialogue searches for improved solutions. Debate defends one's own solution. Dialogue assumes many people know parts of the answer and that together they can create more workable solutions. Debate assumes that there is a single right answer and that one side knows it. Dialogue allows people to admit mistakes. Debate fortifies people in insisting they are right. Dialogue creates openness to change. Debate creates resistance to change. Dialogue assumes both sides can win. Debate assumes only one side can win.

While dialogue forms a part of most mediation processes, it also differs from mediation. Mediation focuses on finding solutions, while dialogue largely ignores solutions and focuses on clarification, deescalation, and improved understanding. In this sense, dialogue is a way of adjusting rather than resolving differences. Together, they form a powerful combination.

Four Forms of Dialogue

There are four dramatically different forms of dialogue that parties can engage in when they are in conflict. First, they can dialogue about *what is wrong*. This includes complaints, criticisms, accusations, and condemnations of others; rationalizations, justifications, and denials about oneself; descriptions of fault or blame and denials of responsibility; hearsay, rumors, gossip, and dramatic exaggeration; efforts to get others to agree to support a "story"; baseless assumptions, unrealistic expectations, and ungrounded judgments; focusing on a fixed past and a foreclosed future; resignations; assertions of powerlessness; and excuses for putting up with or tolerating what is wrong. This form of dialogue often helps people release their frustrations, but does little to solve problems.

Second, they can dialogue about *what is true*. This includes observations or descriptions by careful observers; accurate descriptions and nonevaluative accounts; supported assumptions and grounded assessments; logical interpretations of reality; acceptance of responsibility for mistakes; acknowledgments, validations, and apologies; focusing on the present and on understanding the past; evaluations of what worked or didn't work and why; and nonjudgmental feedback. This form of dialogue moves parties in the direction of problem solving and encourages them to separate facts from interpretations and people from problems.

Third, they can dialogue about *what is possible.* This includes visions, wishes, dreams, and goals; statements of interests; examinations of what is feasible; descriptions of opportunities, possibilities, and choices; creative statements that invent or design; statements of shared values; inquiries, explorations, imaginings, and speculations; focusing on the future; and statements that create possibilities or openings. This form of dialogue elicits interests, values, and visions, in anticipation of a different future, rather than a similar past.

Finally, they can dialogue about *what is going to happen.* This includes commitments and calls to action; strategies, tactics, and action plans; offers, counteroffers, and agreements; statements about achieving or creating outcomes or results; initiations of something new; statements of intention and commitment to action; focusing on the present as a place to begin creating a different future; and calls for partnership, collaboration, and joint action. This form of dialogue emphasizes commitment and specific, concrete actions people are going to take to resolve their disputes or behave differently.

The mediators' role is to walk the parties through each of these different forms of dialogue by asking questions that allow them to transition from one to the other. For example, dialogues about what is wrong can be shifted by asking factual questions, reframing personal answers, inquiring about what happened, and requesting objective criteria. Just asking, "What did she actually do, as you recall it?" and checking back and forth automatically creates a dialogue about what is true.

Dialogues about what is true can be shifted by asking questions about what people want, focusing them on the future, and eliciting their core beliefs or values. When someone states what they believe is true, we can ask, "What would you have liked for him to have done?" which automatically creates a dialogue about what is possible. Similarly, dialogues about what is possible can be shifted by asking, for example, "Who is going to be responsible for making this happen?" In each form of dialogue, multiple questions can be asked that allow the conversation to evolve to a higher state of coherence, self-organization, and resolution.

Questions to Promote Dialogue

There is a powerful, innovative program in Watertown, Massachusetts, called the Public Conversations Project (PCP). The founders of PCP, Laura and Dick Chasen, used their experience as family therapists to prepare community leaders with strongly opposing points of view on highly volatile public issues, such as abortion, the environment, and sexual orientation, to meet and participate in a different kind of conversation.

In PCP's citizen dialogues over abortion, for example, participants are asked not to identify their positions on the issues until after they have eaten together. The process begins with agreement on ground rules. Each participant then answers several extremely powerful questions, such as:

- *What life experiences have energized your involvement or shaped your current views or feelings about this issue?* This starts the conversation with a focus not on what people think, but on the human events and life encounters that led them to their ideas. It also helps rehumanize demonized and stereotyped adversaries.
- *What is the heart of your perspective on this issue, for you as an individual?* This invites people to speak from their hearts, not just their minds, to reframe their positions as perspectives, and to speak as individuals rather than as a bloc.
- *Do you have any mixed feelings, value conflicts, pockets of uncertainty, or discomfort within your overall perspective on this issue that you are willing to mention?* This allows people to present their ideas not as 100 percent true for all times, but as propositions over which reasonable people might differ, and about ares where they may even have second thoughts.

Once these questions have been answered, the room is filled with new information that softens the stereotypes of those with different views, stimulates additional questions participants can address directly to one another, and illuminates areas of shared conviction and concern.

In mediation, I often ask a number of additional questions to advance dialogue, or allow it to evolve to a higher level:

- *Even though you hold widely differing views, are there any concerns or ideas you share with each other? Are there any you feel you may have in common?* This question invites people to consider that their opposing views may obscure a deeper set of shared concerns or ideas that are not in opposition. It asks them to recognize not only what divides them, but what unites them as well.
- *What underlying ethical beliefs or values have led you to your beliefs?* This question allows the conversation to go to a deeper, more principled level, introducing a set of beliefs, ethics, or values over which people frequently agree. It depersonalizes the conversation and encourages great ideas. Even if people do not agree, it reveals the wellsprings of their conflict. Ethical, moral, and value differences are always complex. They are useful in revealing paradoxes, contradictions, gray areas, and deeper issues underneath surface positions.

Here are some additional questions you can ask to promote open, ongoing, constructive dialogue in groups or organizations or with individuals. I encourage you to invent your own:

- What are some of the gray areas in the position you have taken, or the areas you find difficult to define?
- Do the differences between your positions reveal any riddles, paradoxes, contradictions, or enigmas about this issue? Is it possible to see your differences as two sides of the same coin? If so, what unites them? What is the coin?
- What would happen if you won completely and the other side disappeared? What would you lose as a result?
- Can you separate the issue from the person with whom you are disagreeing? Is there anything positive you can say about the person on the other side of this issue?
- What processes or ground rules could help you disagree more constructively?

- Instead of focusing on the past, what would you like to see happen in the future? Why?
- Are you disagreeing over fundamental values or over how to achieve them?
- Is there a way both of you might be right? How?
- Would it be possible to test your ideas in practice and see which work best? How might you do that? What criteria could you use to decide what works best?
- What could be done to improve each idea? Could some of the other side's ideas be incorporated into yours?
- Are there any other alternatives to what you are both saying? Have you left anything out?
- . How could you make dialogue ongoing? How can you preserve your differences so as not to lose sight of their truths?
- What could you do to improve your process for handling disagreements in the future? For encouraging future dialogue?

These questions contribute to a successful dialogue by enhancing the parties' engagement with the issues, each other, and themselves, making it possible to interlace opposing ideas and interests. The role of mediators and facilitators is to initiate, model, encourage, and improve the dialogue by deepening questions and building on answers.

Techniques for Creating Public Dialogue

Two things need to happen for dialogue to become dangerous enough to replace the rights-based process of debate and the power-based process of notification. First, disagreement needs to be accepted as a positive, necessary element in learning, both for individuals and organizations. Learning occurs when we stop and listen to people whose perspectives and experiences differ from our own. Second, we need to understand that we share our disagreements and our uncomfortable feelings, and we are all searching for solutions that will satisfy our interests.

For example, I cofacilitated a task force that was charged by a city council with coming to consensus on a plan for addressing problems of poverty and homelessness. On the task force were homeless people who were experiencing these problems first-hand

and a local advocacy group that proposed offering the homeless an ultimatum to leave town or go to jail.

Weekly meetings overflowed with fierce debates, as angers flared and pain distorted people's perceptions. When advocates made adversarial assertions or personally attacked their opponents, we asked them about the personal experiences that supported their emotions and the commitments, values, and visions that informed their arguments. We uncovered points of agreement and nurtured ideas for resolution, but did not suppress disagreements. We encouraged dialogue over substantive issues and supported give-and-take negotiations between diverse constituencies, all aimed at healing the city and solving the problem. The group finally reached consensus on a plan that was so well thought out and supported that the city council had no choice but to endorse it.

Throughout the process, we used a number of techniques to draw the group into dialogue and encourage people to listen to ideas with which they disagreed. Here are some dialogue-promoting techniques, with sample questions or comments to illustrate each:

Inquiring	What do you think should be done? Why do you think so?
Supporting	I appreciate your willingness to speak up and express your opinions. Here is an example that supports your point.
Acknowledging	You took a risk in making that concession.
Refereeing	What ground rules do we need so everyone can feel we are behaving fairly?
Concretizing	Can you give a specific example?
Exploring	Say more about why you feel so strongly about this issue.
Summarizing	Is this what you are trying to say . . . ?
Challenging	Isn't that inconsistent with what the group already decided?
Coaching	Is there a way you could respond less defensively?
Connecting	That point connects directly with what was said earlier.

Reorienting	I think we're lost. Can we get back on track? Are we talking about the real issue here?
Problem Solving	What are some possible solutions?
Uniting	What do we agree on? Why have we come together to discuss this issue?

This list of methods and phrases is meant to stimulate your thinking. It is not a script to be memorized or woodenly recited, nor is it a technique in what I call "new age manipulation." The most important elements in dialogue are authentic curiosity about differences and recognition that the longer the conversation lasts and the deeper it goes, the more we are likely to learn.

Steps in Creating an Open Dialogue Process

Initiating dialogue between antagonistic groups is inherently dangerous, especially when it takes place openly. Most mediation occurs behind closed doors, privately and confidentially. Yet enormous value can be derived from open dialogue over difficult issues, exploring possible solutions, and negotiating relationships.

Open dialogue is especially useful in addressing complex environmental, diversity, and public policy issues, exploring internal organizational change initiatives, and building genuine, positive community. Some of the purposes of open dialogue, in connection with divisive community or organizational issues, are to:

- Draw everyone affected by the problem together.
- Agree on trust-building ground rules for behaviors.
- Reduce personalization and hostility.
- Encourage listening on all sides.
- Sharpen identification and understanding of problems.
- Raise awareness and understanding of complex policy issues.
- Discuss difficult, polarizing events and beliefs honestly.
- Explore ideas openly without predetermining outcomes.
- Build consensus regarding change initiatives.

Making dialogue open allows everyone to witness and participate in the learning process. It encourages leaders to improve their advocacy, perfect their arguments, and tell their stories more powerfully. Openness educates participants about history, facts, and issues. It facilitates the convening process by encouraging people to come together without demonizing or disrespecting each other. It enrolls people in gathering facts, telling stories, expressing emotional truths, and communicating the results they want or find acceptable.

The steps in organizing an open dialogue process vary, depending on the nature and size of the group, the needs of the parties, the character of the issues, the timing of the process, and other considerations. To visualize the unfolding of a open dialogue, here is a checklist I created in connection with a public policy dispute that pitted ecological preservation against economic development:

1. Identify the principal parties who will participate in the dialogue, including:
   - Primary parties to the dispute.
   - Affected groups in industry, labor, government, and community.
   - Recognized experts and scholars.
   - Leaders of local community organizations.
   - Concerned individuals, such as students, teachers, and officials.
2. Interview key participants in person in advance of the session to discover their issues and interests, build trust in the process, uncover hidden obstacles to moving forward, gather information to assist the facilitators, and fine tune a design for the process.
3. Invite participants to meet and agree on ground rules for the dialogue.
4. As they convene, welcome the participants, review ground rules and the design for the process, and present a list of items to be discussed, drawn from the interviews.
5. Ask each participant to introduce themselves, say who they are, and answer a question that promotes dialogue, such as:
   - Why they agreed to be present.
   - Why they want this issue resolved.
   - What in their experience has led them to feel strongly about this topic.
   - What outcome they want.
6. Introduce a panel of representatives and experts with conflicting points of view. Facilitate the discussion, field

questions from the audience, and gradually shift focus from the panel to audience discussion. Begin by asking each panel member to identify the problem.

7. Draw participants into responsive dialogue, defuse tensions, summarize agreements, and record points of consensus and disagreement on flip charts.

8. Ask each side to present its position, offer back-up information and detailed explanations, and provide ample opportunity for questions and dialogue from all sides.

9. Shift the focus from positions to interests, past to future, personalities to issues, and prescriptions to options. Ask *why* people want what they want, and probe for underlying concerns.

10. Caucus periodically with each side to encourage them to trust and speak freely with you and to bring their interests and hidden issues to the table.

11. Ask representatives of opposing positions to meet in "side-bar" negotiations to come to consensus on recommendations to the group. Select the strongest advocates so others will not question their recommendations.

12. Transition into small-group problem solving and negotiations, identify areas of agreement, disagreement, mutual interest, and consensus. Refocus attention on relationships and qualities the parties have in common.

13. Summarize points of agreement regularly to build confidence in the process and limit the range of discussion.

14. As the parties reach full and final agreements, review each point of agreement.

15. If they have not reached full and final agreement, confirm interim agreements, agree to limit the use of destructive methods between meetings, and encourage continued dialogue.

16. List outstanding disagreements to work on at the next session. Elicit recommendations and agendas for following sessions.

17. Hold repeated sessions, picking up where you left off, and distributing summaries of the last session before the next one.

18. Draw each separate session to a close, not a conclusion. Thank participants, assign homework, and encourage continued dialogue over open issues.

19. Confirm agreements to meet until the conflict is resolved, and to forge a genuine resolution.

20. Reach for closure, acknowledge participants, and celebrate successes. Make the process transparent throughout, explaining what you are doing and why, *while* you are doing it, so everyone can learn skills to resolve conflicts in the future.

Pronouns and Conflict Resolution

Dialogue and conflict resolution can be enhanced simply by shifting the pronouns people use to describe their problem, as depicted in the following chart:

Pronouns and Conflict Resolution

Pronoun	Form	Likely Result
They	Stereotype	Prejudice
You	Accusation	Blame
He, She	Demonization/ Victimization	Hostility/ Disempowerment
It	Objectification	Problem Solving
I	Confession/Request	Introspection/ Responsibility
We	Collaboration/Partnership	Ownership/Commitment

The dialogue facilitator or mediator can actively reframe pronouns used by the parties, ask questions that naturally transition from one pronoun to the next, or simply ask "Could you try saying that as an 'I' statement?" and "What was the difference between those two statements?"

Many of the methods used in dialogue can also be used in mediations and conversations between individuals. While mediation uses private, interpersonal dialogue to search for joint solutions, dialogue by itself is based on the same assumption that fuels debate and litigation—that truth emerges from the clash of opposites. It adds, however, that this effect is increased when opposites acknowledge that they are each part of a greater whole, and have in common not only their opposition, but their search for a higher truth. In this way, dialogue encourages parties to improve the way they fight.

Chapter Sixteen

Improving the Way We Fight

> *Imagine that you are creating a fabric of human destiny*
> *with the object of making men happy in the end, giving*
> *them peace and rest at last, but that it was essential and*
> *inevitable to torture to death only one tiny creature . . .*
> *and to found that edifice on its unavenged tears, would*
> *you consent to be the architect on those conditions?*
> FYODOR DOSTOYEVSKY

While there are profound limits on the efficacy of power- and rights-based processes, interest-based processes do not always result in resolution. Mediators therefore need to ponder not only how to stop people from fighting destructively, but how to *improve* the way they fight. This means inventing and supporting constructive ways of fighting.

This may sound heretical, as mediators are supposed to be against fighting. While it is clearly important to direct our skills and techniques against unproductive, ineffective, cruel, and costly ways of fighting, we can also assist people, through a dangerous mediation process, to engage in constructive forms of combat. In the process, they may discover that transformation depends on the very friction, strife, and contradiction that is sometimes needed for truth to emerge in conflict.

Why Fight?

There are many subtle benefits to fighting, which timid mediations do not adequately address. Fighting can be a way of grieving or coming to grips with loss. It can be a way of discovering the real problem or of generating the energy needed to abandon a dys-functional system. It can be a way of stripping off masks, searching for authenticity, and connecting with one another at a deeper level. And, there are times when none of these can be achieved if we do not permit—even *encourage*—constructive ways of fighting.

When we mediate conflicts that arise out of oppressive rela-tionships, tyrannical behavior, real contests for power, or intense desires for revenge, dialogue and interest-based processes may appear inadequate as vehicles for the expression of intense humil-iation and rage. In these moments, it may be necessary for parties to engage their opponents and do battle. There are times, as Gandhi recognized, when "A No uttered from deepest conviction is better and greater than a Yes uttered to please, or what is worse, to avoid trouble."

When we have done everything we can to reach resolution and failed; when we have taken dangerous risks, spoken honestly, lis-tened empathetically, and accepted full responsibility for our actions; when we have radically improved our skills, mediated, and tried every method we can imagine, yet are still unable to resolve the conflict, it may be time to turn and engage it.

It is possible for us to fight in ways that encourage resolution, learning, collaboration, and transformation. Before beginning, we need to recognize that our ultimate, true opponent in every bat-tle is none other than ourselves. It is our tendency to demonize and stereotype our opponents that fights against our capacity for unconditional integrity and against our ability to always act on our own highest values.

No one should fight lightly, without realizing the brutality that is inherent in the choice and its inevitable, terrible costs. The dan-ger in fighting is that humanity and integrity will be defeated by hatred and expediency, and that values will be compromised in the name of victory. Playwright Bertold Brecht wrote, regarding World War II, that it was time to "embrace the butcher," and accept the realities of war, and Henrik Ibsen wrote that: "One should never put on one's best trousers to go out to battle for freedom and truth."

While difficult, it is nonetheless possible to fight in principled, humane, constructive ways that make future collaboration possi-ble between those who were enemies; ways that allow us to feel we have not sunk to behaviors that are beneath us, or sapped our self-esteem. When we oppose hatred with hatred, hatred wins. Historian Howard Zinn, a combat veteran of World War II, wrote on Veteran's Day 1999:

> [World War I] revealed the essence of war, of all wars, because however "just" or "humanitarian" may be the claims, at the irreducible core of all war is the slaughter of the innocent, organized by national leaders, accompanied by lies. . . . [M]odern war . . . is always a war against civilians and particularly children. . . .

While most conflicts do not rise to the level of warfare, the damage to noncombatants and children is the same. Every conflict involves pain to the innocent, and every conflict is accompanied by lies. The difficulty with any kind of fighting is that it is easy in the midst of battle to let hatred get the best of us. Aristotle wrote: "Anyone can become angry—that is easy. But to be angry with the right person, to the right degree, at the right time, for the right purpose, and in the right way—that is not easy."

All fighting against other human beings brutalizes us. It does so because in order to cause harm, we must disarm our compassion in ways that give us permission to act brutally against a human being we would otherwise be able to appreciate. Novelist James Baldwin described this well: "It is a terrible, an inexorable law that one cannot deny the humanity of another without diminishing one's own; in the face of one's victim, one sees oneself."

On the other hand, avoiding these pitfalls and fighting in a principled way can mean defeat, because our opponent may be willing to fight without being encumbered by them. There is a fundamental rule of fighting, observable in divorces, but applicable to other battles as well: whoever is willing to cause the most damage to innocent third parties and children will win. Yet, in winning, the victors lose their souls and suffer the greatest defeat of all. In the words of Matthew 16:26: "What is a man profited, if he shall gain the whole world, and lose his own soul?"

Value-Based Fighting

If we want to improve the way parties fight based on principles or values, the best way to begin is by assisting them to collaboratively negotiate rights-based ground rules similar to the Geneva

Accords, which mutually limit the exercise of destructive power. These rules fashion an arena of safety within which anger and rage can be released and light can be generated through the heat of confrontation.

We can encourage parties not to waste their hatred and humiliation on something petty like another person, but to dedicate them to solving larger problems, such as preventing future perpetrations or educating future victims. It is possible to combat depersonalization, disrespect, and dehumanization, while at the same time struggling for what is right. The problem for conflicting parties is to act according to ethics or values without preaching or moralizing. Cybernetics expert Heinz von Foerster writes:

> I myself try to adhere to the following rule: to master the use of my language so that ethics is implicit in any discourse I may have. . . . What do I mean by that? By that I mean to let language and action ride on an underground river of ethics, and to make sure that one is not thrown off. This ensures that ethics does not become explicit and that language does not degenerate into moralizations.

Moralizing means preaching to others about how they should behave based on what we believe to be universally applicable, objective principles. Ethics means telling *ourselves* how to behave based on what we believe to be interdependent, contingent, subjectively compelling principles. Dangerous mediation is based on ethics rather than morality. It strives to avoid the seduction of moralizing, lecturing, and holier-than-thou sermonizing. It emphasizes values as the foundation of ethics, and acknowledges that ethics are inherently paradoxical. In doing so, it naturally identifies methods for improving the way we fight.

What are values? Values are priorities. They are choices selected from real, practical alternatives, and based on a consideration of possible consequences. They are openly and publicly maintained, and acted on repeatedly. If we state our adherence to a value but do not act on it, it is not a real value. Values make fighting more human, empathetic, and collaborative.

Mediators can work with parties to specify the values they want to uphold during their fighting. Some of the values that naturally flow from the mediation process can improve the way parties fight. These include:

- Affirmation of conflict as positive; seeing it as an adventure or journey, an opportunity for growth and change, an invitation to intimacy and relationship, and an opening for transformation.
- Affirmation of diversity and difference, rejection of stereotypes, and assumptions of innate superiority, inferiority, correctness, and heresy.
- Affirmation of openness, honesty, and empathy in communication, process, and relationships.
- Affirmation of areas of agreement and commonality, of oneness and humanity; rejection of domination, coercion, humiliation, and suppression.
- Affirmation that cooperation and collaboration are primary and competition and aggression secondary.
- Affirmation of the legitimacy of each side's interests.
- Affirmation of the integration of intellect, emotion, body and spirit, of authenticity and integrity, and the unity of inner and outer.
- Affirmation of the desirability of victory without defeat.
- Affirmation of forgiveness, closure, and transformation; a refusal to leave anyone behind.

From Negative to Positive Opposition

Improving the way we fight can be quite simple. It happens whenever we listen with respect to someone who hates us, or discover behind their hatred a person who is frightened or in pain. We improve the way we fight by asking questions that challenge their stereotype of who we are, shifting from accusations and debate to "I" statements and dialogue, making unilateral concessions, and acknowledging our opponents' interests.

Most fighting assumes the form of *negative opposition,* which is hostile to resolution and contemptuous of compromise. It is fiercely competitive, polarizing, and positional, yet in this way, fortifies the very thing it opposes. Fighting can also take the form of *positive opposition,* which seeks resolution and encourages compromise. Through positive opposition, we reject demonizing and stereotyping, and become *unconditionally* respectful, collaborative, interest-based, and open to dialogue. We accept opposition, but without forgetting unity.

Here are some questions we can ask highly polarized parties or hostile groups and organizations as a way of improving the way they fight. Each suggests possible directions for transformation, openings to dialogue, and ways of resolving the reasons they decided to fight in the first place:

- *How should we respond to conflict, difference, and opposition?* By labeling it as heresy or treason? By silence or ridicule? Or by applause and affirmation—that is, by celebrating the gift of a different perspective?
- *How should we respond to internal divisions and dissent within our ranks?* By preventative measures that ensure mass conformity? By purging and punishing those who deviate? Or by encouraging and supporting criticism, and seeing dissent as information and opportunity?
- *How should we respond to crimes committed in our name?* By justifying them in the name of common ends? By casting their perpetrators out or labeling them liars or false prophets? Or by acknowledging our common subjectivity and taking full responsibility, yet having no name in which one can commit crimes?
- *How should we engage in battle with our enemies?* By trying to win at all costs? By using the same methods they use against us, "fighting fire with fire"? Or by affirming our values in the way we fight, and battling the forces that made us enemies in the first place?

If people are going to fight, it is better that they fight positively, repeatedly invite their opponents to join them in dialogue and collaboration, and fix the problems that generate the fighting. In the moment, they believe deeply in the issues over which they are fighting, but later discover they rarely get what they want by fighting, and only satisfy their interests through dialogue, problem solving, negotiation, and conflict resolution. Sometimes people fight and lose, yet what they fought for takes place despite their defeat. Sometimes they win, yet it turns out not to be what they meant, and they end up fighting for it under a different name.

Having said this, it is important to acknowledge that everything essential in society has been fought for, often by people who were willing to sacrifice their lives in the process. Political democracy, free public education, social security, elimination of child labor, emancipation from slavery, women's suffrage, just cause for termination, racial desegregation, and gender equality all have improved through countless battles, sparked and organized by people who believed in change and participated in organizations that promoted it, even when it became destructive. Yet these battles often sparked a backlash that reduced their gains, and might have been moderated by improvements in the way they fought, and the use of public dialogue to negotiate rules of engagement.

While there are clear limits on the use of dialogue and interest-based conflict resolution, and while it is possible to misuse either, a positive attitude toward process and disagreement can turn conflict into a driver of change and a source of broader unity, within families, societies, and organizations as a whole. The danger for mediators increases, however, and the fighting often turns negative when a conflict or proposed change reaches into or is generated at the very heart of a system.

Chapter Seventeen

Transforming the System

*The people you have to lie to own you. The things
you have to lie about own you. When your children see you
owned, then they are not your children anymore, they are
the children of what owns you. If money owns you, they
are the children of money. If your need for pretense and
illusion owns you, they are the children of pretense
and illusion. If your fear of loneliness owns you, they are
the children of loneliness. If your fear of the truth owns
you, they are the children of the fear of truth.*
MICHAEL VENTURA

Many conflicts are systemic and impossible to resolve without first
breaking the system that generated them. Indeed, conflict can be
defined as "the sound made by the cracks in a system." If we follow
that sound, we will discover that each crack leads us to the heart of
the system that generated the dispute. Surrounding the heart are
a series of defenses, smokescreens, and obfuscating devices hiding
the levers, buttons, and switches that control and maintain it. Anxiety and fear increase exponentially as the possibility emerges that
the entire system might change, and not just some small, insignifi-
cant piece of it. This makes mediating systemic disputes dangerous.

Personal vs. Political Conflicts

Most conflicts in families, neighborhoods, organizations, and
communities appear purely personal in nature. They seem to
stem from people's words, behaviors, and personalities, from

miscommunications, misunderstandings, misperceptions, unsatis-fied interests, differing personal and cultural values, and false expectations. Yet what feels so unique and personal is so common, widespread, and ubiquitous that it can more accurately be described as the byproduct of a larger social, cultural, economic, political, or organizational system.

When we search beneath the surface, we discover that many seemingly individual conflicts have actually been generated or intensified as a result of a systemic dysfunction that is hidden from view. This gives parties the impression that their issues are personal, solitary, and unique, even when they affect vast numbers of people in similar ways, each of whom is unaware of the existence of any others.

For example, in divorce it is common for spouses to complain about each other. If we took all their allegations literally, we would be forced to conclude that the nation is filled with despicable human beings. Worse, we would miss the essential point: that complaining is simply a way of grieving the break-up of a marital system. Once we recognize the systemic origins of their conflict, we can help them lament the loss of whatever the system gave them, and support their search for a new system to take its place.

Another example is downsizing at work. These decisions are nearly always seen by affected employees as personal and directed at them, even though thousands of other employees may have lost their jobs and hundreds of thousands may have been affected worldwide. Not only does this impression result in severely damaged self-esteem, it makes employees feel powerless and unable to affect the larger organizational system that made the decision to relocate the plant overseas, the political system that supported it, and the economic system that made it profitable.

In these examples, the system that generated the conflict is invisible, or present only as backdrop, without apparent relevance to the resolution process. Many personal conflicts are actively created by policies or structures based on ancient systemic assumptions or by unequal distributions of power that are nonetheless *felt* individually.

Many family conflicts can be traced to a lack of employment opportunities or equal pay for women, yet appear as disputes between men who traditionally work for money and women who have been left at home to spend it. Many community disputes stem from racially discriminatory practices that originated in slavery and segregation. Many interpersonal disputes are triggered by organizational hierarchies, unequal distribution of resources, autocratic decision making, and corrupt political processes.

There is a natural, automatic, systemic response to the experience of inequality, which is to push for greater equality. There is also an automatic, systemic counterresponse, which is to resist and attempt to maintain the status quo. These produce conflict, which can either be aimed at individuals and taken personally, or directed at a system and taken politically. Systemic thinking in mediation means transforming systems, be they familial, social, cultural, organizational, governmental, economic, or educational.

Anthropologist Ruth Benedict observed in *Patterns of Culture* that social systems in which people are rewarded for acts that benefit others or the community as a whole experience less hostility, violence, cruelty, crime, and war than social systems that reward people for competitiveness and individual gain. Simply put, whatever systems reward has an impact on what people do. Aggressive, acquisitive, individualistic systems generate conflicts that collaborative, generous, community-oriented systems do not, and vice versa.

Indeed, it is possible to understand conflict as largely a byproduct of aggressive, self-centered systems. It is important to go further, however, and define conflict itself as a system. This does not mean that conflict is not also intensely personal, but that, as mediators, we need to develop the analysis, skills, and capacity for *dangerous* interventions, not only in response to internal and interpersonal conflicts, but external and systemic ones as well.

When we adopt a systems approach to conflict, it immediately becomes clear why it is dangerous to move from settlement to resolution. Settlement and incremental change do not touch the heart of a system, whereas resolution and transformation fundamentally alter it. Personalization of systemic conflicts, or focusing exclusively on the psychodynamics of conflict, can be ways of avoiding its systemic implications. Those who seek resolution and transformation therefore need to understand how systems operate, and why it is dangerous to mediate toward the heart of a system.

The Systemic Context of Mediation

To interpret any conflict, it is necessary to look beyond the words used to the context in which they are communicated. To suppress conflict, all that is needed is to ignore the real context in which it occurred. Systemic conflicts are deeper and more dangerous to resolve—not only because the issues are more complex, but because the context becomes an issue and cannot change without creating far-reaching consequences.

The context of any dispute includes the processes, relationships, and systems that operate in the space *between* the parties, the experiences they have had, and the ground on which they stand. This idea may have led poet Kenneth Patchen to write:

> The best hope
> is that one of these days
> the ground will get disgusted enough
> to just walk away,
> leaving people with nothing more to stand *on*
> than what they have so bloody well stood *for* up to now.

Conflicts are fought, settled, and resolved, forgiven and transcended, not in the abstract or in isolation, but in *specific* cultures, societies, and organizations, in contexts and systems that define the limits of what is possible and acceptable. These limits frame conflicts and encourage or discourage communication at varying levels of honesty and empathy. The context often reveals the hidden meaning of the conflict.

The extent to which conflicting parties are blind to the context of their disputes, or unconscious of their larger, systemic implications, is the degree to which they are trapped and unable to escape their centripetal pull. Yet the only way anyone becomes aware of a context is by stepping outside it. For parties in conflict, this means using outside mediators who are willing to risk revealing its context. These mediators walk a dangerous line between approaching the dispute from outside its systemic context and not stimulating resistance, or approaching it from the inside and not reinforcing the status quo. The outside approach allows for greater honesty, while the inside permits greater empathy.

Indeed, the very mediation processes that help parties feel safe enough to explore their problems can run aground in systemic conflicts. Every system attempts to protect itself, by resisting change and by preventing people from considering options the system perceives as dangerous. Because conflict systems are interdependent, even small changes in minor areas can trigger major shifts in the system as a whole. For this reason, systems generate cultures, rules, and expectations that protect them from change. Yet the context of resolution *is* change—change in personal lives, relationships, society, economics, and politics, in workplaces and organizations, and in how we live.

Conflict and Systemic Change

Mediating dangerously means approaching the heart of dysfunctional systems and facilitating conversations that allow people to change them. Instead of approaching conflicts as merely isolated, personal, and unique, mediators also need to invite parties to recognize the context of their conflicts and discover how to transform the systems that fuel their disputes.

How parties address the context of ceaseless change, for example, can directly influence the meaning and outcome of their conflicts. In mediation, they can see the other side as an enemy or an ally, often as a result of their attitude toward change. Systemic attitudes toward change delineate the line separating suppression from settlement, and these from resolution and transformation.

For example, many personal disputes between employees and managers occur because the larger organizational system in which they work does not encourage upward feedback. Most managers evaluate their subordinates, but are not evaluated in return. As a result, evaluations become humiliating, pointless, judgmental experiences. In addition to working with managers to communicate more carefully and employees to respond less defensively, mediators can encourage organizations to adopt a 360-degree peer-based evaluation system.

It is easy for mediators to lose balance and either ignore systemic influences that lock parties in place or let them off the hook by pointing to outside influences that are beyond their ability to impact. One of the roles of mediation, especially conflict resolution systems design, is not only to resolve individual conflicts, but to point at the systemic causes that will continue to generate new conflicts until they are resolved.

Every flawed or changing system generates a *stream* of conflict. By creating conflict, these systems are in fact trying to reform or repair themselves. Yet every system also erects lines of defense, counterbalance, and compensation to protect themselves against resolutions that might require fundamental change. As these defenses aggregate, they produce a growing sense of insecurity that the whole structure might collapse and a heightened resistance even to minor modifications that could trigger an avalanche. As the fear of systemic meltdown increases, even those who usually favor change may retreat and fight to preserve or roll back the status quo.

The Ecology of Systems

Any system can be understood as a set of interdependent, interacting, interrelated, or responsive parts. These can include ideas, emotions, roles, actions, conversations, and relationships. These systems create coherence in otherwise chaotic families, friendships, neighborhoods, organizations, societies, cultures, political institutions, and economic practices. The potential for conflict within these systems is reflected in subjects that are taboo; secrets that are gossiped about in private; unacknowledged, unfulfilled, false expectations; obvious silences; unclear and ambiguous roles and responsibilities; unrealistic expectations; and defensive maneuvers.

All social systems today are open rather than closed. Their boundaries are semipermeable and subject to outside influence and change. Every system operates in an environment that must simultaneously be adapted to, learned from, and defended against. A balanced ecological relationship between a system and its environment is essential for its survival, yet balance cannot last because systems, together with their environment, make up a larger system, and the whole is affected by changes that take place in any of its parts.

Even the smallest personal systems are deeply affected by dysfunctional changes in family systems, which are directly impacted by social and workplace systems, which are closely regulated by political systems, which depend on economic systems that are global in scope. Together, these create a world system that is dependent on planetary ecology, yet also is increasingly at odds with it.

Every system contains and harmonizes conflict. All systems encompass diverse, contradictory, and antagonistic elements, just as temperature systems contain hot and cold, or family systems contain people who are on time and those who are late. The presence of opposites in a single unifying system permits a magnification and accentuation of differences. Work systems allow one person to excel at one task by encouraging someone else to excel at another.

This unification of opposites encourages their expansion, since separating them into opposing aspects or functions allows their unity to become greater than the sum of their parts. Yet it also creates a constant tension between harmony and discord. Most conflicts in systems are therefore simply expressions of their natural, internal contradictions. In short, it is not differences that cause conflict, but how they are interpreted and handled.

The same is true of change. All systems simultaneously adapt to and resist change, as significant changes alter the internal balance of forces that hold their disparate parts together. Systems strive for homeostasis and balance, which makes it difficult for them to change. Systems that balance internal conflicts and resist or accommodate outside forces achieve dynamic equilibrium. From time to time, however, conflicts cannot be balanced, and the system slips into disequilibrium or chaos.

For this reason, systems require thermostats, or feedback loops, which help them sense the direction of change and adjust without upsetting their internal balance. As conflicts accumulate, these sensors detect a need for transformation. Yet a common response to conflict is to block feedback and resist change. Conflicts are periodic releases or efforts to reestablish equilibrium. Just as earthquakes release accumulated tension between butting plates of the earth's crust, conflicts expose the fault lines within systems. They indicate environmental instability, the need to change, and resistance to doing so. To survive, every system needs to learn to resolve conflicts.

Yet when a system is stable, it cannot be shaken. A balanced, homeostatic system will resist change, even when feedback identifies a problem that threatens survival, because the thermostat that creates the feedback loop is too primitive. The feedback mechanism in any system must possess at best the same complexity as the system it is monitoring. A simple thermostat becomes meaningless in a complex system, and the conflict thermostats used to regulate complex relational systems are hopelessly inadequate.

Responses to Conflicts in Systems

All human systems develop specialized languages and cultures, partly to reduce the possibility of disruptive miscommunications and conflicts. They create rules, prescriptions, secrets, rituals, histories, heroes, villains, myths, rewards, and punishments that differentiate them from other systems, and bind them together. They employ selective intimacy, distancing, command, threat, coercion, manipulation, avoidance, and conformity to reinforce dependency and reduce internal conflict.

Dysfunctional systems manufacture conflict stories that personalize systemic discord, as a way of disguising or repairing holes in the system that are exposed by the conflict. Judgments about the causes of conflict within a system can be used as a defense against insight and change, just as confrontation can be a defense against vulnerability, and rhetoric against the direct experience of reality.

These defensive responses reflect anxiety and an attitude about the system's relationship to change. Conflict encourages anxious insiders to focus on other people's behaviors and attitudes. They personalize, polarize, and create self-fulfilling prophecies that help preserve and protect the system and at the same time ensure its eventual demise. This dilemma makes systemic mediations dangerous.

Blaming as Self-Protection

If either party or the mediator is seen as the primary instigator of the change process or the sole supporter of a systemic analysis of the problem, some may decide to blame the messenger rather than solve the problem. Blaming the messenger simultaneously defends the system against change, instills fear of the consequences of systemic analysis, reflects an inner blaming by people who know they have not been honest, identifies precisely what needs to be changed, and reveals the ecological fragility of the system.

There are many ways of blaming or personalizing systemic conflicts, denying the larger implications and the context of disputes, and resisting the introduction of systemic change. Mostly, these forms of resistance operate by shifting attention from the source of the dispute to the person closest to the problem. Playwright Michael Frayn wrote eloquently of this widespread need for blaming:

> Our desire to blame and to be blamed is often an attempt to impose meaning upon events which offer none, or only an obscure and confusing one. For some impossibly complex conjunction of reasons, a lorry plunges into a crowd; an economic policy fails; a battle is lost. Our instinct is at once to find someone whose behavior can now be reinterpreted as negligent or criminal, so that the event can be read into the world's great underlying pattern of cause and effect.

Once an event is portrayed as having been caused by someone's personal negligence or criminality, the system is off the hook. Some of the more common forms of blaming include:

- Blaming human nature, by focusing on laziness, apathy, and cynicism.
- Blaming the rules, by citing legal and bureaucratic obfuscations.
- Blaming outsiders, by attacking those who appear different or powerless.
- Blaming insiders, by attacking corruption, bribery, or secret conspiracies.
- Blaming victims, by encouraging self-doubt, inferiority, and the idea of personal failure.
- Blaming the structure, by asserting that nothing can be done or that there is no alternative.
- Blaming critics, by attacking troublemakers, radicals, and naysayers.

- Blaming resisters, by punishing those who advocate change.
- Blaming leaders, by finding them incompetent or inadequate.
- Blaming everyone, by indicating we are all at fault, dissolving responsibility through generalization or by forgiving and forgetting.
- Blaming no one, by ignoring, denying, and avoiding issues or escaping through the distraction of "bread and circuses."

Each of these forms of blame diverts attention from the systemic sources of the conflict. In family systems, as in economic and political organizations, blaming diverts attention from underlying truths that many people want to avoid or deny. Each form of blaming also creates conflicts, which often seem to the parties to have nothing to do with systemic issues.

Hierarchy and Autocracy vs. Heterarchy and Democracy

The illusions of authority, safety, and immortality that are ascribed to systems inspire loyalty and a vigilant defense, based on a paternalistic fantasy that the individual will be taken care of by the system. This dynamic impacts marriages as deeply as corporations. There is an implicit bargain in which individuals surrender liberty and become obedient in exchange for sharing the system's power, avoiding the risks that accompany liberty, and basking in its seemingly immortal glow.

This bargain motivates those loyal to the system to deny facts that challenge its organizing principles, justify or rationalize its inconsistencies, attack deviations and perceived disloyalties, and assert proofs of its superiority over competing systems. Failures are viewed as individual, personal, and having nothing to do with the system. Blame for unfairness or inequity is attributed to misguided leaders rather than to the system, which is perceived as paternal and benevolent. In this way, individuals displace their independence and responsibility onto the system, which displaces its failures and conflicts onto the individuals who comprise it. Individual boundaries grow weaker as one approaches the heart of the system. "I" is transformed into "we," "they" defines rival systems, and "you" defines the problem.

Systems encourage individuals to resolve conflicts through avoidance and accommodation. If these methods are unsuccessful, internal cliques or subsystems may be formed that threaten the larger system. In response, a common enemy or purpose can be recalled, mutual compromise can be encouraged, third parties can be brought in to represent the interests of the system in reuniting, or someone can be expelled from the system. Each of these methods heals the system, or preserves it from unnecessary disruption, for which those within may pay a hefty price.

Two entirely different structures and processes have been used by systems to maintain harmony, integrate conflicting individuals, and resolve disputes. These are: authoritarian, hierarchical, power- or rights-based commands; and democratic, egalitarian, interest-based consensus. Any system that seeks to combine fundamentally opposing ideas, functions, tendencies, needs, and personalities faces two fundamental choices. It must either assume an authoritarian structure based on control and coercion, exercised through an accumulation and concentration of hierarchical power or rights; or it must assume a democratic structure based on consensus and choice, exercised through decentralization and collaboration between diverse interests; or some combination.

Systems acquire power because individuals surrender it. Hierarchical power is accumulated and concentrated by authoritarian leaders who extract or coerce it from their ranks, often by selectively allocating scarce resources to supporters and by punishing detractors. This makes hierarchical systems appear more powerful than the individuals who comprise them, leading to further loss of individuation and internal conflicts, which in turn encourage obedience to hierarchical power.

The focal point of power in coercive, authoritarian, or hierarchical systems is at the "top," while its absence is reflected at the "bottom." Dividing top from bottom disrupts collaborative systems in which power is shared and self-regulation is a task of the whole, operating by consensus. In "heterarchical," democratic, consensus-based systems, while the interest of the collective is emphasized, the role of individuals is paradoxically stronger, making the surrender of power to the system more conditional.

Every system resolves internal conflicts in ways that either support coercion, hierarchy, power, and stasis; or collaboration, heterarchy, interests, and change. Voluntary, democratic, consensus-based systems are ultimately more creative, easier to change, and less deeply conflicted than those that rely on coercion, autocracy, and hierarchy. Voluntary systems *require* individuation, honest feedback, and interest-based techniques for resolving conflict. Because they are based on consensus, they encourage power sharing, self-management, teamwork, collaborative forms of negotiation, consensus decision making, democratic procedures, information sharing, dialogue, and an equitable distribution of resources.

Mediating into the Heart of a System

Mediating dangerously, in this context, means making every part of the resolution process collaborative and democratic, including power balancing, empathy building, surfacing interests, building consensus, and reaching closure. More deeply, it means being willing to listen to the sounds made by the cracks in a system. It means revealing the system's heart and soul. And it means revealing and possibly resolving the systemic problems that caused the dispute.

Mediating dangerously means searching for the center and heart of the system that created the conflict. That is where the leverage can be found, not only to end the conflict, but to transform the larger context that triggered, aggravated, and sustained it. Divorce means severing the emotional system that sustained the marriage. Organizational change means altering the operational system that sustained the status quo. Whatever the system, if we want to stop conflict at its source, we need to locate its hidden heart.

By heart, I do not mean a physical location or fixed point in time or space. Rather, I mean the core values, modes of operation, attitudes toward the past, unspoken agreements, hidden expectations, secret rules, and boundaries that influence how people act within it; the circle, center, or hub around which everything important revolves; the energy that is simultaneously everywhere and nowhere. How, then, does mediation reach the heart of a system? Here are some examples:

• The heart of a family system is shattered in divorce when one spouse refuses to play a role that has been important in making the relationship work. It is difficult to know in advance what, when, or how it will be broken. It can be a refusal to accept blame or a willingness to accept it. It can be talking back or remaining silent. It can be deciding to take responsibility for doing something the other person always did or repairing a deficiency in oneself for which the other person always compensated. It can be a yes or a no.

• The heart of an organizational system is revealed in attitudes toward authority, decision making, hierarchy, participation, power, responsibility, freedom, insecurity, self-esteem, and a thousand other issues. Mediating at the heart of an organizational system means examining who participates in decision making, why, for whom, over what, and how. It means uncovering the sources of resistance and working carefully yet inexorably through them.

• The heart of an educational system lies in its assumptions about the nature of teaching and learning. Do schools support the learning of all students, or are they places where adults talk and students listen? What is important for students to learn, and how do they do so? Do the communication systems in schools, from taking roll at the beginning of class to bells that cut off discussion at the end, obstruct or promote learning?

Mediating at the heart of a system requires the development of dangerous strategies. It means peeling away the layers systems erect to protect themselves. These include denial, avoidance, politeness, hierarchy, fixed responsibilities, defensiveness, accommodation, compromise, and counterattack, all waged by people who are frightened of change or are stalwarts of the system.

I recently mediated a conflict between faculty and a principal at an elementary school in a low-income, inner-city school district. The conflict was triggered by the faculty's refusal to select a method of school reform from a predetermined list of choices, and by pressure placed on the principal by the district to encourage the faculty to make a selection. The teachers felt manipulated, disrespected, and disempowered by the principal, who was trying to force the system he wanted on reluctant staff in order to satisfy his superiors.

At the heart of the conflict lay a self-reinforcing system that included teachers' perceptions that the principal was manipulative and untrustworthy; teachers' reluctance to take responsibility for reforming or improving their own school; the principal's need to control faculty decisions out of fear for his job; his inability to trust them with responsibility for decisions regarding education; the district's top-down approach to decision making regarding reform; the superintendent's mandate for reform without support or training in how to resolve conflicts or reach consensus; a hierarchical management structure that motivated people through fear; and teachers so infantalized they had lost the willingness to take risks.

My comediator and I surfaced these issues and encouraged both sides to discuss them. We publicly asked the principal if he thought he could force teachers to accept responsibility for reform, and teachers if they cared enough about their students to accept responsibility for improving education. We asked the principal to send a signal to teachers that he valued their input and would respect their recommendations, and asked both sides to jointly let the district know they did not want to be pressured into making the wrong decision. We asked teachers in small groups to brainstorm what stood in the way of participating in school reform. We asked the principal to say publicly whether he would accept their input and change his controlling behavior. We met with the district administrator to support the reform effort, and the faculty and principal finally reached agreement on a plan for school reform.

It is dangerous to pursue conflict into the heart of the system that created it. Yet we will not achieve lasting results in mediation if we cannot expose the secret places where conflict lies hidden. One of these places is politics.

Chapter Eighteen

The Politics of Conflict

Politics, n. *A strife of interests masquerading as a contest of principles.*
AMBROSE BIERCE

The shift from power to rights to interests is not without political consequence. Indeed, each approach to conflict can be seen as giving rise to a set of organizing principles on which political systems are based. Power results in autocracy, while rights produce electoral democracy. Indeed, it can be argued that the tension between autocracy and electoral democracy is at the heart of most of the political, social, and economic changes that have taken place over the last several centuries. What, then, are the political consequences of an interest-based approach?

It is impossible to litigate the hidden issues at the heart of an authoritarian system without at the same time revealing its core organizational principles, thereby transforming it into a rights-based institution. This is precisely what the Magna Carta and similar rights-based documents did. Rights-based processes such as the law are inherently antiauthoritarian because they are organized to limit the exercise of arbitrary power. In a similar way, interest-based processes are inherently opposed to rights, because they operate through individuating, collaborative, egalitarian, consensus-based processes.

For example, any mediation in a rigidly hierarchical corporation between a high-powered CEO and a cleaning lady has to be conducted, both in style and substance, *only* between people using first names such as Ralph and Sally, with each having an equal voice and an equal right to agree or disagree on proposed solutions. The creation of a joint problem-solving dialogue between them fundamentally shifts their relationship and can thereby impact the entire hierarchical system. It is easy to understand how such mediations become dangerous, because they result in the creation of a collaborative, consensus-driven, positive form of political community that challenges hierarchy and tyranny.

Mediating Electoral Conflicts

Each election year we witness the spectacle of candidates and parties engaged in character assassination, meaningless polarization, trivialization of real issues, false and slanderous advertising, and corruption of the political process through a modern form of bribery called campaign financing. Each of these contribute to a culture of conflict that deemphasizes interest-based options. Gandhi believed the most destructive forces in the world were wealth without work, pleasure without conscience, knowledge without character, commerce without morality, science without humanity, religion without sacrifice, and politics without principle. Yet the political systems we have created undermine and discourage principled political action and nourish unnecessary conflict.

By its nature, politics means conflict. It may therefore seem futile or vain to suggest that mediation might be used to improve the process. Indeed, mediation, interests, and consensus seem the antithesis of politics, and were it not for the divisions between sections or parts of society and the need to overcome them, politics as we know it would not exist. In the centuries-old conflict between haves and have-nots, or between competing controllers of scarce natural resources, politics has always included an element of mediation, a respite from war, and an effort to compromise in order to achieve higher economic or social goals.

Yet political mediation has always been conducted on the basis of an enforced consensus regarding the prevailing system of power and an acceptance of rules regarding the use of force. As I write in election year 2000, it is apparent that the electoral process itself requires dramatic change. In considering how it might be transformed and into what, here are ten mediator's ideas for transforming elections based on interests:

1. Approach elections as consensus-building efforts regarding issues of public policy, using dialogue as a way of exploring disagreements over direction, and uniting around common strategies for addressing them.
2. Restructure and democratize the electoral system to encourage greater diversity and a broader representation of interests. Include easy access to the ballot for independent candidates and "fringe" political parties and universal voter registration.
3. Require candidates to publicly mediate ground rules for their campaigns in advance.
4. Censure, fine, and disqualify candidates who violate ground rules regarding dishonesty and negativity.
5. Remove soft money bribery from politics and reduce incentives for graft, corruption, and politically-motivated appointments; equalize access to media advertising, prohibiting campaign contributions and expenditures in excess of agreed-upon amounts; and disqualify candidates, contributors, and lobbyists who violate the rules.
6. Formulate political platforms as vision statements drafted by facilitated citizen assemblies, and encourage people to support them regardless of who wins. Focus on platforms rather than personalities, on sustained, meaningful, long-term debates regarding social, political, and economic issues, and on instant runoff voting to reduce "lesser of two evils" choices.
7. Openly discuss issues in mediated public policy debates and facilitated, televised town hall meetings, not directed by media reporters, campaign staff, or professional commentators.
8. Decentralize campaigning and allow candidates to be picked electronically by elections at homes and workplaces, reducing the clout of party elites and the Electoral College.
9. Establish a single day for state primaries to reduce costs, hype, hypocrisy, and appeals to narrow sectional interests.
10. Publicly evaluate the process afterwards, and agree on an improved set of ground rules for the next campaign.

In this way, the principal goal of running for office might shift from winning office to improving political relationships and public discourse, which makes a higher form of winning possible. The notion of "winning" in politics clearly implies losing, yet losers include not only candidates, but everyone who voted for them. The losers include those who did not register to vote, those excluded from voting, including felons and "greencard" holders, those who failed to vote, and those whose candidates lost. This amounts to the disenfranchisement of a majority of the population, exclusion from effective citizenship, and encouragement to engage in adversarial conflict-promoting behaviors. Mediation would encourage proportional representation with win/win outcomes in which all significant "stakeholder" interests were automatically represented, as in the European system.

The purpose of election to office might be reframed or shifted from personal ambition and partisan power *over* others to collaborative problem solving and strategic engagement *with* others for the benefit of society as a whole. Jealousy and egotism, pandering to narrow self-interests, obligation to powerful interest groups, personal ambitions, and character assassinations—all are inadequate as methods of selection for high public office.

To identify alternatives to the current electoral process and fully resolve the ecological, economic, social, and political conflicts that make it necessary will require enormous energy, thought, and wisdom. This effort can be aided by ideas drawn from dangerous mediation in confronting power and resolving issues that require systemic change.

Contests for Power

When we mediate contests for power between rival groups, and each side is committed to using coercion or violence to achieve or retain advantage over others, we enter dangerous territory. Power, by its nature, is competitive and a "zero sum game," so that victory for one automatically spells defeat for the other, making it strongly attractive, even addictive. Power is rarely surrendered voluntarily. More often, it is forcibly wrested from its entrenched defenders in ways that encourage abuse and continued conflict.

Power stimulates a strong set of emotions and actions on both sides, particularly when it takes the form of power over others, rather than power over ourselves. For those who possess it, there is arrogance, abusiveness, corruption, fear, and guilt. Those who seek to wrest it from others experience an equally powerful set of effects, including jealousy, impotence, rage, ambition, fear, amorality, greed, internal splits, blaming, brutalization, demonization, and revenge. Power is easier by far to condemn than to exercise fairly, causing many to prefer the safety of cynicism and making it dangerous to translate criticism of what is wrong into concrete proposals for systemic change.

Forms of Power

Mediating power contests requires consideration of the varieties and forms of power that exist not only in government, but in organizations, social relationships, and families. There are countless varieties of power, each of which can be expressed through action or inaction. These include:

- *Physical Power:* The power of physical force and the power to refrain from using it, including nonviolence.
- *Coercive Power:* The power to scare, threaten, or punish and the power that comes from feeling scared, threatened, or punished.
- *Legal Power:* The power to create enforceable rights and prohibitions and the power to break them.
- *Financial Power:* The power to spend and the power to withhold money.
- *Emotional Power:* The power of feelings, including love or hate, and the power of withholding them.
- *Spiritual Power:* The power of consciously directing one's spirit, energy, or life force and the power of withdrawing it.
- *Information Power:* The power to pass information on and the power to withhold it.
- *Collective Power:* The power of organization and the power of individual action.
- *Social Power:* The power of acceptance and the power of ostracism.
- *Empathetic Power:* The power of empathy and the power of insensitivity.
- *Truth-Telling Power:* The power of honesty and the power of lies.

Each variety of power operates in two directions: power for and power against; power of doing and power of not doing; power for growth and power for stagnation. Every day, we face numerous opportunities to use small forms of power to improve our lives and the lives of others, or to ruin them.

Mediating Power Contests

In most power contests there is no clear way of deciding who should win, no escape from the inevitable identification of a loser, no way of avoiding the abuses that flow from one-sided satisfaction of self-interests. Short of abandoning the power game altogether and surrendering to the other side, there are times when mediative approaches seem impossible.

For example, consider the American Revolution, in which the central issue was independence. While mediation might have reduced bloodshed, it could not have, in the absence of a contest for power, successfully convinced either side to compromise over fundamental principles. The only times mediation might have worked were in limiting the fighting or resolving the details of a transfer of power from England to the colonies.

In other words, if we accept that the division of wealth and power between the colonies and England was *intentionally* unfair, and that it was the express purpose of the British government to keep it that way, by force or violence if necessary, what could conflict resolution have achieved, short of either side's surrender? Over time, the only option remaining, short of surrender, was a declaration of independence and revolutionary war. In power contests, compromise acceptable to one side usually means surrender by the other.

But where does this difficulty end? Certainly, between factions in the colonial camp, conflict resolution was essential if a single nation was to emerge from the diverse forces that made up the anti-British coalition. While some sectional self-interests were in conflict with each other, many were shared and held in common, and resolved in ways that increased their unity and chances for victory.

At some point, the British were compelled to recognize, as a result of military battles, international pressure, economic losses, intense colonial resistance, and internal divisions at home, that their bargaining position had eroded. Compromise then became possible as an alternative to complete defeat. This result might have been supported by mediation. But by that time, the balance of political power had shifted. The American revolutionists had increasingly come to speak for the nation as a whole, and to jointly address their common problems without English domination.

Had mediation been used at the beginning, its result would *necessarily* have been either to prevent or authorize a revolution. If the colonists had possessed a vote or veto power, the Stamp Tax would have failed, and the only option left to the British would have been how to respond. Thus, it can be seen that the very act of mediation, by bringing colonizers and colonized together to negotiate their relationship on the basis of equality, independence, and consensus, implies that the revolution has already been won and power has been divided.

Disputes over issues of common concern, such as improved colonial administration or better roads, are examples of conflicts that could have been successfully mediated without addressing the fundamental issue of power. It was disputes over the distribution of political power, economic independence, and the right to tax colonial manufactures, that made each side a threat to the other's self-interests. Still, it was not the contradiction of self-interests between colonizers and colonized, but a historic disequilibrium in the balance of power that prevented these conflicts from being successfully mediated. Disputes over allocation of power can be mediated where issues of inclusion, equality, and fairness have been resolved. In most cases, however, these are precisely the issues that generate power-based conflicts.

Another factor that limited the use of mediation was the perceived trajectory, momentum, and direction of events. Mediation during the War of Independence would have become increasingly possible as forces favoring independence waxed and those of the loyalists waned. A clear direction in power contests suggests compromise to the losing side, while unclear direction stimulates entrenchment. Direction has an objective as well as a subjective aspect, which varies over time. For this reason, mediation is usually proposed too late.

The same factors influence the resolution of personal power contests. Recognition by a neighbor that others are willing to ostracize him for aggressive behavior; acknowledgment by a divorcing spouse that a court will not approve an unequal division of community property; or admission by a company that its expansion will cause ecological damage can significantly impact the resolution process. Clear, objective limits on mediating power contests can result from calculating the likelihood of gain or loss. Mediators can use this information to encourage parties to keep potential losses in sight, and not overestimate imaginable gains.

Nonetheless, peace is temporary where underlying power imbalances are left unresolved. This is why mediators, whether in family, neighborhood, organizational, or political disputes, must act to equalize the distribution of power and its conscious use against others in process, communication, empowerment, negotiation, outcomes, and control over relationships. We do so by sharing power and by building mutual commitment to satisfy the underlying interests it is supposed to serve. In the process, we replace the self-defeating arrogance of power with empowerment, isolation with community, prejudice with diversity, and competition with collaboration, for which power is, and always will be, a poor substitute.

Mediation and Organizations Involved in Change

Organizations that seek to bring about social change, like the Committees of Correspondence created during the American Revolution, are both products and producers of conflict. By joining together to bring about change, they implicitly affirm the positive, creative role conflict plays in calling attention to injustices, pressuring for necessary changes, reinforcing value-based behaviors, encouraging public dialogue, and halting retaliation for criticism. For this reason, they should always be encouraged.

Yet efforts to bring about fundamental change, whether in families, organizations, societies, or governments, are always resisted. The deeper the necessary change, the greater the resistance. Indeed, it is not easy to face the organized opposition of entrenched power, which may include one's spouse, parents, employer, police, courts, media, and everyone who accepts the status quo. Those who oppose change try to divide and conquer, frighten off, and punish those unwilling to accept the status quo. As poet Bertolt Brecht noted:

> Those who take the meat from the table teach contentment.
> Those for whom taxes are destined demand sacrifice.
> Those who eat their fill speak to the hungry of wonderful times to come.
> Those who lead the country into the abyss call ruling too difficult for ordinary men.

The systemic pressures directed against change are matched by internal divisions that, when handled negatively, reduce effectiveness and contradict the very reasons that sparked the desire for change. These conflicts often revolve around goals versus process, or ends versus means. All change efforts are oriented to achieving future goals and simultaneously searching for ways of achieving them in the present with methods that do not duplicate the worst of what needs to be changed. Social change organizations need to adopt procedures for resolving conflicts that do not recreate the negative adversarial relationships that gave rise to them in the first place, but make content and process congruent.

Means Create Ends, Process Shapes Content

Advocates of change often dismiss concerns with process as unnecessary, time consuming, a diversion from substance, or "touchy-feely." Yet to characterize process as unimportant is to ignore its extraordinary capacity to influence content. Indeed, process *encodes* and recreates content. Bowing and saluting have a specific social content, which is to establish relationships of deference through process.

When people stand in line, sit in rows before a speaker, hold hands in a circle, or dance on tabletops, their sense of self and other, their relationships and experiences, their minds, emotions, and spirits are transfigured by form. The content of their communications are affected by form. When the same idea is expressed through geometric proof, footnoted analysis, fiction, rap lyric, and rhymed couplet, different contents are conveyed.

In politics, it makes a significant difference whether we act in obedience to the will of a supreme leader by majority vote or by consensus. It matters whether we resolve organizational conflicts by expulsion, internal power struggles, litigation, or principled debate. It is transformational when conflicting parties clearly articulate fundamental disagreements, clarify issues, and resolve disagreements calmly and openly through dialogue. Agreements become possible when disagreements are acknowledged as legitimate. Problem solving processes then permit solutions based on a mutual recognition of interests.

Change organizations are living organisms that cannot exempt themselves from the cumulative effects of their decisions regarding form and process, or their disregard of dysfunctional relationships. Sooner or later these begin to show, in burnout, fatigue, splitting, cynicism, apathy, destructive relationships, and loss of effectiveness and organizational unity. Valuable contributions in time and effort decline, money dries up, and a cycle of blame and recrimination begins, ending in a hardened outlook among those who remain, and bitterness among those who leave.

Much of this is avoidable. Through internal dialogue, negotiation, and mediation, organizational conflicts can be surfaced, discussed, and acknowledged. In most cases, they can be negotiated or resolved. Communications can be improved and working relationships strengthened, preferably *before* they become dysfunctional. Change organizations can model a collaborative method for resolving conflicts and an acceptance of differing perspectives that represents a significant part of their reason for existence. Cooperative, peaceful, respectful, egalitarian, democratic, honest, and empathic problem solving express the values many change organizations were created to affirm.

In all organizations, unity is paramount. Without unity nothing is achievable, while with unity everything becomes possible. There are several classes of unity. One comes from having a common enemy, which is *unity of opposition*. A second results from ritual and process, which is *unity of form or process*. A third derives from having a common purpose, shared goal, or source of inspirational energy, which is *unity of direction*. A fourth occurs when people interact with each other, through joint efforts, friendship, and empathy, which is *unity of relationship*.

In any organization concerned with the development of internal unity and collective action, it is important to move, wherever possible, from the first to the second, third, and fourth. In goal-oriented organizations, it is especially important to rescue principles of relationship and process from the demands of opposition, expediency, and content.

Building Mediative Systems into Organizations

Whenever we mediate power contests or conflicts that touch the heart of a system, transformation becomes possible simply by pursuing the resolution process. This makes mediation appear dangerous to anyone who sees their livelihood or success as linked to continued dysfunction. This, in turn, encourages denial, trivialization, avoidance, defensiveness, enabling behaviors, aggression, and continued dysfunction as strategies for distracting, frightening, or punishing those who might otherwise critically examine, alter, or exit the system that locks them in destructive relationships.

These behaviors allow flawed systems to continue by making them appear less dysfunctional than they actually are, compensating for the damage they do, and cleaning up after them. Suppressing or settling disputes inside such systems excuses their inadequacies and perpetuates the suffering that flows from their continued existence. Only dangerous mediation and a search for complete resolution can prevent future conflicts by revealing the behaviors that permit the system to work.

Mediators can contribute to transforming systems, for example, by helping parties negotiate expectations, roles, and responsibilities, and give each other frequent, open, honest, empathetic, 360-degree feedback. By normalizing honest communication, collaborative negotiation, and informal problem solving, mediative roles are created that bridge the gaps between diverse goals and constituencies, bringing warring factions together to resolve disputes and implement solutions. Every relationship and organization can expand its mission to include not merely mediating, but *mediative* functions, which integrate conflict resolution principles into ordinary processes, systems, and structures, thereby institutionalizing a dangerous process of learning from conflict, and being transformed by what was learned.

Mediative Values

A strong sense of values lies at the heart of mediative relationships. In an earlier book I coauthored with Joan Goldsmith, *Thank God It's Monday: 14 Values We Need to Humanize the Way We Work*, we identified the core values of mediative, humanized organizations as: inclusion, collaboration, teams and networks, vision, celebration of diversity, process awareness, open and honest communication, risk taking, individual and team ownership of results, paradoxical problem solving, viewing everyone as a leader, personal growth and satisfaction, seeing conflict as an opportunity, and embracing change.

These values can also be used to create systems that actually prevent conflict, promote resolution, institutionalize feedback, and unconditionally encourage collaboration and participation, which allow these systems to renew and transform on an ongoing basis. The emerging field of conflict resolution systems design provides a methodology and approach to building mediative processes into the hearts of systems, including important conflict resolution organizations such as the United Nations.

Chapter Nineteen

Conflict Resolution Systems Design and the United Nations

> *Our systems, perhaps, are nothing more than an unconscious apology for our faults—a gigantic scaffolding whose object is to hide from us our favorite sin.*
> HENRI FREDERIC AMIEL

Mediation is increasingly being used internationally. In countries and cultures as diverse as China, Ireland, Poland, Lebanon, Uganda, Armenia, and Cuba, mediation is bringing parties together, ending bloodshed, and building community. Conflict resolution systems design principles and dangerous mediation techniques promise even greater changes. As problems become more global in scope and solutions become less capable of national resolution, the task of coordinating and harmonizing discordant national and transnational efforts grows rapidly in importance and difficulty.

The end of the cold war marked the beginning of the possibility of transnational consensus. The United Nations (UN) is now the principal organization capable of understanding and coordinating efforts to settle and resolve international conflicts. While there are many international organizations working on individual problems, only the UN is capable of creating solutions that stimulate the full cooperation of the entire world community of nation-states.

The greatest threat to solving world problems, ranging from boundary disputes to hunger, AIDS, the price of oil, human rights, north/south relations, ecological devastation, debt, and global warming, comes from unresolved international conflicts. Conflict has been chronic for centuries between nations, cultures, races, classes, tribes, and trading partners. These conflicts disrupt cooperation, distort negotiation, block communication, and waste precious resources, including human lives. Some hope for resolving conflict can be found by applying the emerging theory of conflict resolution systems design and by considering the lessons learned in mediating crosscultural conflicts.

Conflict Resolution Systems Design

To begin, we need to understand the basic principles of conflict resolution systems design. We start by recognizing that conflicts are not isolated events, but streams within systems that reinforce and continuously generate disputes. While this accurately describes conflict within a system, it is necessary to bolster the resolution process in ways that make it equally systematic. The reasons for this are:

- Once a conflict is seen as a system it can be addressed in multiple ways.
- The emphasis in individual disputes is on discrete resolution procedures, rather than integrated systems design.
- Organizations will respond differently to single disputes than to streams of disputes.
- Some procedures naturally work better in certain kinds of disputes than others.
- Systems are needed to encourage negotiation and deescalation procedures throughout the life-cycle of a conflict.
- A variety of professionals can work successfully on the same problem from different perspectives.
- A systems approach stimulates synergy and improved ideas.

William Ury, Stephen Goldberg, and Jeanne Brett suggest in their seminal work, *Getting Disputes Resolved,* that these systems design principles allow mediators to isolate, identify, research, analyze, categorize, prioritize, and understand how conflict is reinforced and reproduced in relation to the system as a whole. It is then possible to identify predictors of conflict, preventive measures, safety nets, outlets for constructive expression of differences, procedures for resolution, and methods for making them effective. This allows organizations to systematically reduce the risks and costs of conflict, encourage settlement before legal costs and attorneys' fees accumulate, provide a just forum for resolution outside the courts, and learn from internal conflicts.

The goals for any conflict resolution system design process include: promoting expression of differences through constructive dialogue; collaborative analysis of the sources of conflict; reduction of escalation; increasing peer skills and capacities; locating outside resources for resolving disputes; expanding existing options for resolution; examining communication systems for effectiveness; and increasing organizational synergy, teamwork, and partnership.

Applying systems design principles to international conflict resolution means creating innovative approaches that coordinate and harmonize efforts to move disputants from power- to rights- to interest-based solutions. While it may be impossible to completely eliminate use of rights- or power-based options, it is not difficult to rank these from low- to high-cost and offer a broad menu of choices. The methodology of systems design, as developed by Ury, Goldberg, and Brett, includes:

- Placing the focus on interests, rather than on rights- or power-based solutions.
- Building in "loopbacks" to negotiation.
- Providing low-cost rights and power backings.
- Building in consultation before and feedback after intervention.
- Arranging procedures in a low- to high-cost sequence.
- Providing the necessary motivation, skills, and resources to make it work.

In addition to these, others can be added that extend the process in both directions, including:

- Creating a "conflict audit" to assess chronic sources of conflict.
- Analyzing systemic causes and connections to structure, communication, culture, organizational design, values, morale, and staffing.

- Eliciting from within the culture of the organization the metaphors for conflict and mechanisms already in place for resolving it.
- Expanding internally the number and kind of resolution options available.
- Shifting paradigmatic thinking patterns that block the use of new procedures.
- Using collaborative action research before, facilitation during, and evaluation after implementing changes.
- Articulating an expanded set of systems design principles capable of wider application.
- Developing an improved understanding of how these principles fail and why.

The Conflict Audit

The mechanism of a conflict audit allows mediators to ask a number of questions that assess how conflict impacts people, programs, and profits within an organization. Here are fifty questions I use:

1. What are the main types, varieties, and kinds of conflicts?
2. What is causing these disputes?
3. Who are the disputants?
4. How frequently do conflicts occur?
5. What do people do if they have a complaint or conflict?
6. How often do people avoid conflict? How often do they accommodate? Compromise? Become aggressive? Collaborate?
7. Which disputes are resolved by negotiation?
8. When and how often do negotiations break down?
9. What happens when they do?
10. When and how often do power contests erupt?
11. What kinds of power behaviors are used in conflict?
12. What outcomes typically result?
13. Why do people resort to rights and power contests instead of negotiating?
14. When and how often do people turn to lawyers or union officials for help?
15. How much of your time would you estimate you spend each week trying to prevent, manage, or resolve conflicts?

16. What are the primary messages your organizational culture sends about conflict?
17. How does upper management respond to conflict? How might they respond better?
18. What is the cost of stress-related illness and conflict-related turnover?
19. Where might the organization be now if it had not experienced these conflicts?
20. How has conflict impacted clients? Contracts? Funding? Reputation?
21. Which conflicts are constructive and which are destructive?
22. How could the quality or frequency of communication be improved?
23. What is being done to help people build better relationships?
24. What is being done to encourage conflict?
25. Who in the organization is being quiet about conflict? Why?
26. What are some typical responses of people in the organization to conflict?
27. Have you or others in the organization been trained in conflict resolution? If you were trained, what topics were most useful?
28. What are the core values in the organization regarding conflict?
29. What are the organization's goals regarding conflict?
30. Who needs to be involved in the resolution process for it to succeed?
31. Who could veto or block its success?
32. How can public forums and open dialogue be encouraged?
33. How can networking and group learning be improved?
34. What could you do to improve your own skills?
35. What could you do to support others in improving theirs?
36. What steps would an employee have to go through to resolve a conflict?
37. Is there a mediation process? Who is allowed to use it? For which issues? How often?
38. Are some disputes unresolved because there are no procedures to deal with them? Which ones?
39. How satisfied are disputants with procedures that are presently available?

40. Do these procedures allow for venting emotions such as anger and frustration? How costly are they in time and money?
41. Do people know what procedures are available and when?
42. How skilled are people in problem solving? Negotiation?
43. How often do similar disputes recur because they are never fully resolved?
44. How are conflicts affected by formal and informal reward systems? Other systems?
45. What obstacles hinder the use of interest-based procedures?
46. How can people be motivated to use these procedures?
47. What skills do people need to use these procedures successfully?
48. How can learning, feedback, and adaptation be encouraged?
49. How should the successes and failures of the system be evaluated?
50. How can information from the conflict be used to create a learning organization?

Mediating Crosscultural Conflicts

Culture can be seen as a set of understandings, interpretations, and expectations regarding our environment. On this basis, it is possible to see all conflict as crosscultural. Culture produces a broad range of differences, including between precision and ambiguity in communication, open and closed in personal revelation, formal and informal in process, demonstrative and restrained in emotional expression. Some cultures, like those that separate women and men, require a high degree of context in order to understand the meaning of a communication, while others, like law, require very little. Some permit direct feedback, while others allow only indirect feedback. Some are fixed while others are fluid in attitudes toward time, and open or closed in attitudes toward space. These differences often result in conflicts that appear personal, but are actually cultural. It is therefore critical and potentially dangerous for mediators to recognize, reveal, respect, and resolve cultural differences.

In doing so, it is useful to adopt an elicitive approach pioneered by Mennonite mediator John Paul Lederach, which uses a conflict audit to determine the varieties of conflict and resolution procedures already available within a culture, then identify possible additions that supplement what is already done. Here are a few techniques that can be used to bridge crosscultural gaps:

- Begin by welcoming both sides, serving food or drink, and breaking bread together. Ask each person to say what they expect of you and the mediation process, or who they think you are, and how they define your role.
- Ask each side to identify the ground rules they need to feel respected, communicate effectively, and resolve their problems.
- Elicit a prioritization of conflicts from each side. Which are most serious, which are least serious? Compare similarities and differences, and do the same for conflict styles.
- Ask each side to list the words that describe the other culture, and next to this list, the words that describe their own. Exchange lists and ask them to respond. Or do the same with ideas such as time or feelings such as anger, or attitudes toward conflict.
- Ask parties to rank all the available options from war to surrender, and explore the reasons for choosing mediation.
- Ask parties to state, pantomime, role play, draw, or script how conflicts are resolved in their culture. Who do they go to for help? What roles are played by third parties? How do they mediate? Then jointly design the mediation process.
- Invite each side to suggest someone within their culture who may be willing to comediate, and work with them to build consensus on a model for the process.
- Establish common points of reference or values by asking each side to indicate their goals for the relationship or the process.
- Ask questions like: "What does that mean to you?" or "What does 'fairness' mean to you?"
- Acknowledge and model respect for cultural differences.
- Ask each person to say one thing they are proud of about their culture, and explain why.
- If appropriate, ask if there is anything they dislike about their own culture, and explain why.
- Ask them to say the three most important things they have learned in their lives, and explain why.

- Ask them to bring cultural artifacts, such as poems, music, or photographs, and to share their stories.
- Ask each side to identify a common stereotype of their culture, how it feels, and explain why.
- Describe your own culture, list the stereotypes you know of, and explain why they are inaccurate.
- Ask what rituals are used in each culture to end conflict, such as shaking hands, then jointly design a ritual for closure and forgiveness.

Systems Design and the United Nations

If we apply systems design principles and crosscultural techniques to world conflict as a whole, it is clear that the United Nations would be strengthened if it bolstered its mediative capacities in a number of critical ways. One way would be by adopting Harvard law professor Frank E. A. Sanders's "multidoor" courthouse model, which would involve creating an international referral agency to connect conflicting parties with alternative resolution processes and decentralized, specialized services. In addition, I would propose the following "14 Point" program for increasing the UN's effectiveness:

1. Regional Mediation Centers
The UN could establish low-cost regional centers for volunteer, professionally-trained mediators who are familiar with local cultures and languages and skilled in a range of techniques that would be locally acceptable and successful in resolving disputes. These centers would operate on governmental and nongovernmental levels, helping local communities, outside investors, foreign nationals, and minority cultures resolve their disputes.

2. World Arbitration Service
In addition to the World Court, countries and citizens could arbitrate a broad class of disputes, especially those involving commercial transactions and international human rights, using professional arbitrators referred by the UN on a fee-for-service basis.

3. Crosscultural Research Data Base

Just as gene banks collect rare DNA, the UN could research, analyze, and disseminate information on conflicts and conflict resolution techniques to determine their connection with cultural differences and similarities. This material could be fed to regional mediators and arbitrators and to governments to increase understanding of how conflicts happen, how they are handled in diverse cultures, and how they might be more successfully resolved.

4. World Trial and Appellate Courts

The UN could create a regional network of courts specializing in the resolution of a broad spectrum of international issues that separate trial or verdict courts from courts of appeal.

5. Model Treaty Provisions

Standard language could be inserted in all treaties and international agreements requiring disputing parties to take their disputes to mediation first, and then to arbitration, with heavy sanctions for use of force as a first resort.

6. Negotiation Centers

All UN personnel could be trained in interest-based negotiation techniques. Selected participants could become trainers in regional negotiation centers. Disputing parties or countries could be given training, including refresher courses, prior to bargaining.

7. Mediation "SWAT" Teams

A core of highly-skilled mediators could be employed by the UN to travel in teams to hot spots to help reduce conflict. These highly mobile, fast-forming teams could work closely with regional mediators familiar with the background of the dispute and the cultural styles of the participants.

8. Tripartite Panels

In both mediation and arbitration, where conflicts involve two distinct cultures, panels consisting of a mediator selected by each side plus a third party selected by both could have a greater likelihood of success.

9. Regional Conferences and Workshops
The UN could sponsor annual international symposia and quarterly workshops on world and regional problems, bringing together mediators from around the world to compare notes and learn from one another.

10. Practical Solution Sessions
In difficult situations, or when violence appears imminent, mediators and policy makers from both sides could be called together to brainstorm solutions and make consensus-based recommendations to disputing parties.

11. Regional Treaties
The UN could promote the signing of regional conflict resolution treaties providing a variety of alternative methods for resolving local and regional conflicts.

12. National and Regional Ombudsman Offices
Every nation and regional alliance could be encouraged to create *ombudsman* offices to recommend solutions in emerging conflicts without being under anyone's control in a national government. Treaties could create similar offices between conflicting nations or regions.

13. UN Agencies and Systems Design
Agencies of the UN from the World Health Organization (WHO) to UNESCO could examine the principles of conflict resolution systems design, apply them to conflicts occurring in each of their specialized areas, such as health, education, and so on, and develop within their agencies better methods for preventing and resolving conflicts.

14. UN Staff Resources
Every national UN office could be encouraged to appoint experienced mediators to help resolve conflicts taking place internally within the UN. Regional and international headquarters staff could include mediators, arbitrators, facilitators, trainers, and conflict resolution systems designers, who could be made available to members at no charge.

While considerably more might be done, these proposals illustrate the enormous potential for using conflict resolution systems design principles to assist the UN in creating a more peaceful world and enhancing the ability of member states to resolve conflicts without force. Recent wars in Serbia, Iraq, Rwanda, and Somalia, as well as civil wars around the globe, might have been avoided or alleviated had these ideas been implemented.

Using the U. S. intervention in Iraq as an example, it is clear that having a treaty in place with mandatory mediation and arbitration of border disputes; using trained Iraqi and Kuwaiti mediators early in the conflict; sending in UN mediators at the first hint of war; training ministers from the Organization of Petroleum Exporting Countries (OPEC), Islamic leaders, and organizations in mediation; creating regional conflict resolution teams; and convening international conferences with government ministers, professional mediators, academic experts, and representatives from both sides to brainstorm solutions may have reduced the bloodshed. It is never too late to heal past conflicts and begin preventing future ones.

The Globalization of Conflict Resolution

Many conflicts have a transnational character. Neighbors argue about noise, communities complain about pollution, divorcing couples fight over child custody, workers resent being fired or disciplined for poor performance, ethnic minorities confront power elites, schoolyards erupt with arguments, consumers complain about shoddy merchandise, corporations try to get out of unprofitable contracts.

Whether these conflicts occur in the United States, Russia, India, Mexico, Cuba, or Zimbabwe, the outcomes and emotions are often the same. Relationships are disrupted, feelings are hurt, communications are severed, attitudes are polarized, time and money are lost, innocent parties are made to suffer, and everyone feels wounded, depressed, and powerless. Yet these conflicts do not differ fundamentally from society to society, though they clearly differ in how they are manifested, handled, and resolved.

Every culture, family, organization, and society creates its own distinct forms of conflict and continues to produce them as long as their systems are structured to stimulate and suppress rather than resolve their conflicts. Each culture needs to elaborate from within its own set of techniques and procedures for resolving conflicts more successfully and systematically.

Every culture and society can learn how to improve its conflict resolution techniques from other societies. While none have eliminated conflict, many have developed creative ways of minimizing or resolving it. For example, among one tribal community in Africa, it is a common practice to laugh at conflicts and belittle their importance as a way of removing their sting and resetting priorities. Among Native American groups, it is common to use ritual and ceremony as a means of spiritual intercession to resolve conflict. In China, mediators are elected from neighborhoods, workplaces, farms, and schools, with over a million neighborhood mediation committees resolving disputes.

Every society and culture draws on its own traditions in resolving internal problems. Every culture can benefit in reduced costs and increased social unity by understanding conflict as a system and by designing systematic resolution programs. International cooperation and exchange programs allow mediators to share experiences and ideas with one another, from which much can be gained.

As we implement dangerous forms of mediation that address the systemic roots of conflict, not only can we learn new techniques for resolving interpersonal and social conflicts, mediation as a global skill can be enhanced, promoting social peace, healing, and problem solving as a transnational experience. We can then learn better methods for handling crosscultural conflicts and modeling ways of celebrating our differences. When we do so, we create a space where the inner and outer frontiers of conflict resolution meet.

Chapter Twenty

Where Inner and Outer Frontiers Meet

As the least drop of wine colors the whole goblet,
so the least particle of truth colors our whole life.
It is never isolated, or simply added as dollars to our stock.
When any real progress is made, we unlearn and learn
anew, what we thought we knew before.
HENRY DAVID THOREAU

In completing this exploration of inner and outer frontiers in conflict resolution, with their complex interface of limits and boundaries, spirits and systems, we can see that there is no real difference between inner and outer. Inner honesty and empathy are projected externally, while outer dishonesty and prejudgment always echo internally. We can then discern that the true danger lies in not mediating dangerously enough.

Communities of Conflict and Collaboration

Religious philosopher Thomas Merton described community as a "hidden wholeness" that is revealed whenever people collaborate. In probing the inner world of intention, psyche, and spirit, and the outer world of power, society, and systems, we discover that *dangerous* forms of conflict resolution divide communities of conflict from communities of collaboration.

A community of conflict is one in which dialogue remains superficial, simplistic, antagonistic, and based on rage, guilt, shame, denial, or fear. These negative communities are secretive, risk-averse, divided, unstable, and collapse whenever deeply honest, complex, open, and empathetic communication takes place, and whenever people engage in authentic dialogue and collaborative negotiation over issues that divide them.

As false communities of conflict collapse, they reveal stable, positive communities of collaboration that were always possible. Communities of collaboration are fundamentally different from those of accommodation based on civility, and equally different from those of compromise based on rights, or those of aggression based on power. These are simply modified communities of conflict. What differentiates communities of collaboration is the capacity to learn from conflict based on a deep commitment to honesty and empathy. Indeed, each of the chapters in this book describes a number of practical methods for creating collaborative conflict communities.

Imagine communities of collaboration and conflict as invisible intersecting webs consisting of nodes of energy that vibrate at different amplitudes and frequencies, based on our attitude or approach to conflict. Just as on the Internet, conflict creates webs that deliver messages and link individuals and fields. Mediation allows us to enter these webs from multiple pathways and ports. As we do, we discover that we become parts of a system, a holistic ecology of global attitudes toward conflict resolution that is intertwined and self-referential, with collective nodes linking individuals at discrete energy points.

While mediating a divorce, we may confront inner limits of revenge and forgiveness. In working dangerously with these options, we may discover a family system in which oppression and abuse are the norm. It may happen that the parents grew up in families where humiliation was common or that the family resides in a community where inequality and violence are condoned. We may discover that a parent was fired by a company with hierarchical top-down management, that the children attend schools that punish honest criticism, or that government agencies have treated them disrespectfully. Where, then, is the conflict located, and where is the resolution?

Unless we address the outer frontiers of the world in which we live, resolving issues at the inner frontiers may simply adjust but not eliminate the dispute. The fact that conflict is an interconnected system tells us that by altering its vibration in one location, we alter it everywhere. In short, we need to acknowledge that by exploring the inner and outer frontiers of mediation we expand its potential as a system, and subtly alter its energy, spirit, and vibratory quality. In this way, conflict by conflict, party by party, issue by issue, we expand communities of collaboration.

Integrating Inner and Outer Limits

We began this exploration of dangerous mediation with the statement by Goethe that "The dangers of life are infinite, and among them is safety." We end by acknowledging that safety can become a greater danger than escalation and violence. All conflicts exist for a reason, and it is not only the reasons but our *responses* to them that generate dysfunction and violence. Just as pain increases when we ignore our bodies' demands, conflict results in violence when we ignore the underlying issues that gave rise to it. Confronting these issues requires moving toward rather than away from our problems, and transforming the systems and behaviors that sustain these issues, which is dangerous.

In truth, the less difficult path is the one that seems to require more work, while the easier one leads to exhaustion, alienation, and despair. Conflicts are lessons we are asked to learn, problems we are asked to fix, messages we are asked to hear, lives we are asked to live. The true danger is not conflict, but our unwillingness to find out why it occurred in the first place and why it is dangerous to resolve it.

In the first section, we examined the inner frontiers of our ability to reach deep levels of honesty and empathy. We explored our issues and difficulties as conflict resolvers based on our families of origin, our desire for revenge and capacity for forgiveness, and our potential for spiritual engagement, transformation, and transcendence. In the second section, we examined the outer frontiers, the shift from power to rights to interests, how to transcend the rule of law and improve the way we fight, what happens when we mediate at the heart of a system, and how to mediate in the face of fascism and oppressive relationships.

If our inner and outer frontiers are the same, they will merge and join, interpenetrate and mingle, swerve and dance with each other. The inner fear of mediating dangerously and bringing deep levels of honesty and empathy to conflict resolution is increased when the problem originates in systemic resistance to change. In reverse, mediating at the outer frontier of organizational power requires an inner capacity for empathy, spiritual connection, and a recognition of the reasons people seek revenge over forgiveness.

Dangerous mediation thus requires nondual thinking, the ability to perceive hidden wholeness and the *oneness* of all things. This oneness includes our own past experiences and future expectations, the spatial, temporal, and cultural environments in which we mediate, the issues and parties, the political, economic, and organizational systems that created the conflict, and the spiritual, vibratory quality of our attitudes and the ways we choose to manifest them.

Nondual thinking means holding two apparently opposing thoughts simultaneously, including ideas of oneness and opposition, and bringing them so close together that they merge, giving rise to a new, transformed, *transcendent* version that is neither, yet both. There is not just one truth in mediation, nor are there two. There are one and two, and a third, which is greater than either or both.

It strengthens our spirit when we find we can love in the midst of hate, suffer without desire for revenge, serve without remuneration, apologize for mistakes we have made, and forgive those made by others. Our energy increases when we become centered, aware, authentic, and open to our own transformation. In dangerous mediation, we are asked to surrender the illusion of separation between ourselves and others, to be omnipartial and speak, listen, and behave as though we were on both sides of the dispute. We are asked to be ourselves and become one with our opponents; to believe in the possibility of transformational change; to allow everyone to choose, accept people as they are, and ask them to behave differently toward each other; to be ourselves, and revolutionize our way of being.

Unlearning Questions

In completing this exploration at the edges of conflict resolution, it is important to reexamine what we think we know. As mediators, we have undoubtedly learned a great deal. But have we also learned to stay in touch with our ignorance? H ow open are we to the possibility that what we have learned is irrelevant or wrong? Can we live in the present without focusing on the past or the future?

We have learned how to solve problems. Have we learned how to *not* solve them? How willing are we to live with paradox, riddle, and enigma? Do we understand that by solving problems too soon, we might cheat ourselves and others out of learning from them?

We know how to make things happen. Do we know how to allow them to happen? Do we know how to do nothing? Can we let things happen to us or the parties, or watch as they happen? Are we addicted to making things happen?

We have developed strengths and experienced successes. Do we recognize that for every strength, we have developed a corresponding weakness? Do we appreciate that success leads to complacency, while failure leads to learning and change? So which is the success, and which is the failure?

We have helped others transform their lives. So what is the crossroads are we at in our own lives? What is preventing us from transforming our lives? What conflicts have we not transcended? How much of our heart and spirit do we use in mediation? What keeps us from using all of it?

Sublime Mediation

Anything one touches with the right spirit leads to the center of things. In indigenous cultures this is called "thinking with the heart," which is often degraded to "subjectivity" and "irrationality" in Western cultures. The mind is not the only voice or the exclusive arbiter, but often acts to obscure or hide the truth.

The sublime, in conflict resolution as in all arts, emanates from feeling and spirit, as well as from thought. It is a kind of mindful thoughtlessness, a purposeless intention that flows through rather than from us, and speaks to the whole person rather than to any particular part. It is the invisible sap of human connection that flows freely as obstacles are removed from its path. Our task is simply to remove whatever obstacles we can.

A Zen master might demand: "Show me your face before you were born." Mediators ask people in conflict to reveal themselves to each other and delight in what they see and reveal, to release the pain and humiliation of antagonism and reclaim their own true selves. It does not matter if we succeed. What matters is the simplicity of our intention, the skillful artistry of our ceremony, and our impeccable acceptance of this same truth about ourselves. Good luck, and may all your conflicts be dangerous, sublime, and result in transcendence.

About the Author

Kenneth Cloke is director of the Center for Dispute Resolution in Santa Monica, California, where he is a mediator, arbitrator, consultant, and trainer specializing in resolving complex multiparty conflicts, including grievance and workplace disputes, organizational and school conflicts, sexual harassment and discrimination lawsuits, divorce, family, and public policy disputes, and in designing conflict resolution systems for organizations. His consulting and training practice also encompasses issues of organizational change, leadership, team building, and strategic planning. He is a speaker on mediation and conflict resolution and author of many journal articles and books, including *Mediation: Revenge and the Magic of Forgiveness*. He is also coauthor with Joan Goldsmith of *Thank God It's Monday! 14 Values We Need to Humanize the Way We Work, Resolving Conflicts at Work: A Complete Guide for Everyone on the Job,* and *Resolving Personal and Organizational Conflict: Stories of Transformation and Forgiveness.*

Index

Practical solution sessions, resorting to, 228
Preaching, 189
Pride, 69, 91
Principled engagement. *See* Engagement, principled
Problem solver, attorney as, 172
Problem solving: in dialogue, 182; limits on, questioning, 130; moving towards, 177; transitioning into, 122
Problems: defining people as, 93–94, 131; discovering, through fighting, 186–187; separating people from, 94, 122, 177
Process, 192, 215–216, 217
Process fairness, interests in, 143
Professional victims, 88
Professionalism, pose of, 52–53
Promise of Mediation, The (Bush and Folger), 11
Psychotherapy, need for, 67
Public Conversations Project (PCP), 178–179
Punishment: divine and spiritual, 84; questioning, 152, 153
Pythagoreans, 78

R
Rage. *See* Anger and rage
Reconciler, attorney as, 172
Reconciliation: cultivating, 120; encouraging, 19–20; meaning of, 96; practice of, 20; stages in, 105–106; in victim-offender mediation, 85, 151–153
Refereeing, in dialogue, 181
Reflections on the Guillotine (Camus), 21
Reframing, use of, 36, 39
Regional conferences and workshops, sponsoring, 228
Regional mediation centers, establishing, 226
Regional treaties, promoting, 228
Rehabilitation, 152–153
Relational truth. *See* Truth, higher

Relationship improvement, interests in, 143
Relationship, unity of, 216, 217
Relationships, unresolved, impact of, 7–8
Religion, 84, 109
Reorienting, in dialogue, 182
Rescuer role, 33, 43, 51
Resistance: and fear of freedom, 57–58; to forgiveness, 90–94, 99; to systemic change, 199, 200, 214–215; from systems, 197, 198
Resolution: context of, 197; defining, 16, 20, 23; differing approaches to, 16–18; globalization of, 230; mediation as, 19–20; obstacles to, 123–124, 125; resistance to, 57–58; spiritual journey of, 117–118
Resolving Personal and Organizational Conflict: Stories of Transformation and Forgiveness (Cloke and Goldsmith), 70
Respect, 137, 161
Response to conflict, choices in, 116, 140–141. *See also specific choices*
Responsibility, 29; assuming, in divorce, 27; for choices, 30; collective, 98–99, 123, 156, 158–159; to create positive communities, 162–163; for crime, 149–151, 151–153; denying, 98; for education, 155–156; and forgiveness, 95; for labor and management disputes, 154–155; reconciliation and, 105
Responsiveness, 91
Restitution, 77, 85, 151–153
Retaliation. *See* Revenge
Retsinger, S., 91
Revenge: alternatives to, 84–86; defined, 74; empathy and, 75–76; fantasizing about, 73–74; forgiveness and, 74, 103, 133; history of, 76–80; impact of, awareness of, 82–84; limits of, 96–98; mediating, 81–82, 86; nature of, 76; power of ritual and, 103; problem with,